# The Chevalier Noverre

JEAN GEORGES NOVERRE

*Chalk miniature by Roger after Guérin,
in the collection of Miss Josephine Diver.
Photo S. J. Brown, Norwich.*

# THE
# CHEVALIER
# NOVERRE

*Father of Modern Ballet*

A BIOGRAPHY BY

## Deryck Lynham

illustrated

DANCE BOOKS
9 CECIL COURT, LONDON W.C.2
1972

*This is an unabridged republication of the edition first
published in 1950 by Sylvan Press Ltd.*

© *1972 Mrs. May Lynham.*

*Printed by Chameleon Press Ltd.
London S.W.11 1ER*

S.B.N. 903102 01　3

# Contents

# List of Illustrations

# To Miss Margot Fonteyn

Perhaps since I am writing on the eighteenth century, I may be forgiven if, ignoring the modern custom of dismissing a dedication with a telescopic line, I venture to express my admiration for your art and my gratitude for the pleasure you have so often given me.

I feel all the more justification for so grave a break with modern usage inasmuch as I have neither sought nor obtained your consent for, had I done so, your modest disposition might have dictated a refusal.

No one who knows me will see in this a desire to indulge in idle flattery, since I was slow to perceive in your early years the great artist you have become, and I will attempt no panegyric of your talents to which my pen is incapable of doing justice.

If this book were to be graced with a dedication it could only be to one on whom the Chevalier Noverre would have bestowed that praise which he kept for the very few. Because above all else he loved the dance, I feel he would have admired the classical purity of your "Princess Aurora", your "Odette-Odile" and your "Symphonic Variations"; because he laboured his life long for the expressive painting of the passions, he would have been moved to enthusiasm by the "opéra comique" flavour which you alone have known how to impart to "La Fille de Madame Angot".

This book is yours too because so often, when I have been assailed by that weariness of the spirit which wells up inside the writer as the months merge into years and the mass of facts to be transmuted into a book seems endless, I have found fresh inspiration in abandoning myself to the exquisite artistry of your interpretation.

The sincerest form of homage an author has to bestow is his work and nothing less than this book could serve to assure you of the esteem and admiration in which you are held by

Deryck Lynham

# Preface

"HISTORY, if it is to paint freely and portray striking likenesses, must wait for the judgment of posterity which weighs in the balance of impartiality the dead who played in their lifetime the leading rôles on the vast stage of the world. That judgment cannot be equivocal, for it is free and fears neither tyranny nor despotism and aspires to no favours. It takes a century for truth to pierce the tenebrosity with which falsehood, flattery and self-interest surround it; in a word, for truth to show itself in all its radiance, it must clarify itself by filtering as it were through the generations.

It is then that history will be able freely to paint and, forgetting both rank and titles, show us as they were men who are no more and trace, in clear tones and with a bold brush, their vices and their virtues, their weakness and their courage, their mercy and their tyranny. . . ."[1]

Although the "Lettres sur la Danse et sur les Ballets" have withstood this "filtering through the generations" and, to this day, have an important place on the bookshelves of all students and lovers of the ballet the world over, there has been little or no attempt to show us Noverre the man, as he was.

The forewords with which historians and critics have prefaced various editions of the "Lettres" which have appeared from time to time have, in the main, been inspired, directly or indirectly, from the "Lettres sur la Danse et sur les Ballets", the "Lettres sur les Arts Imitateurs" and from Charles Edwin Noverre's "The Life and Works of the Chevalier Noverre", published in 1882. This latter work is of considerable interest inasmuch as the author, a descendant of Jean Georges Noverre's brother, Augustin, had access to family papers, but is limited by his lack of acquaintance with the history of dancing in general and his inability to consult the many Continental records bearing on the life of his illustrious kinsman.

Hans Niedecken's "Jean Georges Noverre, sein Leben und seine Beziehungen zur Musik", published in 1914, seemingly as a thesis, although it has been overlooked for some reason by most dance historians, is an invaluable and scholarly study. The author, who approaches his subject primarily from the musical standpoint, has

9

however, for his English data, been limited to sources not always fully informed.

It has been my aim in this book to correlate the known information on the Chevalier Noverre so as to present a picture of the man and his life and to assess, from the study of his works, the extent of his contribution to the art of the ballet. I have, however, been unable to consult the collection of eleven volumes presented by Noverre to Stanislas-Auguste Poniatowsky, king of Poland, containing, in addition to a condensed version of the "Lettres sur la Danse", programmes and scores of the Stuttgart ballets and 445 designs by Boquet. It is to be hoped a full study of the ballets created at Stuttgart by Noverre will one day be made from the data contained in these volumes now preserved in Leningrad.

In the research which has taken several years, and covered both contemporary and posthumous material, I have been particularly fortunate in having the assistance of my wife, who has undertaken all translations from the German and has collaborated closely in the preparation of my typescript as well as producing the index, and this book is due in no small measure to her efforts.

No words of mine can adequately express my appreciation to Miss Josephine Diver who, drawing on her wealth of family tradition, has, more than anyone else, known how to make the Chevalier relive before me and has very kindly put family records at my disposal and given me permission to reproduce a number of portraits from her collection. I am likewise deeply grateful to Mrs. Jacqueline Arnold, Mr. and Mrs. O. F. Diver, Mrs. Margaret Farebrother, Mrs. B. Noverre and Miss Mary Noverre, who, with that old-world courtesy which the descendants of Jean Georges and Augustin Noverre seem to have made their own, have found time to reply to my exhaustive questions and have given me permission to quote from material in their possession.

Once again I must record my debt of gratitude to Miss Viola Tunnard who, notwithstanding the pressure of her professional engagements, so generously allowed me to draw on her immense knowledge of music for the ballet and brought out many points which would otherwise have escaped me in the scores I have consulted.

For all the data gathered in Paris, I am indebted to Miss O. A. Abbott, who has also afforded me many valuable suggestions.

Considerations of space preclude my mentioning here, as I would like to do, all the many friends who have assisted me, but it would be the deepest ingratitude on my part if I failed to thank Miss G. V

Barnard, the learned Curator of Norwich Castle Museum, for information supplied; Mr. C. W. Beaumont for the loan of the block reproduced,¹ facing p. 122; Mr. S. J. Brown for all the skill he has brought to the photographs taken by him, which are real works of art; Mr. W. D. Cavendish for his many enquiries in Rome; Professor Edward J. Dent for giving me the benefit of his advice on certain musical problems; Mr. Alvaro Fernandes for his research in Lisbon; Miss G. Halcomb for her help in identifying a Japanese Koto; Mr. Barrington Lynham for his research at St. Germain en Laye; Dr. H. M. Ledig-Rowohlt for his help in tracing material in Germany; Messrs. McInerny, Paz, Seignol and Veuillet for their help in combing the municipal records at Lyons; Mr. P. J. S. Richardson for so generously putting me in touch with a number of descendants of Augustin Noverre and for his constant encouragement; Mr. Charles Rosner for his assistance in tracing material in Germany and Austria; "The Dancing Times" for permitting me to use some blocks and the Trustees and Keepers of the Bibliothèque de l'Arsenal, Bibliothèque Nationale and Bibliothèque de l'Opéra in Paris, the Nationalbibliothek, Vienna, the Musée de Besançon, British Museum and Victoria and Albert Museum, for granting me facilities for research and giving me permission to reproduce material and, last but far from least, Miss Lorna Napolitano for her assistance in translating from the Italian.

# CHAPTER I

## Early Years

THE name of Jean Georges Noverre stands forth in bold relief agains the background of the history of the art of ballet. His *Lettres sur la Danse* have been translated into almost every European language and yet, although the idea that he was largely responsible for creating the *ballet d'action*, or dramatic ballet, has gained general acceptance and his name is one of the most frequently quoted in the literature of the dance, scant light has been shed on his life and work.

He was born in Paris on April 29th, 1727, and baptized the same day in the Protestant chapel of the Dutch Ambassador. His mother was French and his father, Jean Louys Noverre, was a native of Lausanne who had served as an adjutant in the army of Karl XII of Sweden, and his presence in Paris was possibly accounted for by his being a member of the Swiss Guard attached to the service of the French monarch.[2]

Jean Georges was destined to a military career and given a liberal education, but he showed little aptitude for tactical exercises or army discipline and was nightly to be found haunting the theatres of Paris, where he was fired with the ambition to become a dancer. Finding all resistance vain, his father placed him under Jean Denis Dupré and the celebrated dancer and choreographer, Louis Dupré, better known as "Le Grand Dupré", of whom Jean Georges Noverre was later to write:—

"Big open movements of the legs and *effacés* positions were without doubt suited to M. Dupré; the elegance of his figure and the length of his limbs were wonderfully adapted to the execution of *dévelopés effacés* and the intricate steps of his dance. . . . This rare harmony in every movement earned for the celebrated Dupré the glorious title of 'Dieu de la Danse' and in fact this excellent dancer seemed a divinity rather than a man. The calm and flowing continuity of his every movement and the perfect co-ordination and control of every muscle made for a perfect ensemble, due to a fine physique and that precise arrangement and well-combined proportion of every part which, resulting less from study and reasoning than from nature, may only be acquired when one is so endowed."[3]

When, in 1743, Louis Dupré was invited to participate in the production of dances in the vaudevilles mounted on the stage of the

Opéra Comique, at the Foire St. Laurent, the young dancer obtained his first professional engagement. The Foire St. Laurent was held every year, from the end of June to September 29th, on the site of the present Gare de l'Est. In the shade of the horse-chestnut trees overlooked by the gardens of the surrounding great houses, the Parisian tradespeople opened their shops which, with the passing of the years, had replaced the booths of the wandering vendors. There were alleys occupied by the *lingères* and the milliners, by the jewellers and goldsmiths, and cafés with tables piled high with cheeses and saveloys and great tankards of wine.

The tightrope dancers, tumblers and other entertainers, introduced by the early merchants to attract custom to their stalls, had early in the century begun to give way to theatrical troupes presenting a medley of dancing and pantomime, somewhat in the style of the Italian harlequinade, which became known as *opéra comique* and in turn gave its name to the theatre in which it was presented. This theatre, situated at the corner of the Rue du Faubourg St. Martin and the Passage de l'Opéra, was dirty and neglected, the orchestra was made up of stray musicians seeking a respite from playing at pleasure gardens and country weddings, the dressing rooms of the actresses were open to all and sundry, and persons of quality mingled at their peril with the audience of lackeys sprinkled with thieves and pickpockets who, by their boos and jeers, virtually dictated what plays should be performed.

On March 28th, 1743, the concession granted in respect of the Opéra Comique by the Opéra, who held the exclusive privilege of authorizing the production of entertainments of music and dancing, was acquired by Jean Monnet, one of the most remarkable impresarios of his day. Monnet at once proceeded to clean up the house and to surround himself with a team of men and women who were later to revolutionize the French musical theatre:—

Jean Philippe Rameau, perhaps the most discussed composer of the time, who had dared, in his ballet and opera music, to break away from the set forms of Lully and who accomplished the first real systematization of harmony, to conduct the orchestra of eighteen musicians; François Boucher, who was later to succeed Servandoni as official designer to the Opéra, to create the costumes and décor; Préville, who had already made a name for himself in the provinces and was later to become one of the greatest actors on the French stage, as his leading man; Marie Sallé, the *danseuse* who, in a period when formal dances and heavy traditional costumes were *de rigueur*, had introduced a new

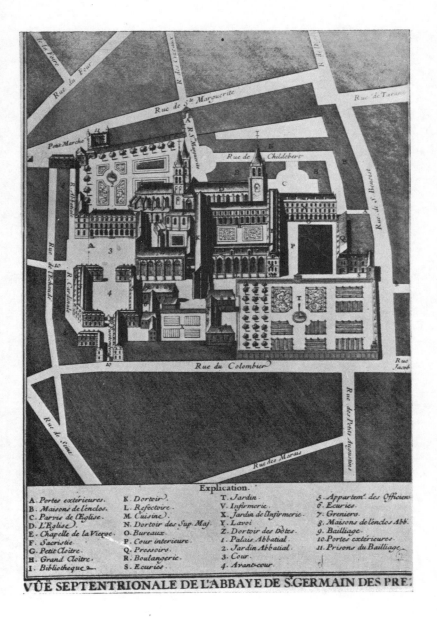

Explication.

| | | | |
|---|---|---|---|
| A . *Portes extérieures.* | K . *Dortoir.* | T . *Jardin.* | 5 . *Appartem.ᵗ des Officiers* |
| B . *Maisons de l'enclos.* | L . *Refectoire.* | V . *Infirmerie.* | 6 . *Ecuries.* |
| C . *Partie de l'Eglise.* | M . *Cuisine.* | X . *Jardin de l'Infirmerie.* | 7 . *Greniers.* |
| D . *L'Eglise.* | N . *Dortoir des Sup. Maj.* | Y . *Lavoir.* | 8 . *Maisons de l'enclos Abb.* |
| E . *Chapelle de la Vierge.* | O . *Bureaux.* | Z . *Dortoir des Dôtes.* | 9 . *Bailliage.* |
| F . *Sacristie.* | P . *Cour intérieure.* | 1 . *Palais Abbatial.* | 10 . *Portes extérieures.* |
| G . *Petit Cloître.* | Q . *Pressoirs.* | 2 . *Jardin Abbatial.* | 11 . *Prisons du Bailliage.* |
| H . *Grand Cloître.* | R . *Boulangerie.* | 3 . *Cour.* | |
| I . *Bibliotheque.* | S . *Ecuries.* | 4 . *Avant-cour.* | |

VÜE SEPTENTRIONALE DE L'ABBAYE DE S.GERMAIN DES PREZ

*The abbaye St. Germain des Près, eastern aspect.   The section in which Noverre
probably sojourned is marked with a 'Z'.   Courtesy Musée Carnavalet, Paris.*

*Danse Chinoise*

*Oil painting by François Boucher
(1703–1770) in the Musée de Besançon*

expressiveness into her art and had had the courage, only nine years previously, to appear in a plain muslin dress without pannier or petticoat, with her hair down and her head unadorned, assisted Louis Dupré and J. B. Lany to create the ballets on a company of fourteen dancers and, as producer, Charles Simon Favart, the baker-boy turned poet and playwright, who was perhaps the real creator of the style we have come to understand by *opéra comique.*

The young Noverre could not fail to be influenced by the great creative artists with whom he was thus brought into contact, and to whom he was later to render homage in his own *Lettres sur la Danse et les Ballets".*[4]

The season opened on June 8th with Favart's one-act vaudeville, *Le Coq du Village,* with *intermèdes,* songs and dances, in which the young Noverre probably made his début. The first time his name is specifically mentioned, however, is on August 31st in *L'Ambigu de la Folie ou le Ballet des Dindons,* in which he appeared, in the *pas de trois* at the end of the fourth act, as "Borée" alongside of Mlles. Puvigné, as "the Rose", and L. M. Lany, as "Zephire". This parody of Fuzelier and Rameau's *Indes Galantes,* then playing at the Opéra, was sufficiently successful to hold the bill until the close of the season.

Noverre then, possibly through Monnet or Marie Sallé, both of whom were not without influence at Versailles, appeared in October before the Court at Fontainebleau, where he seems to have made little impression, although he himself retained a vivid memory of an amusing little incident in this connection. He was to appear, with the little Puvigné, first of all in Paris and afterwards before the Court in a minuet, *Les Jeunes Mariés,* and because Monnet looked after his investments, Marcel, a pompous old dancing master then in fashion who was noted for his teaching of the minuet, agreed to coach the two young dancers. Noverre relates:—

"Marcel admitted us to his school where we made rapid progress. He took a liking to me and said to me one day: 'You can boast of being my pupil and even bill it, but I want to give you a fresh proof of my protection and my good will by devising for you a little rondo to be sung and danced,

*Of Love we follow the laws, etc.*

You are a pupil of the little Dupré, he is an imbecile choreographer and a poor master who dances paper in hand. You go twice a week to the grand Dupré. This one dances pleasingly, but he has jumped with both feet on all principles. I want to give you some and, by following them strictly, you will become, as I have done, the first master of your profession; come and see me tomorrow at seven o'clock.'

I duly called on him and he outlined the little rondo in a closet which, the furniture excepted, did not measure six square feet. Marcel, tormented by gout, could not execute the steps and several times he thought he would crush me. I then said to him: 'Sir, sit yourself in your armchair and perform the steps for me with your fingers and I hope to seize them to your satisfaction.' 'What the Devil', cried Marcel, 'your legs will seize the movements of my fingers?' 'Yes, sir, very quickly, provided, however, you add the name of the steps which your two fingers trace for me.' 'I will try, my young friend, but this seems most extraordinary to me.'

He sketched out the steps for me with his two fore-fingers. I easily understood and, whilst his assistant played the violin, I danced. The rondo learned, he arranged my arms in the antique manner and, pleased with my intelligence, he said to me: 'Come and see me from time to time, I will talk about you and make your fortune!'

I ran to the grand Dupré, who was by nature cold and phlegmatic and to whom I often brought flowers (after women and hunting it was that which he loved most passionately). I recounted to him the story of the rondo and asked his permission to dance it for him. He thought he would choke with laughing. Every time thereafter when he was ill-humoured, I would dance the rondo for him. I have not forgotten it, I have preserved it with the same care with which a curious person keeps an antique medal . . ."[5]

Meanwhile the fashionable audience, bored with the dull traditional productions of the Opéra, had learned of Monnet's new venture and, when he opened at the Foire St. Germain, which was held on the site of the present Marché St. Germain, on a property belonging to the Abbaye St. Germain des Près, from February 3rd to Palm Sunday, they flocked to his spectacle. The season nevertheless was a bad one, owing to very heavy rain, and final disaster came when the artists of the Opéra, jealous of Monnet's success and afraid of the drain on their audience, used their Royal privilege to withdraw his concession and have the Opéra Comique closed by a decree of the first of June, 1744. Monnet and his troupe addressed a prayer to the King, as a result of which they obtained a delay of one month in which to comply, a delay which was several times extended.

We next find Noverre at the Berlin Court, where opera and ballet had as yet but little tradition.[6] The only recreation required by the gross humour of Frederick William from forging the army, with which his son was to establish Prussian military might, were acrobats and mountebanks and one of his first acts, on mounting the throne, had been to draw his pen through the list of pensioners of the royal theatres and to liquidate costumes and décors. Such artists as remained were drawn to Rheinsberg, the residence of the Crown Prince Frederick. When this prince, who was to live in history as Frederick the Great, acceded to the throne on May 31st, 1740, he sought the help of Voltaire to recruit a troupe of French actors and appointed as his chamberlain and director of court entertainments Jean Baptiste Boyer, Marquis d'Argenson, a bohemian adventurer from Aix en Provence. The Marquis engaged a number of dancers with the Sieur Poitiers as *Maître de Ballet*.[7] Frederick, however, was not prepared to pay for his pleasures and in particular would not provide a *corps de ballet*, and Poitiers would not arrange his choreography on amateurs, and so Poitiers was sacked and some of the dancers left with him, whilst Frederick vented his spleen in notes to the gazettes of Paris and London.

Monsieur de Chambrier, Frederick's Minister in Paris, was instructed to find a new *Maître de Ballet* and two *danseuses*. He engaged J. B. Lany from the Opéra Comique, as *Maître de Ballet* and *premier danseur*, at a salary of two thousand crowns, and his two sisters, and they made their first appearance in Berlin in November, 1743. Lany met with Royal approval but his sister, Madeleine, was felt to be too young for a *prima ballerina* and a young Italian, Barbarina Campanini, better known as La Barbarina, was engaged in her stead, and made her first appearance on May 13th, 1744. She was soon the talk of Berlin and the accredited mistress of the Sovereign who gave her a contract, in which she herself filled in the salary of five thousand thalers, and the *corps de ballet* required to show off her graces as a ballerina.

Noverre is mentioned in the cast of Hasse's *Arminio,* in 1745, and probably also appeared in the *corps de ballet* in Graun's ballets, *Pygmalion et Psyche* and *Adriano in Siria* in 1745, and in the same composer's operas, *Catone in Utica* (1744) and *Demofoonte Re de Tracia* (1746), all of which contained ballets by Lany.

He would seem to have been a favourite at Court, where he amused the monarch by his droll imitations of the leading *danseuses* and entertained Voltaire by his wicked stories, for which he was sometimes taken to task by the philosopher who would pull his ear.

All might have been well but for the fact that Frederick treated his players, with the exception of La Barbarina, like soldiers, and, what was more, would not pay them a salary in keeping with what they believed to be their merits, with the result that Lany and a number of his colleagues, breaking their contracts, fled the Prussian Court at the end of 1747.[8]

The Marquis d'Argenson, in Paris with Marianne Cochois, in a letter dated December 3rd, 1747, wrote commiserating with his royal master on their desertion:—

"I have been in Paris for two days and would already have left were it not that Mlle. Cochois asked for four or five days in which to settle some affairs. I granted them to her because I realized that, in view of the desertion of Lany and the other scoundrels who followed him, she would be back in time for the rehearsals of the Opera, Sodi and the other persons we have engaged being unable to leave before the 10th or 12th of the month, by which time the Cochois will be on her way.

Nothing can be quite so dreadful as the action of Lany, he deserves that Your Majesty should make him feel the full weight of his indignation. I have said throughout Paris what I had to say about this low fellow and his companions in desertion and knavery, and I will continue to make them known before leaving here, so that they will repent of their foolishness. . . ."

All of which did not prevent the unrepentant Lany soon appearing in Paris, where he obtained the post of *Maître de Ballet* at the Opéra, and also spread rumours of the meanness of Frederick, to his great annoyance.

On leaving Berlin, Noverre went first to Marseilles as *Maître des Ballets*, to compose his first ballets, and thence to Lyons where, in 1750, he was partnering the famous Camargo. Both the city of Lyons and the Opera House enjoyed a considerable artistic reputation. As early as 1668 ballets, such as *La Prise de Dôle*, had been staged there for the Duc de Villeroy, with brilliant scenery and costumes.

The Académie des Beaux Arts, which enjoyed an uninterrupted existence until 1773, had been founded in 1713, and granted letters patent in 1724, to give musical concerts. Jean Philippe Rameau had been master organist to the City from 1713 to 1715 and his operas were produced in Lyons immediately following on their creation in Paris, whilst Jean-Jacques Rousseau was teaching there in 1739.

The theatre had a history of artistic achievement and financial disaster under successive private managers and under the municipality. Monnet, after the loss of his Opéra Comique concession, had managed the theatre until the end of 1747 or early 1748 but, even though he toured as far afield as Dijon, he failed to cover his expenses. In April, 1750, the theatre was under the direction of another of Noverre's early acquaintances, the actor, Préville, who engaged him as *premier danseur* in a company which included, in addition to Camargo, Mlles. Hyacinthe and Anselin and, as guest artiste, Mlle. Lany, as well as Mlle. Geoffroy and Mr. Bodin, recently returned from Turin.

Noverre lived with his young wife in the fashionable Terreaux district, the residence of the wealthy merchants of the city. Their son, Antoine, was born there, in 1750, as was their daughter, Claudine

Gervaise, on January 24th, 1752, and christened the next day in the church of Saint Saturnin, two notables of Lyons, David Flachat, esquire and ex-magistrate, and Dame Claudine Gervaise Bruyzet, wife of the Sieur Claude Pierre Fuselier, esquire and secretary counsellor to the King, standing as godparents.[9]

The 1751-2 season opened under the management of one Mathieu Belouard, and Noverre, heading an important company of dancers which included his wife, created ten ballets during the year, for each of which he received a sum of one hundred and twenty livres.

Mathieu Belouard was, alas, no more successful than his forerunners and he ended his one and only season with a deficit of twenty-two thousand seven hundred and fifty-one livres, in part accounted for by a payment of two thousand eight hundred livres made to the Noverres as compensation for the termination of their contract.[10]

Monnet meanwhile, after a disastrous season at the Little Theatre in the Haymarket, London, which had been greeted with such violent xenophobia that he had to close down after the fourth performance,[11] had returned to Paris and, through the influence of Madame de Pompadour, had been granted a fresh licence for the Opéra Comique. The theatre in the Rue des Quatre Vents, a cul-de-sac off the Faubourg St. Germain, was redecorated, skilfully rearranged and reopened on February 3rd, 1752, whilst a new theatre was built in the Foire St. Laurent with ceilings painted by Boucher, which were greatly admired and were later taken down by order of the King and transferred to the Hotel des Menus. This theatre also incorporated a number of technical improvements; the ramp leading from the stage to the auditorium was abolished, thus separating the audience from the players, and candles, which customarily illuminated both stage and auditorium, were replaced by oil lamps backed by reflectors. David Garrick was at a later date to see this lighting and order from Paris similar lamps for Drury Lane.

Monnet immediately gathered round him many of his old colleagues, including Noverre who, despite the support of Madame de Pompadour, had failed in his efforts to secure the post of *Maître des Ballets* to the Opéra in succession to the grand Dupré because J. B. Lany, the assistant ballet master, had put forward his traditional right to the reversion.

The opéra comique style now broke away completely from the mould created by Le Sage and d'Orneval and became a genuine musical spectacle, with for only link with the fair the locality in which the theatre was situated. Looking back on this period a contemporary critic, the Abbé de Laporte, noted in 1759:—

"Vallé, d'Auvergne and Noverre long maintained the reputation of the Opéra Comique. The first by his clear and light works beloved of the French; the second by his charming Italian music and arias; the third added thereto superlatively designed ballets and offered the spectacle of a number of living tableaux which the eye considered with as much pleasure as surprise."[12]

The ballet company was made up in 1753 of ten *danseurs* and as many *danseuses,* including Noverre, as *Maître de Ballet,* Lepy and Mme. Noverre-Sauveur, and had been increased by 1755 to eight *danseurs* and thirteen *danseuses.*

Madame Noverre did not, however, remain permanently at the Opéra Comique, for, in his journal for the year 1755, the dramatist Charles Collé notes:—

"The same day, February 7th, the demoiselle Noverre, wife of the ballet master of the Opéra Comique, made her début at the Comédie Française in soubrette rôles. I have not seen her as yet, but I have heard it said that she has talent, although in a lesser degree than Mlle. Dangeville, but that she is intelligent and has warmth; she is neither beautiful nor tall enough for the stage. Saurin who has seen her, tells me she is streets ahead of the Gauthiers and Beauménards. It seems to me she should take on fairly well."[13]

whilst the *Mercure de France* for March, 1755, commented:—

"The Comédiens Français gave on the 7th of the month *Le Tartuffe* and *Les Folies Amoureuses.* Mme Noverre, wife of M. Noverre of *Ballet Chinois* and *La Fontaine de Jouvence* fame, made her début in these two plays in which she takes the rôle of the soubrette. The public gave her a good reception."[13]

This Chinese ballet came at a time when there was a vogue for everything Chinese. Pagodas hung with bells and Chinese bridges made their appearance in formal gardens, Chinese silks and lacquers were eagerly sought after and purchased for fantastic prices and pigtailed Chinese were absorbed into French rococo art. Above all, Chinese porcelain was so highly esteemed that the first porcelain ware to be made in the West, in Saxony, was at first in imitation of the oriental.

Collé in his *Journal* for July, 1754, noted:—

"This month, all Paris has flocked to a Chinese ballet given at the Opéra Comique. I do not like ballets and my adversion to dancing has greatly increased since all the theatres have become infected with ballets; but I must admit that this Chinese ballet is unusual, and at least by its novelty and its picturesqueness it has earned a share of the applause it is given. This ballet has been designed by a certain Noverre, a young man of 27 or 28 years. He seems to have a wide and agreeable imagination for his profession. He is novel and prolific, varied and a painter. It is not by the *pas* and the *entrées* that he pleased, it is by the variegated and novel tableaux that he achieved this prodigious success. If there is anyone who can drag us out of the childhood in which we are still in the matter of ballets, it must be a man such as this Noverre. The Opéra should secure and pay well such talent; but for the very reason that they should do so, they will do nothing of the sort. . . ."[14]

Another contemporary spectator, J. des Boulmiers, has given a description of the ballet which caused such a stir:—

. . . "The stage represents in the first instance an avenue ending in terraces and steps leading to a palace on a height. This first scene changes and uncovers a public square decorated for a festival with, in the background, an amphitheatre on which are seated sixteen Chinese. By a quick change of positions, instead of the sixteen Chinese thirty-two are seen on the gradins going through a panto-mime. As the first group descend, sixteen further Chinese, both mandarins and slaves, come out of their habitations and make their way to the gradins. All these form eight rows of dancers who, rising and dipping in succession, imitate fairly well the billows of a stormy sea. All the Chinese, having descended, begin a character march. There are a mandarin borne in a rich palanquin by six white slaves, whilst two negroes draw a chariot on which a young Chinese woman is seated. They are preceded and followed by a host of Chinese playing various musical instruments customary in their country. This march concluded, the ballet begins and leaves nothing to be desired either in the diversity or in the neatness of the figures. It ends in a *contredanse* of thirty-two persons whose movements trace a prodigious number of new and perfectly designed attitudes, which form and dissolve with the greatest of ease. At the end of the *contredanse*, the Chinese return to their places on the amphitheatre which is transformed into a china cabinet. Thirty-two vases, which rise up, conceal from the eyes of the spectators the thirty-two Chinese one saw before. Mr. Monnet has neglected nothing which could further Mr. Noverre's rich imagination. He has employed in the various *genres* the most able artists. The sets are by Messrs. Guillet and Moulin, painters to the Royal Academy of Music. The costumes were made to the designs of Mr. Boquet."[14]

The Mercure de France, for Monday July 1st, noted that the ballet was mounted with extraordinary luxury and the August number reported that "the multitude flocked to see it with unprecedented furore".

There is in the Musée de Besançon a painting by François Boucher which may have been inspired by the ballet or have inspired the ballet, for the details of the costume are not unlike the designs by Boquet in the Musée de l'Opéra for a costume and a décor for a Chinese ballet, presumably the *Métamorphoses Chinoises*. Against a background of pagodas and exotic trees, on the left of the picture, a mandarin is seated on a raised dais, fanning himself in the shade of an awning of draped and tasselled silk, his robes falling in graceful folds about him, his right arm resting on a cushion. At his feet are a group of musicians, a girl playing a Chinese version of a Japanese koto which rests on her knees, a man crouched over three tomtoms, another beating a gong incrusted in a low stand. On the left a standing figure is discerned playing a long trumpet and, partly concealed by a large stone urn from which a wisp of incense curls lightly into the air, a man can be seen beating a suspended cymbal and another a triangle, whilst a girl is seated at a dulcimer or a harpsichord. In the right foreground, in sharp contrast to the reposing mandarin, four singing men, with linked arms upraised and one leg extended with the toe on the ground, dance round a fifth who wears a large hat of rough straw and has one leg tucked under him while the other is outstretched as in a gopak step.

The décor and costumes, from flowing robes and baggy trousers to shoes with curling toes and pigtailed coiffures, denote a careful study of such Chinese art as was available at the time and a surprising degree of realism when compared to the costumes then usual in ballets at the Opéra and other theatres, based on an eighteenth century version of the dress of a Roman officer with plumed headdress, tight-fitting skirted coat over breeches and buskins for the men, and an adaptation of contemporary court dress with low-cut bodice and panniered skirt for the women. Instead of the usual suite of conventional dances, loure, rigaudon or tambourin, sandwiched between the acts of an opera or play to be idly watched whilst visiting the boxes of one's friends, here was a full length dancing spectacle, commanding interest by its grouping, the pattern of its dances and the picturesqueness of its setting and costumes. There was perhaps nothing very profound in the theme but, for the first time, there was an integrated conception of décor, costumes, properties and movement, subordinated to the development of a stage picture, and people flocked to see a ballet as such, not the virtuoso in vogue.

The various musical instruments used are interesting also, for the triangle, cymbals and other instruments known under the collective heading "Turkish music" did not begin to be introduced into the orchestra much before the seventeen-eighties.[15] We have, alas, no means of ascertaining whether they were actually played or only used as stage properties.

On August 12th, 1754, Favart revived, at the Foire St. Laurent, his vaudeville in one act, Cythère Assiégée", with heroic ballets, but this

time, instead of being an unknown dancer making his début, Noverre·
was the choreographer of the military formations, attacks, etc.[16]

Noverre's next production *La Fontaine de Jouvence* was given on
September 17th, 1754.

"The scene is a garden at the bottom of which is a fountain into which Hebe,
surrounded by a troupe of young cherubs, is pouring the water which has the
power of rejuvenating. On either side, on the steps leading to the temple of
Love, are groups of shepherds and shepherdesses gallantly dressed. Each holds in
one hand a crook and in the other a garland of flowers and one supposes that they
have just recovered their youth. They show their gratitude to Cupid by an *entrée*
of crooks and garlands, followed by another of garlands alone. Two elderly men
and two aged women interrupt the shepherds and join in the games. They are
rebuffed. They sing a verse to pray Cupid to give them back their youth. They
go and drink at the fountain. Their garments of senility disappear with admirable
promptitude and precision and the four old people are metamorphosed of a
sudden into shepherds and shepherdesses who express their joy in song and dance.
Cupid arrives on the scene; he dances himself and then invites all the peoples of
the earth to come and share his favours. The shepherds dance and hardly have
they retired to the wings than they are replaced by the four quarters of the earth,
Europe represented by three Frenchmen, Asia by three Turkish women, Africa
by three negroes and America by three American women. After several individual *pas*, the negroes execute a *pas de trois* with very much pantomime. The
ballet ends with a general contredanse of thirty-two people made up of the
shepherds and shepherdesses and the inhabitants of the four parts of the earth."[17]

Whilst, from this description, this ballet would seem to be in
conception less revolutionary and more in line with the accepted taste
of the time, there is obviously a greater element of pantomime than
was usual and a greater coherence, as well as a definite theme.

Outstanding amongst the other ballets which Noverre created at
this time was *Les Rejouissances Flamandes*, which the Mercure de France
for September, 1755, described as a "pretty painting by Teniers". That
ardent diarist, Desboulmiers, describing the first performance on
August 11th, 1755, noted:—

"Here is the idea of the ballet. When the curtain goes up, the scene is a hamlet.
A hill forms the background sloping down to a big tree around which are set
a number of tables at which people are seated drinking. The two sides of the stage
are likewise taken up with tables and these are occupied by Flemish men and
women who drink and entertain themselves beneath the trellis. The richly dressed
and distinguished gathering of the lord of the manor and his family is in the
centre of the stage. Liveried servants serve them with drink. Whilst mine host
and hostess are serving, the peasants leave their tables to indulge in various games.
Some have themselves weighed, others tilt at a ring, whilst others play skittles.
A hurdy-gurdy player and a musette player cause them to leave their games and
call on them to dance. The ballet begins. After several individual and general

*entrées* the lord of the manor dances a *pas de quatre* with his family and then a minuet. The dances are interrupted by a private quarrel but soon all the men want to join in and all the women try to prevent them doing so. The local judge appears and restores the peace. The ballet ends on a general dance, drawn in a new and piquant manner and executed by a prodigious number of dancers without confusion or turmoil."[18]

If, from this brief description, we cannot glean the nature of the dancing or wherein lay the novelty of the patterns designed, we can get some idea of Noverre's compositions at this period of his career. The ballet opens with a mime-scene which breaks up into smaller characterized by-play, then the ballet proper begins and builds up, through a number of solos and dances by the full company, to the *pas de quatre* by the lord of the manor followed by a minuet. Then the brawl scene, which is pure mime, breaks up the ballet and leads into the finale. The element of mime is obviously much greater than was usual and there is virtually no *corps de ballet*, the development of the theme being carried forward by all the dancers whilst the choreographic pattern departs from the conventional. The theme is slender, but no more so than that of the last act of *Coppélia* or the first act of *Le Lac des Cygnes,* of which it is a forerunner, or even of many modern ballets such as Ashton's *Les Rendezvous* or *Patineurs.* It would seem also that he used a greater number of dancers than was the custom, at least sixty in the *Métamorphoses Chinoises* and thirty-two in *La Fontaine de Jouvence.*

# CHAPTER II

# Noverre and David Garrick

MEANWHILE, David Garrick, presumably on the recommendation of his friend Monnet, had instructed his banker, Mr. Selwin, to offer Noverre two hundred pounds to stage his *Métamorphoses Chinoises* at Drury Lane, but the offer is refused haughtily in a letter to Garrick dated September 21st, 1754:—

"Mr. Silvain has just communicated to me the letter you wrote him regarding me. The proposals which you make cannot be acceptable to me since I earn in Paris in five months two hundred and fifty golden louis without taking into account my students.

If you have a mind to have me in your theatre, I require, Sir, three hundred guinea sand a benefit, without deduction of any expenses, at which, since I know your superior talent bears the palm in your country, my own interest and the pleasure of the Nation have determined me to urge you to appear.

If my proposals are agreeable to you, we will make an agreement for one winter; if I suit you, we will then renew it. Please be so good as to ask about me, and you will see that I do not take advantage of the privilege of appealing to the public to ask you for more than I am worth.

In any case, Sir, this is my last word. Please be so good as to make up your mind because I do not wish to answer the proposals of the Bavarian Court before I know your latest intentions. I await your decision and I have the honour to be, with respect,

Sir, your most humble and most obedient servant,

Noverre.

I have my sister, who is a pretty dancer, for whom I ask one hundred guineas.[19] My address is in the Abbaye St. Germain des Près, Commune des Moines."

In the full flush of the success of his *Metamorphoses Chinoises,* with offers from the Bavarian Court, Noverre, who is living at the Abbaye St. Germain des Près[20] which was by the eighteenth century not merely a monastery devoted to meditation but the brilliant centre of literary culture in Paris, can afford to be high-handed with Garrick.

The negotiations are unhurried and the next letter to Garrick is not until January 10th, 1755:—

"I had the honour to see Mr. Silvain, who communicated to me the letter you wrote him with regard to me. Since the proposals I put to you seem to me to be

25

fair, I cannot reduce them in any way. I will, however, sacrifice my interest by paying the expenses of the benefit mentioned in your letter, not so much to fall in with the customs of your theatre as to give you a proof of my desire to work with you.

I will only bind myself for one season and, if my talents suit you, we will renew the agreement. My conduct in the matter should prove to you that my design is neither to mislead you nor to take advantage of the opinion you have of my capabilities.

Here, Sir, are the clauses of my agreement:—

Primo, three hundred and fifty guineas for my salary and the third benefit, that is to say immediately following the two first which you grant to your two leading actors and actresses.

2. That the play for my benefit will be one of my choice, and that you under-take to appear,[21] as you are so gracious as to promise me in your letter to M. Silvain, and further to overcome any other obstacle or difficulties which might delay or prejudice the said benefit.

3. One hundred guineas for my sister, who will undertake to dance solos, *pas de deux* etc. and even to appear in my ballets for the good of your spectacle, and you will supply her with all things necessary to her employ.

4. As for me, Sir, I will engage myself as *Maître des Ballets en chef* and to compose and have executed at your choice the ballets of invention of all *genres*, as I give them in Paris, procuring for myself (i.e. *you will procure for me*), however, the things necessary both for the execution and the embellishment of the said ballets.

I venture to hope, Sir, that you will be so good as not to tarry in giving me a definite decision through the channel of M. Silvain and, as soon as we have concluded (i.e. *our negotiations*), I will not fail to let you have all the explanations which can contribute to the good of your spectacle. I have the honour to be, Sir, with great esteem, your most humble servant,

Noverre."

Selwin advises Garrick to accept in a letter dated January 11th, 1755, from which it would seem that, whilst Noverre was prudently insisting that the engagement should, in the first instance, be restricted to one winter, when the Opéra Comique would be dark, Garrick had in mind a more permanent arrangement:—

"Nobody could be so fit to manage it as he is, if you could confide in his discretion, which I should, to judge from his countenance and manner of expressing himself. It seems he is of Lausanne and a Protestant[22] and not so much attached to this country, so that it would be possible to fix him with you, if you liked him and could make it worth his while. . . ."

Garrick must have replied promptly and have taken Selwin's advice and decided to trust Noverre with all the details of the purchases necessary for the staging of his ballets. The prudent Noverre, however, did not tie himself down beyond the one season and, on January 31st, he writes to Garrick enclosing the formal agreement:—

26

"You will find herewith my engagement. I would ask you to make an exact copy of it and send it to me by interval of post.

M. Silvain, who read to me your letter, determined me, by all the good he told me of you, not to worry about the time of my benefit and to trust in your equity. I trust, however, that I will not be the last, and that you will have some regard for the care and trouble I will take to earn for you many guineas.

I will undertake with great pleasure to have made all the costumes necessary for my ballets. My intention is to have one made in each character in linen or in taffeta; if this suits you they will serve as samples and will give you an indication of the price, so that you will know exactly what it will cost you to dress your ballet and the advantage you would have in having them made in Paris.

I will also look after all the instruments necessary to my Chinese ballet and the garlands and floral cradles for my *Fontaine de Jouvence*; in any case the transport will not be very heavy and, with a permit from your magistrates or from the French Ambassador, you will pay no dues; the thing seems to me all the easier to arrange inasmuch as this kind of effects are not negotiable and can do no harm to the merchants, the whole being for the use of your theatre. As to the assembly of your dance, you will have to instruct me as to the number of supernumeraries you have, so that I may engage those whom you lack and whom I need. The Foire St. Laurent, which is always well provided with dancing, will give me the opportunity of supplying to you good material all trained in my type of composition.

If you require a very good pantomime dancer, I will engage a good one for you; he is known as Monsieur de Laitre, and gives much pleasure in Paris by his lightness as much as by his vigour. Perhaps you will be good enough to advise me of your intentions in respect of all the articles concerning my letter.

Be assured, Sir, of my desire to know you and to give you some proofs of my zeal and my devotion to your interests. I trust that time will give me the opportunity of convincing you of my sentiments towards you and of the high esteem in which I have the honour to be . . ."

There follows the text of the agreement:—

"We the undersigned, Jean Georges Noverre of the one part and David Garrick of the other, are agreed as follows:—

that I, Noverre, undertake to go to London at my own expense on the fourteenth of October of the current year, to compose all the ballets of invention of the choice of the said Signor Garrick for the duration of the season, that is to say until the closing of his theatre and, if I am in a fit state to dance, I undertake to do so, and likewise to take with me my sister, as second *danseuse* and even, in case of need, to appear in ballets. Signor Garrick on his side undertakes to pay me for the duration of the season the sum of four hundred and fifty golden louis of France in equal portions from month to month, which will be paid to me, as I may desire, either in Paris by M. Silvain, banker, or in London by the said Signor Garrick. The aforementioned four hundred and fifty golden louis will serve as salary for my sister and I, that is to say three hundred and fifty guineas or golden louis of France for me, and one hundred louis for my sister; and further-more, the said Signor Garrick undertakes to grant me a benefit and to appear himself, on the understanding that I will pay the ordinary expenses of his theatre, and undertakes to supply me with all the things necessary for the use of his spectacle and the execution of my ballets. We desire that the present agreement made in duplicate between us at intervals of post, shall have as much force and value as if it were made before a notary, under penalty of one hundred golden louis for the first infringement; and to this end, we pledge as security for the present agreement all our personal and real estate, both now and in the future. If my accident should prevent my dancing this will in no way alter my engagement and I will be paid my salary in full for the composition of the ballets alone. In witness whereof we have signed the present engagement by interval of post. Paris, the fifth day of February, seventeen hundred and fifty-five.

J. G. Noverre."

It would seem from this that Noverre had met with some accident which was likely to prevent him from dancing and he did not in fact appear during the London season, nor can we find that he ever danced thereafter, so that it was probably some injury to knee or foot of the type, alas, all too frequent with dancers. In a further undated letter, which doubtless accompanied the contract, Noverre makes quite clear his reasons for refusing a longer engagement and, at the same time, punctiliously sets out certain, to him, essential prerequisites to a successful season:—

"I send you my contract and I flatter myself that you will send me one signed by you identical in all respects to the original. I have not put in the contract the following matter of the advances I might require to transport me to London, also I would ask you, Sir, in your reply to state that should I need money in Paris during the month of July or August next to arrange for my departure, Mr. Silvain will give me some in Paris.

I have likewise not put in the agreement that, before I can renew (*my agreement*) after this first season, we must know whether I will please in London and if the atmosphere of the country will be favourable to me, whether my talent will be sympathetic to the taste of the country and, in a word, whether I will suit.

Do not doubt, Sir, my anxiety if all succeeds as I hope, to join you. Integrity has always been my guide and we would not quarrel over questions of interest, for I would leave you entirely free to arrange my affairs as you thought best and even to leave them on the same footing as they are now, with the exception of my sister who, in increasing her talent, will increase in salary.

Mr. Silvain will have advised you of the necessity of our meeting (*illegible*) and mine. A journey after Easter seems necessary to me in order to advise you on the spot in your theatre. Also I am prepared to do (*i.e. make the journey*) if you think that it can be useful to you. . . .

P.S. I would be greatly obliged if you would decide at once regarding the journey at Easter because I am in receipt of proposals to go and spend two months at Lyons which I will not accept if you think my presence is necessary in London."

In other words he feels he should come to London to see the theatre where he is to stage his ballets and discuss details with Garrick, but he will thereby lose the benefit of two months' season at Lyons and perhaps Garrick can hardly do otherwise than offer to compensate him in some way. Furthermore, he will need money in advance to cover the cost of transport of himself and his colleagues when they come over for the season.

Once again, Garrick is inclined to haggle over terms and Noverre writes again on February 26th:—

"I received my engagement through M. Silvain who was good enough to read your letter to me. I thank you for the good opinion which you have of me and I venture to hope that time and (*one word illegible*) will prove, more than any words, my sentiments and my way of thinking.

You wish, Sir, that I should go to London, and I ardently desire to do so. M. Silvain offered me on your behalf twenty-five golden louis, but I doubt whether I can undertake this voyage with that sum. The pleasure which I would have of forwarding your acquaintance, and of cementing it, would cause me to close my eyes to the sacrifice I would make to you of my time, since I refuse to go and earn money in the provinces in the interval between the two fairs. You see, therefore, it would not be fair that I lose on both sides and that you must defray the costs of my journey.

I will leave Paris on April 1st and, as I will go by post, I count on arriving in London the 3 or 4. I beseech you to tell me whether you wish me to bring you the models of the various costumes which I will need for my ballets.

I count on arriving sufficiently early to see your spectacle and to remedy the things which you may lack and which may be necessary to me.

M. de Laitre is writing you by this same ordinary (*i.e. post*). He still pleases in Paris and I think he will greatly please in London. I judge by his anxiety to see that Town that he would come down somewhat on his interests. As I find myself entrusted with this negotiation I ask you to finalize it by a prompt decision on your side, so that I do not find myself in a position where I have to reproach myself . . ."

The terms having been agreed, Garrick now has sufficient confidence to write direct to Noverre, who is as eager in defence of his new employer's interests as he was of his own. His next letter, dated March 19th, notes with satisfaction the successful conclusion of the negotiations with de Laitre:—

"I have received the letter you were kind enough to write to me and I communicated it to M. de Laitre who accepted your offers. I am entrusted with his engagement and I have every reason to believe you will be satisfied with this acquisition. I will leave, despite all the affairs I have in Paris, on Sunday afternoon and will arrive on Tuesday morning at Calais, and Thursday in London, or at least I hope so. . . ."

On May 6th, the young French lawyer, Claude Pierre Patu, writes from Paris to his friend Garrick:—

"M. Noverre confided to me that which your letter had told me, and I was inclined to like this young man as soon as I knew you favoured him. I was not in a position personally to judge his talent. I was, in London, (*he had spent some weeks in London in November, 1754*) much more preoccupied with you and with your admirable Shakespeare than with the famous ballets with which our able dancer was enchanting Paris. I congratulate you on the strength of public opinion and the statements of all my personal friends, on the acquisition you have made for the coming season; he seems to me to be imbued with esteem for you and all that belongs to you. All the more reason why I should be his partisan. . . ."

Following his visit to London, Noverre writes on May 7th to confirm the various matters he has dealt with:—

"Although I have had no news from you, Sir, I write to acquaint you with what I have done and, since this letter refers to your affairs, I beg of you to answer me exactly under its various headings:

(1) I paid fifteen louis for your costumes and M. Silvain has the receipts from him who supplied them.

(2) I have seen the sketch for the four décors which will serve both for my Chinese ballet and for my Fontaine de Jouvence, but I would not take them because they seemed too costly; otherwise I found his drawings magnificent.

(3) M. Boquet, who is at the head of the fêtes at the court of France, seeing that I did not accept this proposition, made me another which I did not accept any more than the first one, not wishing to do anything which might not be agreeable and useful to you, this is the matter at issue.

(4) The Sieur Boquet wishes to undertake to go to London, to have executed his four décors and have made before his eyes all the costumes necessary to my ballets, have your theatre arranged without a chandelier and, finally, make it the most agreeable in London. He asks for this, for the journey and for his efforts and the supply of his drawings, one hundred and fifty louis, on the condition that you will supply him with workmen because his time is precious and he could only remain in London for six weeks.

(5) I have engaged three supernumeraries, good, amenable and who will not dishonour our nation; I am seeking for the three others.

(6) It is impossible to find supernumeraries for 40 louis; you know that woman is an expensive, if common, merchandise, and so I await your orders on this subject.

(7) I require a little girl to dance Cupid; I have found one who could appear, do you wish me to engage her?

(8) I saw, on the eve of my departure, twelve children whom M. Levier was making dance. I would ask you not to neglect them. I will need them and will make good use of them. I would like you to give them a master until my arrival, and your French supernumerary would be competent to teach them the steps necessary to the ballet.

(9) I have ordered the chenilles of gold as well as of silk and also the gauze and flowers which you require.

(10) I have no money to pay for all this.

(11) I need some for my own account and I would be greatly obliged to you

*Above, décor and right, costume for a Chinese Ballet by Simon Louis Boquet*
*Bibliothèque de l'Opéra, Paris.*

*Augustin Noverre* (1729-1805), *as a young man.   Portrait in
oils in the collection of Miss Josephine Diver.*

*Photo S. J. Brown, Norwich.*

if you would give instructions accordingly, for I am in difficulty with my affairs and M. Silvain will give me nothing unless he has orders more precise than those you have given me.

(12) I could not live in London without my wife, see if she can be of use to you for your pantomimes; she would dance in my ballets. What is the salary which you could pay her?

Answer me, Sir, under all these headings, and give me news of your health and that of Mrs. Garrick. I have been greatly grieved since my return. I lost two rings of sixty golden louis, which my wife had put on my watch chain without fastening the clasp, and I lost them on the way to M. Silvain's. I had the drum beaten and sent out notes and had posters put up, but in vain. However, one must console oneself and accept philosophically the accidents which befall us. . . ."

On the 17th Noverre writes again:—

"As the Foire St. Laurent does not end until October 8th, I cannot be in London before the 12th, so that it is absolutely essential that the décors, costumes and properties necessary for my ballets should be ready, because I will stage the first *divertissement* in four or five days' time. . . ."

Garrick must have given a favourable reply to most of these requests and perhaps made good the rings lost in his service, for, on the 24th, Noverre writes full of enthusiasm:—

"I received the charming letter you had the friendliness to write me. I am deeply appreciative of your tokens of esteem, your style is admirable and has the approbation of all the persons to whom I read your letter: in a word you are a divine man and all the artists and learned men of this country would like to have the good fortune of meeting you.

I saw Mr. Camus and I went to his house, for he was at the point of death. He begins to enjoy a slight convalescence but his zeal and the devotion he has to England have determined him to leave on Monday. I trust he will arrive safely for he is very weak and in no state to sustain any heavy fatigue. I gave him the works of Fagan and the Année Litéraire of Freron. I did not send you the same author's Letters on the various writings of the time until I knew whether his style appealed to you. I will be careful to bring you the following numbers of the Année Litéraire and to buy it as it comes out.

Mr. de MacMahon has taken charge of the remaining purchases which I made for you and for Mrs. Garrick, to whom I send my respects, as does my poor wife who nearly died of puerperal fever.

Now as to our business, Mr. Monnet, through his negligence, has just lost his *première danseuse* and has none. He has broken with him and so you must be good enough to find a good one, for I find it impossible to get one for you.

I close as postage is too expensive[24] and, furthermore, Messrs. Camus and MacMahon have been entrusted with two letters. Adieu, Sir, I wish you good health, I love you with all my soul and am attached to you as much as to myself. Do not doubt of the sincere sentiments of your honoured servant . . ."

31

C

The terms in which this letter is couched may surprise us today but were not unusual in the 18th century. Neither is it surprising that Noverre should have read Garrick's letter to his friends, for, at a time when newspapers were few, letters were often lengthy epistles and much thought went into their writing with the deliberate intention that they should be read and discussed in public.

From the fact that Mrs. Noverre had suffered from puerperal fever, it would seem that she had recently been with child, although we do not know of any addition to the family.

Patu, although jealous of this ripening friendship between Noverre and Garrick, has become an admirer of the dancer and his wife, for, on the 18th June, we find him writing Garrick:—

". . . You have entrusted Mr. Noverre with the purchase of books for you. I will confess that I am jealous of this favouritism and that I will not willingly suffer any trespass on the rights of my correspondence . . .

P.S. I reopen this boring epistle to thank you again for having secured for me the acquaintance of Mr. Noverre. I esteem all men who distinguish themselves by their probity and their talents in whatever art it may be. He asked me to supper a few days ago and would not let me be until I had given my word, all out of regard for you.

I am convinced that if his wife accompanies him to London, you will be charmed, as I was, by her grace and wit. He has asked me to say a word to you as to the price you want to pay for your supernumeraries. Forgive me if, at his request, I meddle in something which is hardly within the province of a man of letters. I do not believe, in all good faith, that it is possible for you to find supernumeraries at forty nor even at forty-five guineas: the good ones are expensive everywhere, the bad ones have here too many means. Furthermore, were there not three little trollops who were seen in London, engaged by Vaneschi at seventy-five guineas each and who decry that country to their friends as though all London was responsible for the grossness of the Italians with whom they lived, or the incivility of some bailiff. Mr. Noverre also begs me to tell you that he awaits with impatience the young lady whom you announce, and that you must doubt neither the zeal nor the care of his dear wife to show her Paris. I believe in this matter that I can vouch for their good will. I do not doubt for one moment that Miss Pritchard will find herself in very good hands with them. . . ."

When Miss Pritchard, the daughter of the actor, is actually in Paris, Patu is, however, not quite so happy and, on August 23rd, he writes:—

"I believe very sincerely that his daughter (*Pritchard's*) could not be in better hands for dancing and all that concerns corporal education . . . so that I have only been able to see her once or twice, and then it was not at Madame Noverre's but at the Opéra Comique where I went to dissipate my melancholia. Between ourselves, and without its going any further, I could have wished for her good that she were taken more often to our Comédie Française rather than to these miseries of Monnets. . . ."

Miss Pritchard probably returned to London with the Noverres, for on September 27th, Patu wrote to Garrick:—

"You will soon be enjoying the company of Mr. Noverre, for the season (*i.e. the Paris season*) is approaching its end. You will have reason, I hope, to be well satisfied with his care of Miss Pritchard and with the progress this young lady has made. These ladies sent an express letter to Passy (*a district of Paris in which Patu was resident*) to ask me to supper the next day. I was in despair, for I was expecting a company of seven persons . . ."

When Patu did finally go to supper he would seem to have been shaken by the passionate vehemence of Noverre, for, although he gives the ballet-master a letter for Garrick, he writes from Geneva on November 1st:—

"I wish Mr. Noverre every success vis-à-vis your (*one word illegible*), for he seems (between ourselves) to be somewhat sadly, not to say laughably, outraged with the Paris public. He has not been given a large number of students, his great reputation has not caused his liqueurs to be bought (who the devil would imagine that a dancing fellow would at the same time be a distiller!). These are his dreadful grievances and the really tragic causes of a scene of oaths, imprecations and fury, in the style of those of Orestes or of your good King Lear, which was the soul of a dinner to which he invited me 3 days before leaving France. I must confess, my friend, that this scene and so ardent a character gave me too much cause to fear for my situation, my humour and all that I owe to myself, for my ever to enter into any sort of *intimacy* with him. I warn you beforehand because, to be quite truthful, I accepted many courtesies for your sake and, in the sad obligation under which I find myself to reply to them somewhat coldly in future, I am well pleased that you should find here my real reasons. I cannot be suspected of any desire to do him an ill turn where you are concerned, since the young man is useful to you by the genius, the invention, the design, in a word all that concerns the dance, qualities which he possesses, it is said, to a very eminent degree, and there is only in my reproaches a question of a lack of savoir vivre.

Another matter which pained me is that they should have crammed the head of your amiable Miss Pritchard with a hundred little prejudices which are bred in the husband and wife concerning many things and especially our actors (*i.e. of the Comédie Française*). You do not know perhaps that Madame Noverre presented herself (*i.e. to become a member of the Comédie Française*) and was refused after a few trial weeks. The bitterness which she has conceived therefrom towards several members of the company seems most unjust to me. It was necessary to appeal to the public and this she could not succeed in doing. Failing talent for the stage, sweetness, graciousness, affability, all these things make a person amiable in private, but in the theatre this is not enough. Mlle. Clairon, despite anything Madame Noverre may say, is the most astonishing actress we have seen."

33

Noverre, therefore, would seem for a time to have added to his activities as a ballet-master the gentle art of distilling liqueurs, although we gather that no great success attended his efforts, financially speaking.

That Patu, who was, perhaps, not personally acquainted with many professional stage folk, should have been amazed at their open criticism and apparent bitterness towards their fellow-artists is something we can well understand, for, even today, artists have been known to refer to their colleagues in terms sometimes acidulous! Noverre himself was probably already angered at the failure of the authorities to offer him the position of ballet-master at the Opéra which was for so long the height of his ambition.

Patu would seem to have taken a kindlier view on further reflection, and also to have had no hesitation in making use of Noverre, for on November 28th he writes to Garrick and tells him he has asked Noverre to pay Garrick for certain books he has sent to him, and he continues:—

"I hope my friend that your friendship and good sense kept you from showing my last letter to Mr. Noverre, as I am not to forget this gentleman's politeness, the severe, the unfeigned description of his temper, is a thing I would by no means have him acquainted with."

In fact, so much importance does he attach to Garrick fully understanding this, that he breaks with his usual practice of writing in his native French and pens his letter in English.

Noverre's season was doomed to failure before it ever opened. It was the eve of the Seven Years War and the papers were filled with articles calculated to inflame the jingoism of the masses. *The London Evening Post* went so far as to report:—

"We are assured that the French are gathering together a great number of small craft at Boulogne, Calais and other Northern ports of France for a descent on England."

No sooner was it known that Garrick had engaged a company of dancers from France than, in the words of Arthur Murphy, actor and dramatist and an intimate friend of Garrick with whom he was acting at the time, "the scribblers, the small wits and the whole tribe of disappointed authors, declared war against the manager. In newspapers, essays, and paragraphs, they railed at an undertaking, calculated, they said, to maintain a gang of Frenchmen. The spirit of the inferior classes was roused and spread like wildfire through London and Westminster."[25]

The season at Drury Lane opened on Saturday, September 13th, and the programme for Monday, November 3rd, included "a new dance by Signor Baletti, Mr. Lauchéry, Mrs. Vernon and Miss Noverre", which was repeated without incident on the fourth and fifth. On the sixth and seventh there was given a dance called *The Lilliputian Sailors* with a cast including Miss Noverre.

Garrick, in the hope of averting the threatening catastrophe, applied to Lord Grafton, the Lord Chamberlain, requesting that he might have the honour of appearing before the King, George II, who had never seen him act, and, on Saturday, November 8th, the papers advertised for 6 p.m. that night, "By His Majesty's Command, The Fair Quaker of Deal with a new grand Entertainment of Dancing, called the Chinese Festival, composed by M. Noverre". The press also carried an announcement by Garrick:—

"Mr. Noverre, whose Entertainments of Dancing have been celebrated in almost all the Courts of Europe, exhibits this Evening his Chinese Festival, at the Theatre Royal in Drury Lane, in pursuance of a Contract made above a year ago with the Managers of the said Theatre: The Insinuation that at this Time, an extraordinary number of French Dancers are engaged, is groundless, there being at Drury Lane at present as few of that Nation, as any other Theatre now has, or perhaps ever had. Mr. Noverre and his Brothers are Swiss, of a Protestant family in the Canton of Berne, his Wife and her Sisters Germans: there are above sixty performers concerned in the Entertainment; more than forty of which are English, assisted only by a few French, (five Men and four Women) to complete the Ballet as usual. As the Intention of the Managers on this Occasion is to give Variety to the Entertainments of the Town; it is not doubted it will meet with the public Approbation."[26]

On the opening night the nobility, who had many connections in France and whose women folk, war or no war, would continue to receive from across the Channel a doll dressed in the latest fashions[27], flocked to the theatre to applaud and, since there were as yet no police, they carried a sword by their side. His Majesty's loyal poor on the other hand were, saving his presence, not going to let the hated French get away with this, and possibly too there were amongst them a goodly sprinkling of the footpads and pickpockets, lured by the scent of turmoil from the country lanes bordering on Tottenham Turnpike or the road leading to the village of Kensington.

A description of the scene is best given in the graphic terms of an article dated November 25th by an anonymous correspondent, perhaps Noverre himself, of the *Journal Etranger* for December, 1755:—

35

"I will satisfy, Sir, the curiosity you manifest to me to have an exact account of the disorders which have taken place in London over the ballets of the Sieur Noverre. He began by presenting his little sister for her first appearance in *La Provençale* with the young *Pietro*. They were both received with considerable applause. Next he gave a small ballet of six male dancers and six French *danseuses*, in which the Sieur Baletti junior and the Sieur Lauchery made their first appearance, the first in a mime scene, the second in *demi-caractère*. Both these dances and the ballet as a whole were received with pleasure, despite the fact that there were no English dancers.

On Saturday November 8th, the Fêtes Chinoises was given and the name of the author was billed. The manager of the theatre, the celebrated Garrick, had omitted nothing which could possibly be done to ensure the success of the Sieur Noverre. The sets were superb and the costumes magnificent. Ninety persons appeared in the march. The palankeen and the cars were richly decorated. All the wings were embellished with balconies filled with Chinese men and women spectators of the Fête. The *Corps de Ballet* were well composed and well grouped, the individual *pas* agreeably varied and the *contredanse*, danced by forty-eight persons, was executed with a precision and neatness unusual in *grands ballets;* finally these Fêtes Chinoises, which had such a brilliant success in Paris, were nothing compared to those in London, which cost two thousand Louis to produce. The King of England, attended by his entire court, honoured the first performance with his presence; the people received this Prince with as much joy as indecency; the comedy was given after which the ballet began. The applause started immediately and was continued until the end but was however broken by three or four piercing calls and as many voices from the gallery echoing the cry 'No French Dancers'. The Nobility and all honest folk shouted to throw them into the Pit and applauded the louder to drown the sound of the catcalls. The King left, well pleased with the Ballet and very ill pleased with the lack of respect of his people.

On Wednesday the 12th, the second performance was given. By three o'clock the auditorium was full. All the Nobility were there to contain the demonstration, now increased in strength and fomented partly by the minor English actors and dancers and partly by the management and staff of other theatres. When the curtain went up there was general applause and catcalls were forgotten for a few minutes, but the people paid to this end, who would have felt dishonest had they remained silent, created a frightful uproar. This was the signal. First a man was thrown into the Pit and another into the Stalls. All the My Lords leaped into the Pit, some with staves others sword in hand, and descended upon a group of demonstrators whom they covered with blows. The English Ladies, far from being afrighted by the horrible scuffle, gave a hand to the gallants that they might leap into the Pit and pointed out to them the people to be knocked out. A number of innocent people paid for the guilty. The outraged Nobility struck right and left regardless, breaking arms and heads, and blood was running everywhere; the ballet ceased until finally the Nobility turned out the mutilated rioters. The ballet began once more; all the spectators flourished their hats on high crying 'Huzza', a term of applause corresponding to the Italian 'Bravo'; the clapping was general and there were no more catcallers, they were all round at the surgeons.

On Thursday the 13th, the third performance was given and the house was fairly quiet. There were, however, a few hisses from the gallery. The Nobility went up there with the ordinary arms of the country, in other words sticks, distributed a few blows and brought the unruly to order. One of them, who attempted to resist, was cast down the stairs, rolled down the three flights, broke his skull and shattered all his limbs. It so happened that this man enjoyed an income of 600 golden sovereigns; he had disguised himself as a hooligan to create a disturbance; this unhappy business coupled with blows bestowed on the innocent served but to inflame and increase the cabal.

On the day of the fourth performance, Friday the 14th, the furious riff-raff took advantage of the absence of My Lords (it was the first sitting of Parliament) to wreak their revenge and booed the ballet at leisure; thus it was given to the sound of applause, shouts and hisses, for it was impossible to hear the music.

On Saturday the 15th, the ballet was given for the fifth time. There was no Parliament that day but the Italian Opera, supported in part by the Nobility, were opening their season and had attracted all the My Lords. The Blackguards (that is to say the rag-tag and bobtail of London) triumphed and made a horrible row; they tore up the benches and threw them into the Pit on the opposing party; they broke all the mirrors, the chandeliers, etc. and tried to climb onto the stage to massacre everybody; but, as there is a magnificent organization in this theatre, in three minutes all the décor had been removed, all the traps were ready to come into play to swallow up those who might venture up, all the wings were filled with men armed with sticks, swords, halberds, etc. and, behind the scenes, the great reservoir was ready to be opened to drown those who might fall on the stage itself. All the public called for Garrick who had very good reasons for not showing himself. His partner appeared and promised that the ballet would not be given again and the *Blackguards* retired well pleased. This scene lasted until midnight.

There is no theatre in London on Sundays but, by way of compensation, there are taverns which are much frequented. This revolt thronged them with customers and a number of tragic scenes were enacted between the two parties which, far from healing the trouble, envenomed it more and more.

On Monday the 17th, faith was kept with the public. A tragedy was played and the ballet was not given. At the commencement of the fifth act, all the Nobility in uniform interrupted the show and requested 'The Chinese Festival'. A goodly proportion of the audience were in their favour but the opposing faction, still small in numbers but still obstinate, shouted 'No French Dancers'. The Spectators were unanimous in calling for Garrick. At last he appeared. His position was delicate inasmuch as he had to be circumspect both with the Nobility and with the people. Everybody talked to him and he answered everybody. A thousand small details were gone into. He offered to cut out all the French dancers, to pay them and dismiss them, but this was not acceptable. Seeing that there was no means of reconciling the parties, he wanted to withdraw but the audience recalled him. The Nobility and their party wanted the ballet to be given the next day, that is to say on the Tuesday; the opposition did not want it until the Wednesday, undertaking that there would be no more row if they were granted this slight satisfaction. The Nobility made it a point of honour not to give way and loudly forbade Mr. Garrick to give this promise; the Public were equally obstinate and began shouting afresh. The My Lords leapt sword in hand into the Pit and drove out the most factious. As they had seized hold of a man, who was one of the leaders of the rabble, and were holding him suspended in the air to strangle him, Mr. Garrick cleared the orchestra and threw himself into the pit shouting:—'Gentlemen, do not hurt him, he is a friend of mine.' He was let go there and then and this incident proves the way of thinking of Mr. Garrick and the esteem in which he is held. The My Lords, who had carried the day, proposed as a compromise that if those who shouted 'Huzza' hat in hand were more numerous than those who said not a word, the ballet would be given on the Tuesday, and the proposal was accepted. The My Lords began and were imitated by all for when they turned towards somebody who was against, fear made him shamefacedly raise his hat. So it was decided that the ballet would be given.

Therefore the sixth performance of the ballet was given on Tuesday the 18th. By three o'clock the theatre was packed. The 'Blackguards' had turned out all the servants from the first row of boxes. The Nobility arrived at five o'clock in frock coats and with rapiers and loaded sticks of an enormous size. The rabble gave up their seats and, since all the Nobility of England were in the House and that there were not enough seats, several of them hid in the wings. It would be difficult to record all that happened before the show. Hissing and horrible cries, bawdy songs repeated *in chorus*, in fact if one can picture all the indignities which an inflamed crowd can be led to commit one will have some idea of this dreadful prelude. The music began, fresh demonstration. The 'Blackguards' demanded Roastbeef, a common tune but one which flatters them, and they sang all the choruses. The play was heard in comparative peace, then the overture to the ballet was played and the noise of boos and handbells was redoubled. The My Lords jumped from the Circle on to the stage the surface of which was covered with iron tacks, too small to be seen, which pierced their feet. One of them defied the public and received an apple in the face. Furious, he threw himself into the Pit followed by all the others. Broken arms, legs and heads, people half crushed under the benches, the Chinese dancers hiding in the corners, etc; such was the spectacle offered in an instant to the eyes. The refractory are evicted, the Pit empties itself completely, the My Lords return to the stage and stretch out a hand to those remaining in the Pit, who were of the party, so that these may climb up too and all seems appeased. However, as the My Lords rally the Chinese dispersed by their fear, the pit fills up with fresh combatants come down from the gallery. The ballet begins, the stage is covered with several bushels of peas mixed with tacks. The My Lords sweep the stage with their hats, fresh peas are thrown; the My Lords jump once more into the Pit, the doors of which are forced open by a troup of butchers who declare themselves for the Nobility hitting right and left at the demonstrators. Meanwhile two people had formed the plan of breaking down the door in a corridor, to gain access to the stage and take the My Lords in the rear, but the plot was discovered by a little girl. Ten or twelve stage-hands, warned in time, posted themselves in ambush by this door, let it be broken in and then fell furiously on the besiegers who, not expecting this manoeuvre, lost their heads and were belaboured unmercifully as the corridor being very narrow, they could only turn tail by falling over each other.

At the same time Mr. Garrick's own house was being besieged by the populace; all the windows were broken and, had it not been for a guard which was hastily despatched and expected to be massacred, the house would have been pulled down and set fire to.

The ballet was executed all the same, but without music. The triumphant Nobility indecently mocked the Pit. The show over, the riff-raff broke everything they could. The windows of the coaches were broken and a Milady thought to be stoned to death and had to take refuge with a merchant and spend part of the night there. The butchers, on the other hand, had taken up positions by the doors of the Pit and all who emerged, talking against the ballet, were soundly trounced. Finally, for the preservation of the inhabitants of London, the ballet has been withdrawn. It has occupied the whole town for a fortnight. Mr. Noverre and his family have had to go into hiding for fear of accidents. Had the Nobility and the honest folk taken up his interests with a little less ardour all might have passed peacefully over.

It would be too long to go into the platitudes which have been circulated in London on this occasion by way of songs, poems, lampoons, etc., etc. Imagination has been stretched so far as to print that the French dancers were officers and the *Maitre des Ballets*, Prince Edward."[28]

The pamphleteers added fuel to the flames. On November 15th there was published *The dancers damned or the Devil to Pay at the old House*[29], in which the writer, in an attempt to vindicate Garrick, represented the party who so violently opposed the staging of the Chinese Festival as a "blind, ignorant and tasteless mob, deaf to the voice of reason and determined on the riots they raised, rather for the sake of rioting than from a laudable principle of public spirit or generous resentment against the enemies of this country".

There was also a *Lettre de M. Voltaire au Peuple d'Angleterre sur les Ecarts qu'il a fait paraître, au sujet des Balladins Français* which, "by comparing the conduct of our ancestors with that of their sons on this occasion, endeavours to show us to the world in a despicable light". It subsequently turned out to be written by a certain Roger, a poor French scribbler who, having come over to London a year before with a letter of introduction to Garrick from his friend Patu, had failed to see him and hoped by this manner to ingratiate himself.[30]

Boquet's costly décors and machines were all destroyed in the riots and the damage to the theatre and accessories amounted to the considerable sum of four thousand pounds and effectively precluded any revival of the ballet. Had it not been for the generosity of Garrick, the entire Noverre family would have been in dire stress. As it was, they had to go into hiding, for, in the general mêlée, the Balletmaster's brother, Augustin, had run a man through with his sword and he would have received scant justice whilst anti-French feeling was at fever pitch, even though the man subsequently recovered.

Augustin Noverre ultimately settled in Norwich where he, and his descendants after him for several generations, taught the Norfolk nobility how to dance, a happening which is recorded in a rhyme until recently current in Norfolk,

> "Mr. Noverre came from France
> To teach the Natives how to dance."

and still to be found as a skipping tune in the East End of London as

> "Dancing Froggy came from France
> To teach the ladies how to dance."[31]

Noverre and his wife would seem to have remained in England for some time after the Chinese Festival riots, for, on February 13th, 1756, Patu writes complaining that he has no news from anybody and does not know whether or when Noverre is returning to Paris. Possibly the ballet-master continued to supervise the production of such dancing spectacles as were put on at Drury Lane where, after the play, it was customary to give a farce, harlequinade or spectacle of dancing. What is certain is that he used his time to record with his keen sense of observation and his analytical mind, every aspect of English life.

Nearly ten years later, in a letter to Voltaire on David Garrick, he explains that:—

> "the English deploy in their country seats the greatest magnificence and stay there as long as possible because they love the country, horses and hunting. I know several noblemen who have in their pay all the inhabitants of the village except a few tradesmen. At two o'clock a bell is rung; the tailor, the saddler, the surgeon, the apothecary, the barber, the carpenter, the locksmith, the coachmaker, etc., etc., shut their shops; they arrive at the castle where they are served with a very good dinner; at three o'clock each one returns home to take up his work again. At eight o'clock they return once more to the castle to sup."[32]

He takes a poor view of English pantomime, which he describes as "mean and disgusting", but English stage machines he regards highly:—

> "It is in the theatres of Paris and London that the best resources in this line (*i.e. stage machines*) are to be found. The English are ingenious; their theatrical machines are more simplified than ours; also the effects thereof are as quick as they are subtle. With them every part concerned with the working of the machines is highly finished and of great delicacy; the cleanliness, the neatness and the precision which they bring to the smallest parts can, without doubt, contribute 10 the speed and precision (*i.e. of the machines*). It is principally in their Pantomimes, a trivial style lacking in taste, devoid of interest and with low plots, that

the chef-d'oeuvres of the mechanism are unfolded. One may say that this Spectacle, which carried in its train enormous expense, is designed to appeal but to eyes which nothing can offend and that it would meet with but mediocre success on our Stage, where pleasantry is liked only where it is coupled with decency and is subtle and delicate and wants neither morals nor good taste."[33]

He was especially impressed with one particular piece of mechanism in the form of:—

"a funnel from the centre of which was projected a jet of water to a height of twelve feet, whilst from the sides arose eight further jets which, as they dropped into the shining waters of the pool, formed a kind of bell. Had all this remained immobile nothing would have astonished me; but these jets were endowed with a rapid and continuous motion. They were made of silvered gauze and the effect of water was given so as to create a real illusion."[33]

He offered, in vain, to buy "the ingenious machine" for twenty-five guineas.

His friendship and admiration for David Garrick ripens apace. He is present at some of Garrick's Sunday lunches in London where, remarks Noverre, the actor lived frugally and the guests were few, for most of the nobility did not keep house in London but, when in Town, ate at taverns leaving their family in the country. He has the run of Garrick's vast library where the chefs-d'oeuvre of French literature are side by side with the most learned English works. He goes also to the country house at Hampton where Garrick lives on a much larger scale with many servants, horses and dogs. At the bottom of the garden, from which it is separated by a road, is a large field and Noverre suggests that Garrick should have built a bridge of one single span, with at either end a gentle slope which will give an agreeable and varied view. Garrick adopts the idea with alacrity.

At Drury Lane he found "a large troupe of actors, singers, choruses, a large orchestra but a somewhat mediocre *corps de ballet*. Apart from this great assembly there were painters directed by the famous Lauterburg (or de Loutherburg), a modeller and an ingenious stage carpenter who was entrusted with the running of the scene docks and machine rooms. The wardrobe was all the larger inasmuch as all the actors and actresses were dressed from head to foot and therefore had no expenses in this connection."[32]

Noverre returned to London and Drury Lane for the season of 1756-7 against, it would seem, the advice of David Garrick, who may have felt that anti-French feeling ran too high, for hostilities between England and Prussia on the one side and France and Austria on the other had now openly begun.

His copy of the contract, under which he was to receive four hundred and fifty guineas for himself and his sister, is retained in London by Garrick's brother, possibly for fear it would create difficulties for the ballet-master if it were found in his possession in France.

Patu, writing to Garrick from Naples on the 15th November, envies the ballet-master for,

"if Noverre is now with you, and he was resolved to come to you, I find him fortunate indeed to be able to enjoy in freedom a conversation after which I sigh. Give him from me a thousand tokens of my friendship and tell him that I would be greatly obliged if he would act as your secretary when your business does not permit of your writing me. . . ."

Both Noverre and his wife succeeded in crossing the Channel but, although Noverre's sister is there for the opening of the Drury Lane season on September 18th, 1756, he himself does not appear until December 1st and, whilst he supervises the production of the ballet company, his name does not appear on the bills or in advertisements.

Some time towards the end of March, he petitions the Managers for permission to return to France. His letter, signed but undated and bearing no address, was preserved by Garrick:—

"I have communicated to my wife the kind proposals you were good enough to make to me this morning; she is as appreciative as I am of the interest you condescend to take in the state of my affairs and we are determined to avail of the permission you give us to leave, since the interest of my child would seem to depend on this voyage which we have fixed for the beginning of next week, provided, however, I am no longer of use to you.

I send you herewith, Sir, my proposals. I have not included the most important clause, that which is the most agreeable to me and which flatters above all my ambition, that which finally I beseech you not to forget (it is your friendship). I venture to say that I am worthy of it and that I would die in England if I were deprived of it for a single moment. You will not refuse me its continuation and be assured that no one in the world is more truly devoted to you than I am; I would be too happy if I could give you convincing proofs of the sentiments of esteem and friendship with which I will all my life . . ."

There follow the proposals for the settlement of Noverre's account:—

"(1) He petitions the Managers to permit him to leave in order to settle his affairs in Paris, provided, however, that he is no longer necessary to them this season.

(2) He begs that these Gentlemen, in the event of their accepting this proposal, will give orders to the Treasurer to make up his salary and that of Mrs. Noverre.

(3) He leaves it to the Managers to arrange his benefit as they will and whatever

they do will seem·right to him; he relies on their probity and their generosity of which he has had many proofs.

(4) As the Sieur Noverre has every reason to be pleased with the methods of the Managers, he would be delighted to renew his agreement for two seasons according to the old proposals which were made to him by the Managers and which he did not accept out of delicacy, wishing to make himself known first of all; he prays these gentlemen to let him have a reply in this matter so that he may arrange his affairs in consequence and dispose of his store.[34]"

Finally, he prays these gentlemen not to judge his talents by the poor sample he has given and he is mortified to have been of so little use to them and to have been unable to give them proofs of his zeal and goodwill.

There follow, on a separate sheet, details of his accounts. He has drawn to date two hundred and three pounds, ten shillings, including twenty-five pounds paid to his sister; he needs to clear up his affairs a further three hundred and thirty pounds, making a total of five hundred and thirty-three pounds, ten shillings. If he is paid in full the amount agreed for the season, and any deductions for his late arrival and premature departure are left until the following season, he is owed four hundred and seventy-two pounds, ten shillings, plus fifty-two pounds, ten shillings for his sister, a total of five hundred and twenty-five pounds, and he adds a postscript:—

"It would put him at ease if Mr. Garrick would do him the favour of paying him in full for this season, failing which he would be greatly embarrassed and quite unable to honour his engagements. The deduction (i.e., *for the unfulfilled remainder of his contract*) and the loss of his benefit would amount to something like one hundred and eighty pounds, so that, should Mr. Garrick refuse him this sum, it would be quite impossible for him to procure the necessary things (i.e., *for his journey*) and to have sufficient money to return to France."

Business, however, is business and Messrs. Garrick and Lacy, the joint managers of Drury Lane, cannot, as a matter of principle, pay an artist for a whole season when he leaves part of his contract unfulfilled. His contract provided for a payment of four hundred and fifty guineas for his sister and himself, calculated at the rate of fifty-two shillings and sixpence a night, but from this they deduct for his own absence forty shillings and tenpence a night for fifty-five nights, making a net amount of three hundred and sixty pounds, four shillings and two-pence, out of which he has already drawn two hundred and twenty-six pounds, six shillings and eight pence, leaving a balance due to him of one hundred and thirty-three pounds, seventeen shillings and sixpence.

They agree, however, to allow him his benefit performance and engage him for the following season.[35]

Noverre is in indifferent health and Madame Noverre feels that an unfair advantage has been taken of him and she leaves no doubt as to her feelings in the matter, in an undated letter to Garrick, sent from France presumably some time towards September, 1757.

Noverre's letters are couched in the flowing style affected in the eighteenth century and are written with a well-inked quill in a bold, if somewhat hasty, hand ending every word in a flourish. With the passing of the years the flourishes, if they do not disappear, are greatly attenuated and the lines become finer but the words are run into each other with little or no punctuation. His letters are those of an educated man and spelling mistakes are rare. His wife, however, writes in the cramped hand of one unused to the pen, and the syntax and spelling suggest a person expressing herself in an adopted tongue, or of little education.

She vents her spleen on Garrick's partner, Lacy, in four closely filled pages:—

"Having written you several letters which have remained unanswered, I am writing this to advise you that it is impossible for Mr. Noverre to join you this season and these are the reasons. Firstly his health does not permit of his travelling and since one is not paid when one is ill and he has already suffered the rigours of a law so unjust and which perhaps was only made for him, he must not again put himself in a position in which he will meet with a proceeding which you would certainly not have adopted had your partner Mr. Lecy (*sic*) been as right minded as you are.

Secondly, Sir, the present circumstances further determine me not to leave my husband. I want to travel with him and will not suffer him to expose himself in any way. Passports are absolutely refused and furthermore I feel that his talents would be a charge on you at the moment, that he would meet with public and private unpleasantness, that he would be obliged to bury his talent to be in safety and that it would be much more flattering for the management to enjoy his talent in time of calm; when the public will see everything with a tranquil eye and will applaud merit without considering from whence it comes. Thirdly, I think it would have been seemly that Mr. Noverre should have a copy of the undertaking you had him sign and that the undertaking be written in a language known to him and to me so that I could have taken note of it. I do not know, Sir, why you have not sent it to him. Your silence in this matter, and that which you have observed concerning the letters I have written to you, have made me think that perhaps circumstances have caused you to alter your sentiments and, as we have no (*one word illegible*) towards you, I prevented Mr. Noverre from leaving as, despite his poor health, he wished to join you. I will not conceal from you that I had him given orders so as to overcome his obstinacy; thus it will only be after receiving letters in your hand and an agreement, identical to the old one and

44

written in French, that I will make up my mind to go to London to settle there with my family if, however, it is your desire and your interests and mine can be reconciled.

You refused to my husband an agreement for six years. You would not engage me at a salary of 100 guineas. Truly, Sir, I cannot reconcile your friendship for us and your methods. They hardly agree with the philosophy to which I know you subscribe. My husband and I, however, are truly attached to you and we would, without regret, leave the advantageous lot which can be ours throughout France to exile ourselves, to settle near you despite all the troubles Mr. Noverre met with in England and especially the dire need in which he found himself of having to pledge his effects in order to live at a time when he had a good contract signed by you and Mr. Lecy.

He saw himself despised by the man he loves and esteems above all others in the world and he was with good reason sensitive to these methods, because he is used to consideration and is esteemed in his country as much as you are in yours.

It is regrettable that circumstances did not permit him to show all his talent and it is that perhaps, Sir, that led the management to treat him with such contempt.

The period of his illness was used to write a book on dancing and the theatre; he satisfied his inclination in praising your virtues and your talent. He gives you all the credit you so well deserve, and which all who know you owe to you, and if he has reason to complain of the sorrows and the losses he was made to suffer in England, he attributes them only to the complaisance which you have to have towards Mr. Lecy, who is a man devoid of taste and knowledge and who weighs everything in the light of his petty genius.

Finally, Sir, it will not be thought, if I have to hide it from the whole world, that you are so unjust in London as to humiliate a man of talent and take advantage of his illness to make him lose one hundred and fifty louis and his benefit. I would blush were I to complain, convinced as I am that you will be good enough to make good this loss, as to when I will come to London, it is up to you alone to settle us there or to keep us away for evermore; your reply will decide of my conduct and awaiting . . .

*femme* Noverre

P.S. You would greatly oblige me, Sir, by presenting my respects to Mrs. Garrick and assuring her of my devotion and my appreciation of her many kindnesses to me during my stay in London."

Just what were the orders which the irate Madame Noverre had had given to her husband to overcome his determination to cross the Channel, despite the fact that the two countries were at war and he would have to travel by clandestine means without a passport, we have no means of telling; were they doctor's orders or perhaps even those of the King's officers?

Her indignation at her talents not being considered worth a modest one hundred guineas and, above all, the fact that the contract was drawn up in English, a language which she could not understand (although presumably her husband could) is the crowning indignity, for how is she to know what is going on and she would not be a true French wife if she were not fully acquainted with her husband's affairs! She heaps coals of fire on Garrick's head with a promise that no one shall ever know just how shabbily her husband was dealt with.

None the less, through all this wounded feminine vanity, we glimpse a tale of very real hardship: the exuberant and ambitious ballet-master having to sell his clothes in order to live and yet, on his sickbed, working away at his book on dancing and the theatre in which he will praise the acting of Garrick.

Garrick's reply, undated but presumably written towards the end of 1757, of which we have a draft in English in his own hand and a translation into French, probably by another, is dignified and a little hurt:—

"Madam,

If I have been a little surpriz'd that I have not yet received a letter from Mr. Noverre, how much more am I that I have received one, and so extraordinary a one, from you, without Date, or even mention where you are!

You say you have wrote several Letters to me, without any Answer; this is still more astonishing; for I have not receiv'd a single line from France, since your Husband left us, with the name of Noverre to it before; and He himself makes mention in a Letter to his Brother, of his intention only of writing to me. How is this to be reconcil'd?—and what is the Subject of the Letter I am honour'd with from you?—a very lively and severe Remonstrance against the Injustice of the Managers (which you'll permit me to say is entirely Groundless) and not the least mention made of some other things, which I shou'd rather have expected from your Justice and your Delicacy.

I am almost convinc'd that Mr. Noverre cannot be privy to the Letter you have sent me; he wou'd never have permitted you to represent the Facts so partially and so injuriously.—But to Answer your Letter in Order and as briefly as I can.

You complain that the Managers oblig'd Mr. Noverre to forfeit part of his Salary for not attending his business—but sure nothing can be more equitable.— What, Madam, wou'd you have ye Managers pay for the Services of three months, what they are bound to pay only for nine? Is there Reason or Justice in this? Indispositions that keep the Performers from their Duty for two, three, four, or even five weeks, are always overlook'd; and I will venture to say that no Managers ever consider'd their Company with more Indulgence in these Particulars—but to convince you that this Law was not made on Purpose (as you hint) for Mr. Noverre; Mrs. Cibber, our first Actress, paid three hundred Pounds the same Season, by the consent of her own Lawyer, on Account of her inability to perform her Contract.—Besides, it was left to Mr. Noverre's own Option, whether he wou'd come to England or not, with a Promise from Us that his Agreement shou'd stand good for the next Year, and for the same Term. But he chose rather to come, contrary to my most friendly Advice, and the repeated Letters of his Brother.

*The Assembly Rooms, Norwich*
*Augustin Noverre taught in the left wing.*

D

*Francis Noverre
(1773 - 184?) Water
colour by I. B. Ladbrook
after the portrait by
Lovett, in the collection
of Miss Josephine Diver.
Photo S. J. Brown,
Norwich.*

*Frank Noverre
(1806–1878). Portrait in
oils in the collection of
Miss Josephine Diver. Photo
S. J. Brown, Norwich*

Mr. Noverre was not depriv'd of his Benefit; it did not, indeed, turn out equal to my Wishes and Expectations, for Mrs. Cibber falling sick disappointed the Public of their Entertainment, and tho' I play'd for him, and a capital character, The Weather and the change of the Play Hurt the House.—But was that my fault? or was my friendship less ardent or sincere; and does a Lady of Mrs. Noverre's understanding, judge and determine by Events? Besides, when I engag'd to perform a Character for his Benefit, I did not engage likewise that the Weather shou'd be favourable, and the House full—but I must say more— Mr. Noverre is the first Person that ever had a Benefit Play and was not in the Kingdom himself to take care of it.

As to the Necessity he was under of pawning his things for subsistence, I am amaz'd to see this Circumstance mention'd, for the very Moment that his Brother told me of it, I sent him Money to redeem his Things, and told him often that he shou'd never want for Money, if I had it, and he wou'd apply to me; and this, Madam, I said at a time when Mr. Noverre had in some measure forfeited his Engagement to Mr. Lacy and Myself.

The part of yr Letter which speaks of another Agreement, and that to be made in French, and for six years, with several other things equally Astonishing, appear to fall so severely upon your Husband that I cannot make an Answer to it.

The Contract he sign'd was given to him to consult his Friends upon, which he sign'd with the greatest Pleasure at that time, and which I thought wou'd have been the most substantial foundation for his future Interest and Happiness and which I am sorry to say he has lost by his most unaccountable irresolution.

My Brother, by his desire, kept his part of the Contract for him, which he will immediately deliver to Mr. Selwyn, as he little imagin'd that His probity too was to be call'd in Question with ye rest—As for myself, if you and Mr. Noverre will please to consider of my Behaviour and Friendship (notwithstanding my Losses and the disagreeable Oppositions I met with) I flatter myself you will think that I have not been well treated—there has been no act of Friendship or Kindness that I wou'd not have done, but as one of our Company, he was oblig'd to abide by our Rules and Laws, which were less severe upon Him than any of the Rest.

And what were my Motives to engage and fix Mr. Noverre in England? Why merely my great Regard for a Man of his Merit, and to do all in my Power, to promote and establish his Interest Here.—Don't imagine, Madam, that I engag'd him from lucrative views, for let me assure you, tho I am certain our Dances would be the better with Mr. Noverre than without him, yet I am as certain our Receipts will be the same in either Case.

As to the Excuse of waiting for more calm and undisturb'd times, Mr. Noverre is very sensible that all opposition was at an End, and that he met with the most unfeign'd Applause for the little he did for us, when he was here last winter; and at this time your Brother and Mr. De Latre are highly approv'd of, and their Names are in our Bills at large, every time they Dance.

As to Mr. Lacy, I must confess that he did not at first see Mr. Noverre's extraordinary Merit as I did; but is that any Reason you shou'd attack him so unmercifully while you remain indebted and engag'd to him?—This he shall never know from me, and I am sorry that it ever came from you.

I cannot possibly give you, Madam, any Answer to the last Paragraph of your Letter,—When Mr. Noverre pleases to write to the Managers, they will answer

him, and indeed I think in delicacy that he shou'd have written to 'em before.—
Tho' we honor the Ladies as much in England as in France, and I particularly
have the greatest Regard for you, yet Business of this Nature is always transacted
with the Husband, and by the Laws of our Country the Act and Deed of the
Wife, in such Cases pass for Nothing.

I am, Madam,

Yr most obedient

humble Servt

D. Garrick.

Mrs. Garrick returns her best Complts to You."

Madame Noverre's acknowledgment is dated from Lyons, January
18th, 1758, where the ballet-master was once more attached to the
local opera house, and is somewhat more conciliatory:—

"I received your letter ten days ago and Mr. Noverre will answer it as soon as
he returns, I expect him in twelve days time at the latest and I do not doubt he
will be anxious to reply under the various headings of your letter and give you
satisfaction on the various points in all that you say. As for me, Sir, I have never
doubted your courtesy and your chivalry; I know that you are the Anacreon of
England and the Roscius of your country; this is something I acknowledge in all
fairness and with pleasure.

You will however permit me to say that there is a certain singularity in wishing
to constrain opinions and that I did not imagine I was sinning in giving you mine
on Mr. Lecy. It is no fault of mine if he is not amiable. My little philosophy is
tender and allows my heart to have its every wish, yours is more severe because
it is more reasoned and more political; I hold mine from nature and yours is
perfected by learning and scholarship. . . ."

Noverre retained his admiration for Garrick, whose friendship he
valued throughout his life and whose praises he sang in his *Lettres sur
la Danse et sur les Ballets* and also in two letters to Voltaire dated
March 1765, which are in fact two lengthy essays in which he traces
a vivid portrait of the famous actor on the stage and in private life.[36]

Garrick never succeeded, however, in bringing about a reconciliation
with Lacy, whom the ballet-master persisted in regarding as a boor.
As late as 1765 Noverre writes to Garrick:—

"I thank you most sincerely for all the trouble you have taken to reconcile me
with Mr. Lacy. I am as appreciative of the assurances of your friendship and the
proofs of your esteem as I am indifferent to all the disobliging things which he
(*Mr. Lacy*) may think of me. I am in despair that you should have wearied
yourself in making approaches which have gone unheard. A man such as you,
Sir, should obtain everything but there are in this world certain species of people
who have no merit other than that of having gold and who, puffed with the pride
of seeing themselves in easy circumstances, impudently insult the benevolent
source which in enriching them washed them of the mire in which they were
plunged.

I am mortified to learn that your health is not fully restored; if the wishes of all those who love and esteem you, who worship your talents, were granted, you would enjoy health equal to your merit and for this reason would be equally immortal.

My attachment to you, Sir, invites me to urge you to cure yourself of this sensitiveness (source of both your good fortune and the ills and to which you give yourself too easily). You will correct this fault so harmful to your health, when you make use of your philosophy and, in casting your eyes on all that is unpleasant around you, you say to yourself, I see no Garrick in that direction.

You are returning to the stage and I congratulate your country; it was only deprived of your talent by (*one word illegible*) led on by caprice, jealousy and intrigue. She (*?your nation*) will cease to raise altars to you, the artist can find no better revenge over the caprice of the public than by delivering it wholly to its inconsequence.

Your fortune, your country house and the love which scholarly Europe bears you assure you of a tranquil vengeance if the apes, who try in vain to imitate you, should attack you or seek, by their low tricks, to divide the number of your admirers; look upon their intrigues with a philosophical eye; in thinking on what you are, you will feel what they are and you will give yourself weapons against injustice; all these counsels, Sir, are dictated by friendship. I fear your Nation as much as your sensitiveness and I trust you will be the dupe of neither the one nor the other.

You have a peculiar advantage which few men can claim to enjoy; you are the accomplished model of your art: you have frayed new paths which none other will be able to follow: you have given a new form to stage spectacles and your taste and genius, always inspired by the imitation of nature, have shaken the geniuses of the old declamation. You have established new principles and you have astonished your country; it is in vain that men will seek to imitate you; you will always be inimitable; you are one of these phenomena of which the centuries are sparing and to which Nature only gives birth with economy. Were we living in the days of fairies, I would be tempted to believe that the Muses and the Arts had presided at your birth and that they endowed you with their precious gifts to the envy of mankind; so, Sir, enjoy once more the pleasure of seeing yourself adored by your learned Nation. The air of your country, and especially that of your country house, will restore your health.

I end my much too long epistle by beseeching you to retain your sentiments towards me; I will ever glory in the fact that I have a place in your recollections and in the esteem of a man whom I honour, respect and admire. . . .

P.S. My homage, I pray you, to Mrs. Garrick, my wife is greatly appreciative of the honour of her kind wishes.

P.P.S. I am weary here as the unhappiest of men. Sorrow and misery keeps me company; would you speak to my brother and tell him that ingratitude (*two words elligible*)."[37]

# CHAPTER III

# The Second Lyons Period

WHEN Noverre left London about March, 1757, he returned to Lyons where the old converted squash court, known as the "Salle du Jeu de Paume de la Raquette", which had been the scene of his first choreographic efforts, had been replaced by a new opera house built by the municipality which, with its vast stage and splendid decorations, was the finest in France. The theatre, too, had at last found managerial stability under the actress Michelle Poncet, better known as Destouches, who married the singer Lobreau in 1759 and presided over the destinies of the theatre from 1752 to 1760.

During his stay in London and the months which have elapsed since, Noverre has had leisure in which to clarify his ideas and work out the principles which he incorporates in his *Lettres sur la Danse et sur les Ballets*. The acting of Garrick and his vivid mime have provided the stimulus which will finally shake the ballet-master out of the conventional mould and cause him to break with traditional forms. His ballets cease to be spectacles for the eyes alone, pleasing by their pattern and their colouring, to become eloquent paintings of the human passions, appealing to the heart.

*Les Caprices de Galathée* and *La Toilette de Vénus ou les Ruses de l'Amour*, his first works in the new style, create a sensation by the introduction of mime and the heightened drama of the various scenes.

News of his activity soon reaches the Paris papers and in November the *Affiches, Annonces et Avis divers de Paris* report:—

"We have been sent from Lyons, a description of two ballets composed by the Sieur Noverre, the celebrated artist in this *genre*. The first given in the theatre of that City on September 21st is entitled *Les Fêtes du Serail*, *Ballet sérieux Héroï-pantomime*. The other, entitled *L'Impromptu du Sentiment* was executed in the presence of Madame la Duchesse d'Aiguillon and Madame la Comtesse d'Egmont, on the occasion of the victory over the English of Monsieur le Duc d'Aiguillon off the coast of Brittany on the 11th of September."

"If the ballet is in its realization as it is painted in the programme it is without doubt one of the finest spectacles in this *genre* we have seen for a long time."

"*L'Impromptu du Sentiment* is described as 'a kind of poetic tableau of the second attempt by the English on the coast of Brittany' and of the good reception with which they met at the hands of the troops commanded by Monsieur le Duc d'Aiguillon. It is in the nature of a vaudeville of the time which draws its merit from the circumstances."[38]

The victory of the Duc d'Aiguillon, one of the few bright interludes in the Seven Years War so disastrous to France, was particularly pleasing to Madame de Pompadour, whose protégé the Duke was. In singing his praise, Noverre sought possibly not only the local support of Madame d'Aiguillon but also the patronage of the Royal Favourite, whose influence over the Arts was all-powerful.

Of *les Fêtes ou les Jalousies du Serail*, Noverre has left us a detailed description:—

"The stage represents in the foreground a part of the Seraglio; downstage is a peristyle embellished with cascades and fountains. Upstage an arbour in the form of a circular colonnade the intervals of which are crowned by garlands of flowers and embellished by fountains and groups of columns joined together in twos and threes. The décor merges at the back of the stage into a cascade which falls through several levels into an ornamental lake with, in the background a distant landscape. The women of the Seraglio, engaged in various pursuits followed by Turkish women, are lying on rich divans and on the tiled floor.

Superbly dressed white eunuchs and black eunuchs enter and proffer sherbet and coffee to the Sultanas whilst others hasten to present them with flowers, fruit and perfumes. One of the Sultanas, more concerned with herself than with her companions, refuses everything for a mirror which a slave brings to her. She admires herself complacently and arranges her gestures, attitudes and bearing. Her companions, jealous of her graces, endeavour to imitate her every movement and from this emerge several *entrées*, both general and single, which express only voluptuousness and the ardent desire which they all have to please their master.

To the charms of soft music and the murmur of the water in the fountains, succeeds a proud and well-marked air danced by mutes, black eunuchs and white eunuchs who herald the coming of the *great lord*.

He enters precipitately followed by his Aga, a crowd of janissaries, several Bostangis and four dwarfs. At this moment the eunuchs and the mutes drop to their knees, all the women bow their heads and the dwarfs proffer him baskets of flowers and fruit. He selects a bouquet and with one single gesture commands all the slaves to disappear.

The noble lord alone in the midst of his women seems uncertain as to the choice he should make. He walks round them with that air of indecision which a multiplicity of pleasing objects inspires. All the women strive to captivate his heart but it seems Zaïre and Zaïde must obtain his preference. He presents the bouquet to Zaïde but as she is about to take it, a glance from Zaïre delays his decision. He considers her, allows his gaze to wander afresh; he returns once more to Zaïde, but an enchanting smile from Zaïre finally decides him. He gives her the bouquet which she accepts with rapture. The other Sultanas express by their attitudes spite and jealousy. Zaïre now enjoys the confusion of her companions and the dejection of her rival. The Sultan, perceiving the impression his choice has made in the minds of the women of the seraglio and wishing to add to the triumph of Zaïre, orders Fatima, Zina and Zaïde to fasten on the favourite Sultana the bouquet he has bestowed on her. For all the alacrity with which they seem to respond to the Sultan's command, they obey reluctantly, and their movements betray spite and despair which they appear to stifle when they encounter their master's eye.

The Sultan dances a voluptuous *pas de deux* with Zaïre with whom he withdraws.

Zaïde, to whom the Noble Lord had seemed to offer the bouquet, abashed and despairing, gives herself up in an *entrée seule* to the most frightful rage and spite. She draws her dagger and wishes to end her life but her companions stay her arm and hasten to turn her from this barbarous design.

Zaïde is about to give way when Zaïre proudly reappears. Her presence reawakens the fury of her rival. She darts suddenly on Zaïre to deal her the blow she had destined for herself. Zaïre adroitly evades her, seizes the dagger and raises her arm to strike Zaïde. The women of the Seraglio break into two groups and each runs to one of the antagonists. Zaïde, disarmed, takes advantage of the moment when her enemy has her arm held to throw herself on the dagger which Zaïre carried at her side, intending to use it against her, but the Sultanas, watching over their well-being, ward off the blow. At this moment the eunuchs, roused by the noise, enter the Seraglio. They doubt their ability to restore the peace and they go out hurriedly to warn the Sultan. Meanwhile the Sultanas part and draw away the two rivals, who make incredible efforts to free themselves. They succeed but hardly are they free, than they furiously grip each other.

All the terrified women fly between them to stay their blows.

At this moment the frightened Sultan enters. The change which takes place on his arrival is highly dramatic. Pleasure and tenderness succeed there and then to grief and rage. Zaïre, far from complaining, shows, with a generosity common to lofty spirits, a serenity which reassures the Sultan and soothes the fear with which he was tormented of losing the object of his tenderness. This calm brings renewed joy in the Seraglio and the *noble lord* then permits the eunuchs to organize festivities for Zaïre. The dancing becomes general.

In a *pas de deux*, Zaïre and Zaïde are reconciled. The *noble lord* dances with them a *pas de trois* in which he still shows a marked preference for Zaïre.

The festivities are concluded with a *contre-danse noble*. The last figure presents a group disposed on a throne at the top of a tier of steps, composed of the women of the Seraglio, the *noble lord* and Zaïre and Zaïde who are seated at his side. This group is crowned by a large canopy of which the curtains are supported by slaves. The two sides of the stage present another group of Bostangis, white eunuchs, black eunuchs, mutes, janissaries and dwarfs prostrated at the foot of the *noble lord's* throne.

There, Sir, is a poor description of a series of scenes all of which really arouse interest. The moment when the *noble lord* makes up his mind, that when he leads away the favourite Sultana, the fight between the women, the group they form on the arrival of the Sultan, that sudden change, those contrasting feelings, that love of their own persons which all the women show and which they each express differently, are so many contrasts which I cannot make you feel. I am equally powerless in regard to the simultaneous scenes which I introduced in this ballet.

The pantomime is a shaft which the great passions unleash; it is a multitude of lightning flashes which rapidly succeed each other and the resulting pictures are of fire and last but an instant immediately to give place to others."[39]

Despite the condemnation of the armchair critics in Paris who, on the reading of the printed programme and without having seen the work on the stage, objected that Bostangis and Janissaries were introduced into the Seraglio whereas, the indignant ballet-master pointed out, in fact, they never penetrated into that part of the harem in which were the women, but were only introduced into the garden to give added pomp to the arrival of the Sultan. The ballet was an outstanding success; so successful, in fact, that when the *Metamorphoses Chinoises,* now renamed *Ballet Chinois,* was given, on a better stage than it had ever had before, it fell flat.[40]

Such indeed was the popularity of Noverre's work at Lyons that, three years after he had left the city to take up his appointment in Stuttgart, one of his successors, Jean Baptiste Hus,[41] could think of no better claim to fame than to announce: "The Lyons theatre will see revived the brilliant days of the celebrated Noverre. The ballets will come back into their own under the direction of the Sieur Hus already known and applauded in the capital . . .". Noverre too, in years to come, was to return again and again to stage revivals of his ballets.

His fame had now spread far beyond the frontiers of France, and Favart, in a letter dated January 24th, 1760, to Count Durazzo, whom he kept regularly informed on all matters artistic, wrote:—

"I do not doubt the ballets are perfectly designed and executed at Vienna, but as the Sieurs Noverre, Pitrot and Dehesse have distinguished themselves in France in this art which they have raised to the highest degree of perfection, I think an able composer could still enrich himself from their ideas. I will therefore also send you their programmes. . . ."[42]

If there had been criticism of the novel aspects of Noverre's ballets, it was nothing compared to the reactions to the *Lettres sur la Danse et sur les Ballets* when they appeared, at the end of December, 1759, in Stuttgart and Lyons, in an edition dedicated to Karl, Duke of Wurtemberg. In this book, which to this day remains one of the most remarkable treatises on dancing and ballet, Noverre expounded, in fifteen letters addressed to an unknown or imaginary correspondent, his ideas on every aspect of his art.

*Les Affiches de Lyon* gave up two columns to an enthusiastic review of the book concluding with:—

". . . it is certain that all who have seen him at work on the stage and rightly applauded him, will find it difficult after reading his *Lettres* to decide whether he carries out his ideas on the stage better than he describes them", and noted "The advice he gives to the children of Terpsichore is full of good sense and it is to be hoped that it will be followed. It would free the stage, as he himself remarks, of an immeasurable quantity of bad dancers, and poor *Maîtres de Ballets* and would enrich the forges and the shops of the artisans by a large number of workmen better employed in catering for the needs of society than they were in supplying its amusements and pleasures."[43]

These "bad dancers and poor ballet masters", imbued as they were with the old traditions and to many of whom any general acceptance of Noverre's ideas would have spelt ruin, since they were incapable of the degree of artistic expression which he demanded, could hardly fail to be violently critical of his work.

His critics even stooped to the suggestion that the *Lettres* were not the work of Noverre himself but that of Claude Bourgelat, son of a Lyons Magistrate and founder of the famous veterinary college in that city, whom Noverre held up to dancing masters as an example for his knowledge of anatomy and with whom he had, in all probability, often discussed this very subject.[44]

The *Affiches de Lyon*, for Wednesday, April 23rd, 1760, published an exchange of correspondence on the subject:—

"The letters of Mr. Noverre on Dancing and ballets have been generally appreciated; envy has however endeavoured to take from him the glory of being their author. The humour, the purity and the elegance which fills them, have induced some jealous people to spread the rumour that M. Bourgelat, who was nominated as censor of this work, had lent him his pen. But the honour of truth is involved and M. Bourgelat, who would not disdain to admit he was the author of these Letters, if such was really the case, is distressed to see reflected on himself a glory due to M. Noverre alone. To put a stop to all suspicions, he has sent us the letter from this celebrated *Maître de Ballets*, and the answer he has made thereto. We might add that most of these Letters were made by M. Noverre before our eyes, and that they passed through our hands before they were seen by M. Bourgelat; but in confounding the envious, they will cause the true Author to be recognized."

"Letter from M. Noverre to M. Bourgelat, Master of the Kings Horse Correspondent of the Royal Academy of Science of France, and censor of the work entitled *Lettres sur la Danse et sur les Ballets*:

Sir,

In despair at being unable to have the honour of making you my reverence, I am taking the course of writing to implore you to doubt neither my gratitude nor my respectful attachment to your person. Permit me, Sir, to assure you sometime of the sentiments which I have vowed towards you for life. I am going away, and I leave here fewer friends than persons eager to do me ill. These, to whom I give little account, make it known that you are the author of my letters. Perhaps they will be able to tell you that I am lacking in gratitude and that I deny the obligation under which I am to you. Far from forgetting it, Sir, I will publicize it everywhere, and my Letter will serve to confound my enemies, when you show them that I have expressed to you my sincere thanks for the excellent correction which you have made to my work. I regard anything it may have of agreeable as something which belongs to you, and I will never lay·claim to it except to offer it to you in most sincere homage.

I am, etc."

"Reply from M. Bourgelat to M. Noverre:

"Whatever may be, Sir, the honour which your enemies do me, I cannot be gratified by the opinion they have conceived of me at the expense of that which they should have of you. If no more is required to silence them than an authentic declaration on my part they will soon hold their tongues. I am not, and I would not know how to be, the Author of your Letters on Dancing. It is sufficient to consider the manner in which you have conceived in this work the different parts of your art to recognize the genius with which you are gifted and the luminous shafts to which only a great Master can attain. But amongst the number of readers, to whose criticism one becomes exposed in making public one's work, there are few capable of sane judgement and jealousy enlarges all too often the multitude of decisions pronounced through ignorance. The reading of your manuscript enlightened me on an infinite number of points which I had neither unravelled nor felt even though I admired your theatrical productions. It is only after being instructed by you that I was enabled to pick out, in the composition of your Ballets, beauties which that tact or that instinct known as taste, and which is not granted to all men, will not cause one to see unless it is assisted and supported by a certain background of principles and knowledge. I think that the sincere admission which I make here, Sir, will shelter you from the effects of the imputations of which you complain. Furthermore do not concern yourself with those persons who in vain have endeavoured or will endeavour to harm you; the surest way of triumphing over them and of being happy is to be sensitive only to the attachment of those who love you. You know, Sir, that which I have vowed to you, and with which . . ."

If his fellow dancing masters did not at once acclaim his work, it met with a gratifying reception from many of the leading writers and aesthetes. L'Abbé de Voisenon, poet and author friend of Voltaire, wrote to Noverre on February 10th, 1760:—

"M. Baletti gave to me, Sir, a copy of your *Lettres sur la Danse*. I find the title most modest. It is real poetics and many of our authors who make up plays but of much detail, would do well to read your book to learn how to make plans. It would be good that all ballet masters should have studied their art as you have done, Sir. They would see that any ballet is a genuine poem and so made that the deaf could imagine they were spectators of a comedy or a tragedy, but it requires your genius to treat the dance in this manner. They save themselves by *pas de deux* and *entrées seules* which have no logical sequence, nature or link; bad authors do the same, saving themselves with antitheses and tirades. I could wish that, having given us a book on the precepts of choreography,[157] you would come here to give us some examples. Your *Ballets Chinois,* your *Fontaine de Jouvence* are the cause of my seeing the others as *tours de force* and not as *tours d'esprit.*

I regard the gift of your work as a distinction which flatters me greatly. This favour makes me add to the admiration which I have for you, the gratitude and sincere esteem with which I have the honour to be . . ."

Neither the popularity of his ballets with the general public nor the letters of esteem he received from a literary elite could, however, compensate Noverre for the bitter attacks of his critics and the lack of any sign from the administration of the Académie Royale de Musique that they had appreciated the importance of his reforms. He determined to seek abroad a recognition denied him at home and accepted an invitation to go to the Court of Wurtemberg.

# CHAPTER IV

## *Stuttgart Period*

KARL EUGENE, Duke of Wurtemberg and Teck, Prince of Montbeliard and Seigneur of Heydenheim and Instingue, having dismissed his prime minister and divorced his wife was free to spend the taxes paid by his dutiful subjects and the subsidies received from France, for the services of an army of six thousand Wurtembergers, on the gratification of his love of the exotic and the beautiful.[45]

Through the halls of the Duke's fantastic castles moved the Janitor of the Chamber, a Swiss of immense stature attired in Turkish dress, and the ducal bodyguard of light cavalry, in green uniforms with red facings and gold trimmings, and hussars, in scarlet richly embroidered with gold, waited at table whilst picked men aged between thirty and forty, in red uniforms liberally enriched with silver, with red velvet sword-belts over one shoulder, and carrying halberds adorned with a large silver tassel, mounted guard. The Duke and his guests, princes and nobles from many lands, divided their time between hunting parties—three or four hundred of the finest horses in Europe filled the ducal stables—and reviews of the Wurtemberg troops commanded by an officer in the prime of life attired in a Hungarian uniform with a tiger skin over his shoulders and mounted on a superb charger. Priceless paintings and sculpture filled the castles and free instruction was given to all who could profit by it in an Academy of Fine Arts under the direction of the painter Guibal.

Above all, Karl Eugène loved and encouraged the theatre. Plays alternated with operas, ballets and concerts. Vast sums were spent to attract the finest artists Europe could offer and theatres were built, and pulled down again if the acoustics were not perfect.

The Opera House at Stuttgart was one of the finest in Europe. Some four thousand spectators could be seated in the stalls and in the three rows of boxes placed one above the other to form a vast amphitheatre of beautiful proportions with, in the centre, the ducal box, a chamber lined with mirrors. Several thousand chandeliers cast a scintillating illumination over the masses of flowers with which the auditorium was decorated.

The Opera House at Ludwigsburg was equally grandiose, whilst a third and smaller "Théâtre de la Solitude", part of a hunting lodge in the midst of a mountain forest near Graveneck, was used during the summer months.

The magnificent décors were the work of Innocenz Colomba and the illustrious Servandoni, one of the greatest scenic artists of his time, whilst Boquet, designer in chief to the King of France and the Paris Opéra, came every year to Stuttgart to create the rich costumes.

The operas were under the direction of Niccolo Jomelli, a Neapolitan of a size so immense that he could only move with difficulty who, engaged as Kapellmeister in 1758, remained for twenty years to compose his greatest works and rule over the orchestra of forty and more musicians.

Noverre was engaged as *Maître des Ballets* and his wife as *Comédienne* on the first of March, 1760, at a joint salary of five thousand florins, plus two hundred florins each for travelling expenses. Little attention had so far been paid to the ballet. The first ballet master, Michele del Agatha, appointed in 1758, had a company of but six *danseurs*, five *danseuses* and eight supernumeraries, whilst François Sauveterre, who succeeded him in 1759, fared little better.

Noverre at once proceeded to take stock and reorganize, promoting here, dismissing there and engaging new dancers. Gaetano Vestris paid a yearly visit to appear at the special festivities attendant on the Duke's birthday. His brother, Angiolo, was engaged as *danseur sérieux*. Jean Dauberval, who was in later years to prove himself so apt a disciple of Noverre, was the *premier danseur sérieux* from November, 1762, to Easter, 1764. Charles Le Picq was taken out of the *corps de ballet* to be specially instructed by Noverre as a *danseur sérieux*.

A number of the dancers who had been with Noverre in London and had been trained in his methods, such as Baletti, Delaitre, who lead the *corps de ballet* with Lépi, and the Pietros, father and son, were engaged to fill the ranks until, by 1764, he had a company of some fifty or sixty artists, including seven leading dancers and a *corps de ballet* of twenty-three men and twenty-one women. At the same time as the ballet company grew in importance, his personal fortune prospered and his joint salary, with his wife, was now eight thousand, eight hundred florins with one hundred florins for shoe money and free lodgings and stabling.[46] He now drove his carriage and pair and had his ballet copyist in attendance.

Jomelli had never taken much interest in the ballets between the acts of his operas, but now, although he continued to leave to others the composition of the ballet music, for which possibly he felt himself unsuited, the co-operation between *Kapellmeister* and *Maître des Ballets* became of the closest. The ballets were no longer treated as of secondary importance but formed a whole with the opera, which they strengthened and helped to carry forward. It is probable, even, that Noverre was called in to supervise the movement and grouping of the singers in the opera proper and that each new production was preceded by conversations between ballet-master and *Kapellmeister.*

The form which this co-operation assumed is evident from their first work together, Jomelli's opera *L'Olimpiade,* given for the Duke's birthday on February 11th, 1761, in which the pastoral setting of the first act, with the two loving couples constrained to change rôles and constantly changing in disposition, is paralleled in *Les Caprices de Galathée* which Noverre revived at the end of this act. In the second act of the opera, the hero, Migades, puts the ties of friendship above his passion for Aristia which is thereby broken whilst the ballet, a revival of *Rinaldo et Armida,* deals with the same conflict of emotion, with Rinaldo's sense of honour finally rising above his infatuation with Armida. The final act, in which Jomelli brings his opera to a conclusion with the betrothal of the faithful woman, Noverre followed with a new ballet, *Admete et Alceste,* in which he adopted the same theme.

Each of these ballets, although an entity complete unto itself, echoed as it were the emotional drama of the previous act of the opera. The spectator who, through the subordination of words and mime to music in the opera, had failed to grasp the *leitmotiv* saw it repeated and strengthened in the pantomimic ballet executed before his eyes.

For the purposeless medley of dances and music, which until now had divided the acts of opera, Noverre substituted a genuine danced drama in which everything was subordinated to the development of the theme and pure dance forms to dramatic expression, thus applying to opera ballet those principles which Gluck and Calzabigi were later to advocate for opera itself. How successful he was in putting these principles into practice is shown by the comments of a contemporary spectator, Joseph Uriot, librarian and official chronicler to the Duke, who noted:—

"in the last ballets the dancers have known how admirably to express in their movements all the passions. They are no longer strictly speaking dances, they are great happenings represented by movements of the body alone without the use of speech and yet they are very different from ordinary pantomimes . ."[47]

Later the same year Noverre created a heroic-pantomime-ballet, *Amors Sieg über die Kaltsinnigkeit*, interpolated in Jomelli's *Isola Disabitatta* and, the following year, Jomelli revived his opera, *Semiramide*, with two new ballets, *Psyche et l'Amour* and *La Mort d'Hercule*, both to music by Rodolphe, who again created for the latter an expressive score for a large orchestra.

The festivities surrounding the celebration of the Duke's birthday in 1763 were particularly brilliant and lasted fourteen days. They were fully chronicled, at the request of the Duke, by his librarian Joseph Uriot.[48]

The influx of visitors from other lands was such that they could not all be accommodated in the Palace and lodgings, often most exiguous, had to be found for many of them in the town.

The celebrations opened on February 11th, with an investiture, in the Chapter Hall of the Military Order of St. Charles, at which the Duke created two knights. Meanwhile a picked corps of infantry in three lines on one side and cavalry on the other had been drawn up in the great square outside the Castle where the Duke, preceded by fourteen adjutants and forty halberdiers of giant stature and followed by his pages and household dignitaries, reviewed them.

Changing his uniform for one even more gorgeous, the Duke then gave audience to his ministers from twelve to one, after which he showed himself to his people at a balcony whilst, on his instructions, money and food were distributed to the populace and the fountains ran with wine.

After dinner in the Knights' Chapter Hall, the Duke and his Court proceeded to the Opera House, where their entry was the signal for a concert of kettle drums and trumpets.

The opera was a new version of Jomelli's *Didone Abbandonata*,[49] in eighteen or twenty scenes, with scenery by Colomba and costumes by Boquet. To follow on the first act Noverre had composed, to a score by Rodolphe, *Médéa et Jason* which was to prove one of his most popular works and to be given again and again in the capitals of Europe.

The role of *Médée* was danced by Mlle. Nency who, according to Uriot, "apart from her amazing dancing talent succeeded in showing in her acting all the soul and the expression of that incomparable actor, the celebrated Garrick, in England, where this dancer, trained by Mr. Noverre, was born." Gaetano Vestris, who had come from Paris for the purpose, danced *Jason* whilst the part of *Créon* was taken by Angiolo Vestris.

The second ballet was *Orpheus und Eurydice,* for which Florian Deller, a violinist in the Court orchestra, composed a vivid and imaginative score in a free form. *Orpheus* was danced by Lépi and *Eurydice* by Mlle. Toscanini.

In the final ballet, *Der Sieg des Neptun,* to a book by Uriot and music by Deller, all the nine divinities of the sea were ordered by Neptune to crown the *divertissements* of this great day with dances.

On the second day, the Duke entertained two hundred of his guests to dinner at a great horseshoe table, magnificently decorated, after which they assisted at a ridotto which probably owed not a little to Noverre. The third day opened with attendance at Mass and in the evening there was a comedy followed by revivals of Noverre's *Psyche* and *La Mort d'Hercule.*

Jomelli's opera, with the ballets, was repeated on the fourth day and, on the fifth, there was a ball. On the sixth day, the company removed to Ludwigsburg. On the evening of the seventh day, after dinner in the Palais de la Magnificence, Cupid, who with Venus and other mythological figures had graced the festivities with songs and recitations, taking up his bow loosed an arrow at the wall which parted in twain to reveal a hall sixty-two feet by fifty-eight and forty feet high with, at the far end, a stage fifty-six feet long on which there was enacted Jomelli's pastoral, *Le Triomphe de l'Amour,* introduced by a ballet in which the fifteen-or sixteen-year-old Mlle. Toscanini junior made her first appearance in a *pas seul* and a *pas de trois.* The evening concluded with a display of fireworks which, despite several set pieces having become damp from the heavy rain which had set in, was worthy in every respect of so lavish a host as the Duke Karl Eugène.

On the eighth day, there was a performance of Voltaire's tragedy *Zayre,* followed by a Persian ballet by Noverre. The ninth day was devoted to the hunt with a concert in the evening and, on the tenth, Jomelli's opera was again repeated. On the eleventh day there was a ridotto, on the twelfth a concert, and on the thirteenth a revival of *Le Triomphe de l'Amour* and *Rinaldo et Armida.*

The festivities were concluded on the fourteenth day with a horse ballet in the great square at Stuttgart, led by the Duke himself in a costume of Turkish blue with trimmings and coat of flaming red embroidered in gold, with a hat to which the plumes were fastened by a diamond clasp, astride a magnificently caparisoned chestnut horse with a long tail and a white mane parted to fall on either side to its knees, and escorted by twelve halberdiers, halberd in hand, led by the two lord lieutenants in uniform of scarlet and silver.

Noverre considered creating a ballet drawn from the *Henriade* and, on September 1st, he wrote to Voltaire to ask his approval to certain alterations which he felt to be necessary to make it more suitable to interpretation in terms of dancing. He took the opportunity to enclose a copy of his *Lettres* and explain that he had left his homeland because of the refusal of the Directors of the Opéra to recognize his talents, even though he had offered his services free.

Although Voltaire gave his consent, the project was never realized, but this was the beginning of an exchange of correspondence in which Voltaire expressed his esteem for Noverre and his admiration of his work. Noverre, in 1765, sent at Voltaire's request a description of Garrick, in two long letters, real essays on the actor and life in England penned with the vivid prose and acute observation which characterized the dancer's writings.[36]

The last full scale opera to be given at the Stuttgart Opera House, which was afterwards to remain dark until 1775, was Jomelli's *Demofoonte* on February 11th, 1764,[50] a great favourite which was to remain in the repertoire until 1778. The ballets were *Der Tod des Lykomedes* and *Hypermnestra*.

In the autumn the construction of the new opera house at Ludwigsburg, where the operas were to be given in future, was begun but the burghers made representations to the Duke at the squandering of the finances of the Fatherland, to which he replied "What Fatherland? I am the Fatherland!"

The new opera house, which had a stage so large that it saw Mexico conquered with more soldiers than Cortes had in fact at his disposal and in extravaganzas whole regiments of horse could pass over it, opened on February 11th, 1765, with a revival of Jomelli's *Demofoonte*. Visitors to Ludwigsburg at this time included Voltaire, whilst Leopold Mozart with his young son, already a child prodigy, passed through in July on their way from Vienna to Paris.

The following year the work chosen for the ducal birthday celebrations was *Il Vologeso*, produced in a particularly lavish manner. The cast for the amphitheatre scene (Act I Sc. II) included no fewer than five hundred and forty-nine actors of whom seven were singers, eight pages, twenty-four counsellors, two hundred soldiers and three hundred and

*Marie Antoinette dancing in a court ballet at the Imperial Palace in Vienna. Painting by de Vinck, c. 1765, presented to Marie Antoinette by the Empress Maria Theresa on the completion of the Trianon where it is still to be seen. It suffered considerable damage from damp during the last war. Photo J. & R. Whitmann, Paris.*

*Chapter-heading 'Les Jalousies du Serail' designed by Simon Louis Boquet for an edition of collected programmes of Noverre's ballets in Leningrad. From a copy in the Bibliothèque de l'Opéra, Paris.*

ten "onlookers". The ballets were Noverre's *Das Fest des Hymenaüs* and *Der Raub der Proserpine*.

Shortly afterwards the Duke went, as was his wont, to the Carnival at Venice, taking Jomelli with him. During his absence public indignation at his lavish expenditure, which is said to have attained to three hundred thousand gulden in one year, on a theatre to which the people were often denied admission, and at the fact that so much of it went to foreign artists and producers, who sent it out of the country, whilst local artistes and artisans went in need, reached fever point and even the Duke's own musicians began to show signs of restlessness. On his return from Venice, the discontent of his subjects was made clear to him in no uncertain manner and, to retain his crown, he resolved to cut his expenditure, a resolution in which he was aided by his mistress, Franziska de Bernadin, later to become his consort as Countess of Hohenheim. Jomelli's opera-buffa, *Il Matrimonio per Concorso*, given at Ludwigsburg on November 4th, 1766, would seem to have been the last work produced for the Duke with the collaboration of Noverre.

Apart from the ballets specially created for the annual birthday celebrations, Noverre, in the course of his stay in Wurtemberg, must have revived a number of his earlier works in addition to many new creations on which we lack precise information.[51] During one of them, *Les Danaïdes*, it has been said the scene in which *Death, Parcae* and a number of spectres appeared, was so terrifying that a number of the audience, seized with a sudden terror, hastily left the theatre.

Another, *Diane et Endymion*, was imitated in Paris and caused Baron Grimm to write to his sovereign the King of Prussia:—

"This . . . was followed by a heroic pantomime, in three acts, *Diane et Endymion* in imitation of the ballets which M. Noverre creates for the fêtes of the Duke of Wurtemberg. I have also seen some in this Style, some very beautiful, at the Mannheim Court. These ballets have a completely different system from those of the French opera. One sees many fewer *pas* and symmetrical dances than gestures and groups. The two lines of dancers drawn up on either side of the stage are unknown. This ballroom-like arrangement can at the best take place only after the *dénouement* when all that is left is to end the play with a general divertissement. I have not yet been able to ascertain the effect of the ballet *Diane et Endymion* or whether they have conformed themselves to the general protocol of French opera or whether it has genuinely been designed following the principles of M. Noverre. What I do know is that, apart from the beauty of the décor, this style requires a delicious music. . . ."[52]

Noverre's contract at Stuttgart was formally terminated by decree of January 24th, 1767. There arose immediately a number of difficulties and misunderstandings out of his own engagement and his relations with the composer Deller and one of the dancers, Simonet. These are consigned in a report made by his minister to the Duke Karl Eugène and preserved in the Wurtemberg archives.[53]

Despite these difficulties, Noverre retained the esteem of the Stuttgart Court and negotiations for his return were started on a number of occasions but never came to fruition.

# CHAPTER V

## *Vienna Period*

On the termination of his Stuttgart contract, Noverre accepted an engagement as dancing master to the Imperial family and ballet master to the two great Viennese Theatres, the Burgtheater, often referred to as the "French Theatre" because French plays and operas were usually given there, and the Kärnthnertor, or German theatre. In the former capacity he gave dancing lessons to the young Marie Antoinette who was later to become his Royal Patron in France.

He found at Vienna an encouragement of the arts and a cultural life second only to that of Versailles. The Imperial Household and most of the noble families of the realm produced gifted amateur musicians and employed their own *Haus Kapellmeister*, and music played an important part at Court festivals.

The theatre in particular was still of great brilliance. For a number of years the general direction of the arts had fallen to Count Durazzo, a man of wide culture who had gathered around him many of the greatest artists of his time and especially had had the courage and the foresight to see and encourage genius in the embryo and to foster new trends and ideas.

In the field of music, light operas by Pergolesi, Paisiello, and Cimarosa and operas by Wagenseil, Jomelli, de Mayo, Scarlatti and, of course, Haydn were in the repertoire, whilst Hasse was resident in Vienna, where Gluck was preparing his musical revolution and creating some of his finest operas.

The ballet already enjoyed a solid tradition and considerable popularity, indeed Noverre's two immediate predecessors had both experimented with ballet-pantomimes.

Franz Hilverding, who had ruled over the destinies of the Viennese ballet until 1758 when he was sent by the Empress Maria Theresa as Ballet Master to the Empress Catherine of Russia, was possibly the first to attempt to introduce a greater element of expression into stage choreography. We have no precise details of his work but, from some of the themes he attempted such as Racine's *Britannicus* and Voltaire's *Alzire*, it is obvious he must have used a greater dramatic element than was usual in the stereotyped dances of the formal French classical ballet.

His pupil and assistant, Gasparo Angiolini, who succeeded him at the Burgtheater, created a number of ballets in which he sought to put into practice his ideas and possibly also those of Noverre, whose *Lettres* he must have read and whose work he had seen on a visit to Stuttgart. He was fortunate in working with Gluck and the librettist Ranieri Calzabigi, both of whom were endeavouring to widen the field of opera by the subordination of the purely musical development to the dramatic requirements of the theme. In particular, he arranged the dances in Gluck's *Orfeo* in 1762 and Gluck wrote the music for his ballet *Le Festin de Pierre*, based on Molière's comedy of *Don Juan*, in 1761. Following on the death of the Kaiser Franz I in 1765, the Burgtheater being closed for a time and the Empress having withdrawn from all diversions, Angiolini replaced Hilverding as Ballet Master at the Russian Imperial Theatres.

It was, however, with the coming of Noverre that the ballet attained its greatest brilliance. He arrived at the height of his creative powers and with a reputation already assured, as many testimonies of his success at Stuttgart had been brought back by eye-witnesses and, in addition, Gaetano Vestris had, on February 25th, 1767,[54] for his first appearance in Vienna since he had danced there as a young boy, revived at the Burgtheater Noverre's *Jason et Médée*. With Noverre had come many of his dancers and pupils from Stuttgart who were added to the well-trained company which he found awaiting him to make up a company of seventy-two, thirty-five at the Burgtheater and twenty-seven at the Kärnthnertor, with a total wage bill of forty-nine thousand, five hundred and nineteen gulden. Noverre himself was in receipt of one thousand, eight hundred dukats yearly and, in addition, he was allowed to give an annual ball for his benefit, as a reward for his services in the organization of Court dances, and this brought him in a further two thousand florins. Besides this, his private pupils amongst the nobility gave him a further six hundred dukats.

The orchestra of twenty-four musicians at the Burgtheater was directed by Josef Starzer, a well-known violinist who played an important part in Viennese musical life, whilst the thirty-four musicians at the Kärnthnertor came under the baton of Franz Aspelmayer, besides which seventy-eight artists were attached to the operatic side, twenty-two at the French theatre and thirty-six at the German.

Italian opera was given twice a week at the Burgtheater and once in the Stadttheater, and there were ballet performances every night, either to divide up the acts of the operas or the plays or in addition to these.

It was obviously impossible for one man to provide so great a repertoire and Caselli, Guglielmi and Rosay, who formed part of the company of dancers, were also entrusted with the creation of ballets.

Noverre's first production was for the betrothal of the Archduchess Maria Josepha to the King of Naples. The third and last day of the rejoicings, September 10th, 1767, was concluded by a dinner followed by a performance at the Burgtheater which included, in addition to a German comedy, a new machine and pantomime ballet by Noverre, *L'Apothéose d'Hercule*, with Gaetano Vestris, absent by royal leave from the Paris Opéra season. The Court, who attended in full pageantry, found the comedy dull and insipid but greatly applauded the ballet. The veteran Franz Hilverding, but recently returned from Russia, was also amongst the audience and it is regrettable we have no record of what he thought of it.

On December 26th the theatres reopened, after the forty hours of prayer at Court, with a performance at the Kärnthnertor of a new opera by Gluck, *Alceste,* which was deemed too lugubrious but was saved by the extraordinary applause which greeted a ballet by Noverre in the grotesque style with which it was concluded.

Noverre relates an amusing anecdote in connection with the choruses which Gluck had introduced for this revival:—

"The libretto was written in Italian and he had only been able to find a small number of singers in the town, so he had to make up the numbers with choristers from the cathedral. These choruses required action, movement, expression, gestures. It was asking the impossible for how can you move statues? Gluck, alive, impatient, is beyond himself, throws his wig on the ground, sings, gesticulates but all in vain, statues have ears and hear not, eyes and see not. I arrive on the scene and find this man of genius in the throes of that disorder born of despair and anger; he looks at me speechless then, breaking the silence, he says to me with certain energetic expressions which I do not repeat: Deliver me my friend from the sorry state I am in, for pity's sake give some movement to these automata; here is the action, be their model, I will be your interpreter. I asked him to have them sing but two verses at a time but having spent two whole hours in vain and used every means of expression, I said to Gluck that it was impossible to use these machines, that this would spoil everything and I advised him to give up the idea of choruses altogether. But I need them, he cried, I need them, I cannot do without them. His distress gave me an idea, I suggested he should break up the choruses and conceal them in the wings so that the public would not see them and I promised to replace them by the elite of my corps de ballet who would perform the gestures appropriate to the song and so dovetail the action that the public would believe that the moving figures were in fact the singers. Gluck nearly smothered me in his excess of joy; he found my project excellent and its realisation created the most perfect illusion."[55]

Noverre's ridottos and balls were the most brilliant Vienna had seen and, for the Carnival in January, 1768, he arranged a *contredanse* in which sixty *danseurs* and *danseuses* took part, which was so popular that it was repeated again and again on successive days and sometimes twice in an evening.

Despite the high esteem in which Noverre was held in Vienna and the great amount of money he earned, neither he nor his wife were really happy there. Perhaps the narrow and almost puritanical outlook of the Empress with her *police des moeurs* seemed oppressive to artists accustomed to the freedom of Stuttgart? What is certain is that their heart was still in Wurtemberg, and that they several times flirted with the idea of returning there is shown by the exchange of correspondence preserved in the Stuttgart archives.[56]

An unsigned copy of a letter from Stuttgart, dated October 28th, 1768, invites Noverre to come in time for the birthday celebrations and suggests the terms of his engagement can best be discussed on the spot but that Noverre can, if he wishes, send his proposals by return, bearing in mind that the Duke has considerably reduced his expenditure on the theatre. Noverre, in reply, confesses his pleasure at hearing that the Duke has not forgotten him and explains that he cannot come to him except with the certainty that his services are really required, and he could not in any case arrive in time for the ducal birthday festivities.

Another unsigned copy of a letter, dated January 4th, 1769, expresses the desire of the Duke to see a ballet by Noverre to conclude Jomelli's opera *Fetonte,* for which décors already in existence could be used. Noverre replies without delay, on January 7th, to say he cannot give a formal promise as, although he has permission from the Director of court entertainments to absent himself, the consent of their Imperial Majesties will be necessary as they have not yet made known their wishes regarding the Carnival and, furthermore, there is the question of the interruption of the lessons he has the honour to give to the Archduchess Marie Antoinette to be considered. In any case, if matters can be arranged, he will need money for the journey and perhaps the Duke will issue instructions for two hundred dukats for his travelling expenses to be put at his disposal. Alas! arrangements could not be completed in time and, since the two hundred dukats were not forthcoming, Noverre wrote, on January 22nd, regretting that it was now too late for him to obtain leave of absence in time for the Duke's birthday.[57]

On March 25th, 1770, he writes again to notify the Duke that his contract at Vienna will shortly expire. He could renew his lucrative engagement but offers his services to the Duke from October to March each year and intends to spend the remaining six months in his countryside of Lorraine,[58] where he would however be at the orders of the Duke if circumstances should arise such as would require his presence. His terms are six hundred dukats salary plus one hundred for the journey, and free lodging, wood, wine and forage, or a corresponding allowance in cash. As to his unsatisfied claims, he will forgo these but ventures to hope the Duke will have the generosity to bestow on him the honorary title of his Agent in Lorraine, together with a small pension payable during his lifetime and that of his wife should she survive him.

The Duke was favourably disposed and asked for further details, at the same time enquiring whether, since the allowance for lodging, wood, wine and forage had now been discontinued for all members of the company, Noverre would himself forgo it.

Noverre, replying on April 18th, points out that in Vienna he is in receipt of one thousand, eight hundred dukats salary, plus approximately six hundred from his pupils amongst the nobility and the presents he receives from the Court, and that he can renew his contract on the same terms, if he so desires. Lest it seem extraordinary that, despite this, he seeks an engagement elsewhere, he points out there is method in his madness. His savings enable him to put his freedom and his love of the countryside before pecuniary interests. He has been offered six months' leave every year from Vienna with a corresponding reduction in his salary, but this he has had to refuse because the journey to and from Lorraine would be too tiring for his wife. He had thought to give to the Duke a fresh proof of his devotion to his person by offering him his services at very modest terms and he is pained to see that His Serene Highness is so little anxious to have him at Court that he would cut out the allowances and lengthen the period for which he would be required to work for the sum proposed. Furthermore, he notices the Duke remains silent on the matter of the pension arising out of his claims, most of which are based on letters from His Serene Highness and therefore above contestation. He renews his offer on the same terms as before, but reducing his travelling expenses to twenty-five dukats for every journey, and he expresses his willingness to bind himself to ask for neither increase nor bonus so long as he might remain in the service of the Duke. He will, however, only engage himself for one year. The Duke's acceptance must be definite or he will have to accept one of the offers he has received from Vienna, Turin and also from a Court in the vicinity of Stuttgart.

The Duke having enquired through his Counsellor, Bhüler, the amount of the allowance required in lieu of food, wine, wood and forage, Noverre assumes an almost regal tone to reply on May 9th.

He would have thought it unnecessary for him to stipulate the amount of the allowance before negotiations were concluded, for was it not evident that he would have accepted whatever His Serene Highness decreed reasonable. All these delays would greatly prejudice him were he not in a position (he ventured to say) to be sought after. The Counsellor would remember that, on the strength of his letters, Noverre had made ready to start for Stuttgart to compose the ballets for the Duke's birthday when the instructions had been countermanded, and he had had to bear all the expenses connected with preparations for his departure. He could and should remain in Vienna and all his offers to enter the service of the Duke, from which he was dismissed like the least subaltern of his theatre, must be seen only in the light of his devotion to the person of His Serene Highness. Since it is insisted that he ask for that which should have been dictated by the Duke's generosity, he requires one thousand florins in lieu of lodging, wood, wine and forage.

Although His Serene Highness has remained silent on the question of his claims he believes him too just not to grant him in any case an indemnity such as will console him and be worthy not of the munificence but of the equity of a sovereign.

He adds in a postscript, designed perhaps to shame the Duke, that he has just received from "Madame la Dauphine" a present of six hundred dukats and his elder son has been placed in the Caroli Regiment, Her Imperial Majesty having presented Noverre with a lieutenant's commission for him.

Bhüler replies on May 21st. The Duke accepts the salary of three thousand florins for six months, fifteen dukats for each journey and one thousand florins allowance. He will not, however, agree to the request made in Noverre's last letter for an advance, payable in Vienna, of three hundred florins, as this was not stipulated in the conditions originally put forward.

It is on this comparatively minor point that the negotiations break down. In the absence of her husband, who is at Presburg directing the fêtes which Monsieur de Palfy is to offer next month to their Majesties,

Madame Noverre replies on June 2nd. She has forwarded Monsieur Bhüler's letter and will transmit her husband's reply which she should have within three days. She doubts, however, whether he will accept, because the three hundred dukats on account are essential to him to set up his son who, when they leave Vienna, will lose his powerful protectors and will therefore need money to make him independent. She feels sure His Serene Highness will remove this little difficulty, the more so as he will appreciate that they will need money for the journey and for their living expenses during the six months they will spend in the country. She will not hide the fact that she would be more than sorry if such a petty matter should cause her husband to renew his engagement in Vienna, a city which she does not like at all despite all the advantages and all the money her husband earns there, and she will do her best to persuade Mr. Noverre to await an answer to her letter. Let this answer not be a delaying one like the last or they would be forced to accept a contract at one thousand, eight hundred dukats which they are daily pressed to sign and which has been delayed only by the question of the leave of absence for which Mr. Noverre applied that morning. It has been agreed (*i.e. by the Director of Court Entertainments*) that it shall be of three months' duration and that she shall sign on behalf of her husband, but this she has refused to do. She trusts therefore Mr. Bhüler will second her desires by persuading the Duke to grant the payment on account, the more so as, knowing her husband's devotion to His Serene Highness, this lack of trust will offend him all the more. She begs him to assure the Duke that she will hold herself responsible in this matter.

On the sixth, Madame Noverre writes again enclosing a letter from her husband dated from Bude (?) the day before. He is desperately sorry that the refusal to grant him an advance deprives him of the pleasure of serving the Serene Duke for a second time. In other circumstances he would be more fortunate and such a bagatelle would not become a major difficulty. He could have wished that his means permitted him to do without this sum and await a fresh decision from His Serene Highness but he has for some time amused (?) the management by his delays and he cannot and must not further play (?) the Prince of Kaunitz or the Count of Koarij. Since he is uncertain as to the Duke's real wishes and since he is being pressed to conclude the matter, he will sign the contract offered to him in Vienna.

Madame Noverre, in her covering note, comments that her husband's answer is as she had foreseen, knowing the arrangements he had made and also that, with his susceptibility, he would feel the seeming distrust in the protracted negotiations. He has sent her his contract which she will give to Count Koarij, the new director. Her husband could not have continued the struggle (*with the Duke*) any longer without risk of losing once and for all the esteem and the consideration with which he is honoured by the nobility. She is as annoyed as anyone that the affair has failed because of a petty matter which was no favour but a custom which one can refuse but to subjects of doubtful honesty and unknown talent.

Throughout the correspondence we see Noverre's reluctance to renew his Viennese contract, above all perhaps because of his wife's dislike of the city and his obvious desire to return to the Wurtemberg Court where they were both so happy. At the same time he is no longer the little ballet master from the French provinces but the creator of works which have become the talk of Europe and whose services a royal Court, second only to that of Versailles, are anxious to retain. He is prepared to make some sacrifice in order to lead the life of his choice but, with memories of the unsettled claims arising from his previous sojourn in Stuttgart, he is unwilling to make a move until his terms have been accepted and embodied in a formal contract. The gift of a lieutenancy for his son, perhaps made with the design of keeping the parents in Vienna, created the need for a sum of money to set him up in style. That the Duke should have let so small a matter stand in the way of a happy conclusion to the negotiations may surprise us, but Noverre, except for a small concession in the matter of travelling expenses, had held out finally for the conditions set out in his first letter and His Serene Highness, obliged to take Noverre on his own terms, may have felt it a point of honour not to give way on a stipulation introduced half-way through the negotiations.

Meanwhile Noverre is actively engaged, producing ballets to Gluck's *Paride et Elena* and *Orpheus et Eurydice,* organizing masked balls and festivals and directing the theatre school he had created, in which a number of young children of both sexes are trained by the ballet-masters Frickman and Helvin and also given stage experience by small parts in the theatre ballets as well as in charity productions specially choreographed for them by Noverre himself.

He accompanies the Kaiser Joseph II to his camp at Neustadt and stages his *Diane et Endymion* before Frederick the Great. Coming out of the theatre, the Kaiser, catching sight of Noverre, turned to Frederick:—

" 'There is Noverre, the famous composer of ballets; he has been in Berlin I believe.' Noverre thereupon made a beautiful dancing-master bow. 'Ah I know him', said the King, 'we saw him at Berlin; he was very droll; mimicked all the world, especially our chief dancing women to make you split with laughing.' Noverre, ill content with this way of remembering him, made another beautiful third-position bow; and hoped possibly the King would say something further, and offer him the opportunity of a small revenge. 'Your ballets are beautiful', said the King to him. 'Your dancing girls have grace; but it is grace in a squattish form. I think you make them raise their shoulders and their arms too much. For, Monsieur Noverre, if you remember, our principal Dancing Girl at Berlin wasn't so.' 'That is why she was at Berlin, Sire', replied Noverre. (Satirically all he could.)"[59]

He is in Milan for the wedding festivities of the Archduke Ferdinand of Austria with Maria Ricciarda Beatrice of Modena on October 17th, 1771, for which there were performed Metastasio's festival opera *Ruggiero,* to music by Hasse, Noverre's *Les Fêtes et les Jalousies du Serail*[60] and *Roger et Bradamante,* and Abbate Parini's festival play *Ascanio in Alba* in two acts, set to music by the fifteen-year-old Mozart and linked by a ballet by Noverre.

Parini's opera was designed to further the royal union, which had not been consummated without difficulty, for the Princess, although of an amiable disposition, was far from beautiful and it was common knowledge that the Empress was not without misgivings as to whether she would meet with the favour of the Archduke. In the first act Venus, with an attendant chorus of genii and graces, descends from heaven with her grandson Ascanio and intimates her desire to unite him to Silvia, a lovely and virtuous nymph of this her beloved land, that they may found a new city with their progeny.

In the ballet which follows, the nymphs and Graces astonish the shepherds by changing the grove of the first scene into a splendid temple, the first building of the newly founded city.

The second act of the opera sees the meeting of Ascanio and Sylvia, to whom he has previously been revealed in a vision, and their final betrothal at the hands of Venus.

The arias of the opera are full of unmistakable allusions to the ducal couple and to Maria Theresa and, as in the operas of Jomelli, the ballet is an integral part of the whole and contributes to the unfolding of the theme.

Back in Vienna early in 1772 Noverre stages, at the beginning of March, a "Chinese Ball" as part of the court festivities. In June Prince Esterhazy gives a festival in honour of the French Ambassador extraordinary, Louis René Edouard, Prince of Rohan Guéménée, Cardinal Archbishop of Strasbourg, and for five days, from June 12th to 16th, banquets, masked balls, plays and operas in the castle, fireworks and folk dancing in the park, and hunting and shooting in the forest bear witness to a magnificence comparable to that of Versailles. Noverre is invited to stage his *Das Urteil des Paris,* created the previous summer in the Burgtheater, but the performance, although brilliantly successful, brings in its train a tragedy, for Mlle. Delphine, the "delight of Vienna" and Noverre's favourite pupil, catches a chill of which she died in Vienna on the 18th of June in her fifteenth year. Thus was the world deprived of a genius in embryo, for she was already acclaimed as the equal of any dancer in Vienna and, although she had been denied beauty, she had strength, speed and vivacity in her dancing and grace in her deportment and was equally successful in the heroic and the comic styles.[61] Her acting ability had been particularly praised in *Die Gerächte Agamemnon,* the first of the great dramatic ballets in several acts with which Noverre attained the full realization of his ideas and the peak of his choreographic achievements. This latter work, to a score by Aspelmayer, was followed by a sequel, *Iphigénie en Tauride,* and by *Apelles et Campaspe* by the same composer, and *Les Horaces et les Curiaces* and *Adéle de Ponthieu,* to scores by Starzer. They are epic tragedies in the heroic style of Racine and Corneille in which pantomime and strongly programmatic music combine with pageantry to provide an entertainment complete unto itself.

These ballets met with considerable success and greatly pleased the Empress so that, although the Imperial Theatres were not covering their expenses, with the result that at the end of February, 1772, the troupe of French Comedians was disbanded and the Burgtheater closed, the ballet was permitted to continue. Such indeed was the favour in which he was held that on one occasion he was called forth to be congratulated by the Empress, an honour only bestowed on one other artist, the actor Bergopzoomer.

His second contract expired at the end of 1774, but he remained in the service of the Imperial family, taking up an appointment in Milan at the Teatro Reggio Ducal, whither a number of dancers, including the darling of the Viennese public, Mlle. Vigano, followed him; which made it extremely difficult for his successor in Vienna, Angiolini.

Angiolini, who had returned from Russia in 1773 and had been producing ballets in Venice, Padua and Milan, had for some time been engaged in a bitter literary struggle with Noverre. In the forewords to his ballets *Le Festin de Pierre* (1761) and *Semiramide* (1765) he had set out at length his ideas on the dramatic possibilities inherent in the ballet as derived from the pantomime of the Ancients and rediscovered by his master, Hilverding. These ideas, he considered, Noverre had usurped for himself, a fact which he made known in pamphlets, circulated privately, in which he also attacked Noverre's use of lengthy programmes and his disregard of the rules of Aristotle and of the three unities.

Noverre retaliated by staging, in Vienna in 1773, a work satirizing the ballets of Angiolini and, in January, 1774, he openly quarrelled with Calzabigi, who was in fact the author of Angiolini's programme notes to *Le Festin de Pierre* and probably also of his other written attacks on Noverre.[62] This artistic fray, which seems to have caused a certain scandal, may have hastened the departure from Vienna of both Noverre and Calzabigi. The incensed Angiolini replied in his *Lettere al Sr. Noverre sugli Pantomimi, Riflessioni sopra l'uso de Programmi ne' Balli Pantomimi"*, published in Milan in 1773 for private circulation, but neither this nor his campaigning in Vienna did him any good, for, after the ballets of Noverre, his productions in Vienna found little favour and the Empress Maria Theresa writes to the Archduke Ferdinand on April 12th, 1774:—

"Angiolini treated us to two very bad ballets which were booed; I do not approve of this impertinence, perhaps the same thing will happen to Noverre in Milan."

On August 11th, she writes again:—

"I am well pleased that Noverre has been so successful in Milan; the contrary had been spread about here and it was said Angiolini was as much regretted in Milan as Noverre is here. The former is producing abominable ballets here and Madame gives herself the greatest airs. I cannot say that Noverre is as perfect in everything else; he is unbearable especially when he has had a little wine which frequently happens to him, but I find him unique in his art and his ability to get something out of the most indifferent material."[63]

Noverre brushes aside these attacks as he might flick a fly from his sleeve in his *Introduction to the Ballet des Horaces or little answer to great letters of the Sieur Angiolini:*—[64]

"Connoisseurs have always felt that tragedy should end on the fourth act as the fifth is without action. Corneille preferred to adhere to convention rather than adopt reasonable licence. It is absurd to claim that a subject which can provide but three acts of animated intrigue and action must be extended to its detriment to five acts. One should have the courage to break away from rules which are arbitrary. It is the nature of the subject which must determine its form and its length.

Doubtless the Ballet des Horaces et des Curiaces will be subjected to the criticism of the Sieur Angiolini and his petty oracles.[65] . . . They will say I have sinned against the rules of Aristotle and the three unities . . . I say the rules of Aristotle were not created for the Dance. . . .

Ballet being an imitative art can borrow in order to please, now the graces of the drama with its regular development, now the brilliant variety of the Poem. In any case as in all *genres*, it should paint and imitate, it should trace with accurate tints the sentiments and the passions and the affections of the soul. To succeed one must study nature, the artist must follow nature step by step and be capable of appreciating the signs which the soul expresses on the features and in the eyes; he must learn to calculate the effects of the passions, the impression which each one of them traces on the face and in the gestures; it is they who are the faithful interpreters: they reveal all inner feelings. A man who studies his fellow may often be misled by his speech but let him carefully observe his features, let him read in his eyes, watch his bearing, consider his gestures and he will find confirmation or formal denial of his speech."

He goes on to explain that the "Sieur Angiolini, whom I only know by sight" would seem to object to the fact that he did not strictly comply with all the rules and especially those of Aristotle:—

"Rules are excellent up to a certain point. It is with them as with principles in general. They must be known, followed, abandoned and then taken up again; it is the work of taste and genius; the urge of the moment, the instant need which must determine the manner of the Composer. The mercenary man by way of imitative art slavishly follows his subject ad nauseam: he is a greyhound whose prey always eludes him when he loses sight of it. Such a being is coldly regular and boringly methodical: he is continually chasing after fleeting and passing Beauties which his slow imagination can never fix.

Does one want to seize on the divine and harmonious shades of a beautiful sunrise? One must have in one's hands the varied brushes of the Graces; the facility of genius and the activity of an ardent imagination which, without stopping at small points of detail, takes in in a flash the united parts of the whole; if one reasons instead of doing, the cloud flees and is eclipsed, the luminous shades fade imperceptibly and the sombre veils of night envelope both the brilliant phenomenon and the obscure artist.

Woe betide those cold composers who cling tremblingly to these petty rules of their Art, they resemble those unfortunates who, to escape shipwreck, cling to a piece of cork; the imitative arts demand a certain daring which genius alone can give; taste must be the compass and I would say with one of our modern critics, that such boldness are the wings of the Fine Arts: but it often happens that imbecility gives them inverted wings which far from raising them to perfection drag them in the mire.

More, might I not apply to the strictly methodical composition of ballets that which Boileau says concerning the Ode?

Son stile impetueux souvent marche au hazard.
Chez elle un beau désordre est un effet de l'Art.
Loin ces rimeurs craintifs, dont l'esprit flegmatique
Garde dans ses fureurs un ordre didactique,
Qui, chantant d'un Héros les progrès éclatants,
Maigres historiens, suivent l'Ordre des temps.
Ils n'osent un moment perdre un sujet de vue, etc."

(Its impetuous style often proceeds haphazard,
With it a beautiful disorder is a manifestation of Art.
Far from those timid rhymers whose phlegmatic soul
Retains in their furies a didactic order,
Who, singing of a hero the shining progress,
Petty historians follow the order of time.
They dare not for one moment lose sight of a subject, etc.)

He goes on to deprecate Angiolini's criticism of his work, compares him to "one of those learned Doctors who, not knowing Greek, carry their Hypocrates in their pocket," and suggests he, Angiolini, may in the same way carry Horace.

He then defends the use of a programme as a means of outlining and fixing the aims of the composer which is what he has tried to do and, speaking of Angiolini, he states: "but I would have him know that whilst he was spelling out barbarous caricatures of dances from across the mountains, I was forming Dauberval, Asselin, Pantaloncini, Lolly, Nency . . . le Picq, Binetti, Rossi, Derossi, Vigano, Ablectscherin and many others besides who have carried my name and my ballets to Italy, Spain and Portugal." He states that Angiolini, when he came to Stuttgart, saw him composing and returned to Vienna where he shouted his praises . . . "he (*Angiolini*) then tried his hand for the first time in the tragic style (Semiramide) and my pupil Madame Trancosa, who for mime is the Ampuse of our century, endeavoured in vain to sustain this pantomime without dances."

As a parting shot he suggests Angiolini has been soured by failure and must fain have his letters circulated privately by underhand ways instead of coming out into the open.

Angiolini meets with so little favour that by the end of the year Noverre is invited by the Empress to return and, although he refuses, his ballets, to the mortification of Angiolini, are staged by one of his pupils, Gallet.

He was now at the very pinnacle of his fame and his works were becoming known throughout Europe. In Paris he had been made a member of the Académie de Danse[66] and Vestris had staged *Jason et*

*Médée* at the Opéra on December 11th, 1770, with the celebrated Guimard, who appeared in the third act as a shepherdess in a dress which at once became the rage of Paris.

Le Picq had gone with Binetti to Naples where he staged *Armide* in 1773 and *Orfeo ed Euridice* and *Adèle de Ponthieu* in 1774.[67] For the Carnival of 1776 *Les Horaces et les Curiaces* was given simultaneously in Milan by Noverre himself, in Naples by le Picq, in Vienna by Gallet and in Venice, where Noverre had also refused the offer of an engagement, by another of his pupils, Franchy.

News that the famous Noverre had left Vienna soon spread to London and David Garrick promptly started negotiations to secure his services for Drury Lane, through his old friend Monnet in Paris. On July 10th, 1775, Monnet writes to Garrick giving a list of books he is sending over by Noverre junior, who was on a visit to Paris, and adds:—

"You will see from the enclosed letter that the elder Noverre promises to give you preference over any other engagement. I was careful to make him see the advantages to him of joining your theatre but I do not know how you will settle the question of salary. . . ."

The handwriting of the enclosed letter from Noverre, dated July 3rd, 1775, has less flourishes than of yore but the sentences run one into another without stops or capitals as though the writer were even more impetuous and eager to get things done than ever. He assures Garrick of his devotion to him and gives his word that he will not enter into any definite engagement for the following year and suggests that he should keep Garrick informed of the dancers he has available. He goes on to ask Garrick to have him written to by somebody who "will put greater clarity and precision in his letters for my brother (although I love him with the greatest tenderness) always confuses me."[68] Nevertheless it is his brother Augustin who writes to him on September 26th.[68] He has seen Garrick who bids Noverre send contracts for three years, for himself and five dancers, and leaves it to him to fix their salaries as he is certain Noverre will settle all the details as well as he could himself. As soon as these contracts are to hand, Garrick will send his signed agreement. Augustin has been to see Drury Lane which has been transformed beyond recognition. The painting, the mouldings, the gilding are perfect, the auditorium has been lengthened and widened and the height increased in proportion. The columns supporting the boxes are beautifully varnished; in fact, it is a charming theatre and a credit to the artists and to Mr. Garrick.

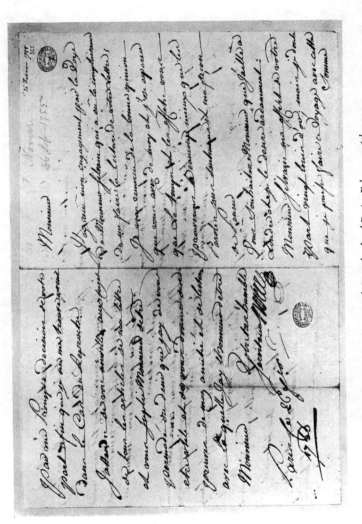

*Letter from Noverre to David Garrick, dated Paris, February 26th 1755.*
(From the Forster Collection, Victoria and Albert Museum, London).    Photograph S. J. Brown, Norwich.

*Augustin Noverre (1729 -1805) at the age of eighty.  Portrait in oils by Clover in the collection of Miss Josephine Diver.  Photo S. J. Brown, Norwich.*

Noverre, however, despite his very real friendship and admiration for Garrick, has not forgotten his previous misfortunes in London and is not prepared to return there until every detail has been settled and will not bind himself for a longer period than one year. He writes to Garrick, on December 8th, and makes it clear that he regards himself as engaged for the 1776 season. He would contract for life if he was sure of pleasing but "faced with the doubt which a becoming modesty inspires in him" he will only bind himself for one year and that on the condition that he has the good fortune to be successful. He is writing to Mr. Greville in detail and regrets that during the last two years talent, like all scarce merchandise, has gone up in price. He will do his best for Garrick to engage dancers at a lower figure provided they do not question him as to the cost of living in London, for he would then become the instrument of their poverty and this he would regard as dishonest.

He has shown Garrick's letter, "which is charming and in very good French, to the Archduke Ferdinand and the Archduke Maximilian who know Garrick as one knows Newton."[68]

On the same date he writes to Mr. Greville and points out that he can only succeed in London provided he is given dancers capable of carrying out his ideas. There is no doubt that the first year, and even the second, will be costly by the need to acquire dancers who are few and are becoming all the more expensive inasmuch as the best of them have left him, not to fly with their own wings but to follow in his tracks, for they have a devouring desire to compose; they indulge in slavish imitation of his work but they are earning money. He deplores the delays in settling the matter as, whereas a few months ago the dancers at Vienna were going begging, with the revival of his ballets there for the Carnival they are all engaged and their price has gone up in consequence; furthermore, the Paris Opéra is setting a very bad example by the prodigious salaries paid to dancers. By founding a school it will be possible in time to form good dancers. Garrick must look on the whole thing as a throw of the dice, if he (*Noverre*) is as successful there as he has been everywhere else, Drury Lane Theatre will be amply repaid and if he was not hopeful of success he would not risk going to London. He attaches a list with details of the salaries of the dancers he proposes to engage and who will enable him to stage every type of ballet, except the low and trivial for which he has not much use.[69]

He is not anxious to have anything to do with the payment of the dancers as he has always sought to avoid such business calculations which cannot be reconciled with his own occupations. If, however, Garrick will indicate what he is able to spend, he will do his best in consequence. As far as he is concerned, he will not discuss his salary but is happy to leave it to the discretion of Garrick, for "who can better appreciate talent than the god of all talent." Garrick can count on him and nothing but an order from the Empress, which is out of the question short of the marriage of the Emperor, could oblige him to return to Vienna.

He would be happy to place his son for the composition and arrangement of the music of his ballets as well as for his own rehearsals. As he will only be in Milan for two more months, any engagement must be made before he leaves. He will spend the spring and summer in Paris and could make a trip to London to make final arrangements for the staging of his ballets with Garrick.

In Vienna, meanwhile, it had been decided to disband the ballet and the Italian opera and close the Kärnthnertor Theater, the Burgtheater becoming the *Hof* and National Theater. Noverre, who had always befriended the humble members of the *corps de ballet* by whom he was held in veneration for the added interest they had found in his ballets, offered to take over the ballet company for two months to give the artists time to find other engagements. He undertook to pay all expenses and, with the consent of the Emperor, he opened at the Brunnerhof Theater on April 17th. Thirty-two operas by Gossec, Monsigny, Grétry, Philidor, Hiller, Wolf, Gluck, Bickler, Holly and Baumgartner, and forty-nine ballets were given during the season, which ended on June 17th, and, although the singing left much to be desired, so many flocked to the ballets that the Burgtheater was deserted. At the conclusion of the season, Noverre had detailed accounts printed and distributed free to the public with a foreword in which he stated:—

"Thus I took upon myself the sour and troublesome office which humanity imposed on me. I did not omit to follow all those precautions which prudence and honour prescribed to protect myself from all attacks which ingratitude and calumny might invent to sully the brightness of a good deed. For this reason I had my accounts examined by a notary and a merchant in the presence of the leading dancers and I had them signed and printed and left them in the hands of the said notary so that in case of need they might be open to inspection: on the one hand I thereby showed the public a picture of their generosity and on the other I made them acquainted with the manner in which I had made use of the funds provided by their support. One can thus convince oneself from the whole calculation of the expenses of my ballets, of the exaggeration fanned by hatred which has led to their being termed high, and one can see the return they have produced in a season supported only by a moderate spectacle. Thus will one be able to judge the revenue they would have produced in a fashionable season in conjunction with a good company of artists capable of winning and retaining the taste of the Nation.

One will find in these accounts no portion which concerns me. Philanthropy and a particular inclination for Vienna had guided my steps and I am amply rewarded if I take with me the sympathy, esteem and commendation of the whole nation."

For the prodigious activity which such a programme must have involved, Noverre had not taken a florin, but the company of dancers staged a performance in his honour and for his benefit and the Kaiser honoured him by the appointment of Honorary Dancing Master to his Person. Thus he left for Paris surrounded by the honour and esteem of the capital which had been the scene of his greatest triumphs, and perhaps in the bitter years to come he sometimes looked back regretfully at that Vienna he had been so anxious to leave.

# CHAPTER VI

## Paris Period

HIS work in Vienna finished, Noverre made his way to Paris. His erstwhile pupil, Marie Antoinette, had but a short while before acceded to the throne and was at the height of her popularity. She had extended her patronage to the arts, of which Paris had, since the reign of Louis XIV, been the centre, and especially she encouraged music which in a short time attained to a perfection it had never before reached in France.

Amongst all her playing with exaggerated fashions, Marie Antoinette always found time to make a constant study of music and La Garde, the composer of the opera *Eglé*, was her singing master. Piccini and Sacchini were attracted to Paris in turn and were treated with the greatest distinction at Court, whilst, immediately on his arrival, Gluck was admitted to the Queen's toilet and she talked to him of his work the whole time he was with her.

She also took great interest and often participated in private theatricals. In the little journeys to Choisy performances of grand opera and French and Italian comedy often took place twice or three times in a day. At eleven at night parodies would be staged by the best artists from the Opéra in whimsical parts and costumes. The celebrated dancer, Guimard, was the leading spirit and, whilst she danced better than she acted, her excessive thinness and her hoarse voice added to the burlesque in her parodies of *Ernelinde* or *Iphigénie*.

Noverre, who came to the French Court with recommendations from the Empress Maria Theresa, was at once honoured by being given the entry to the Queen's toilet and his son, Antoine, was given an appointment as Comptroller of the Royal Farms and with it, the Barony of Séricourt. Soon rumours began to circulate that Noverre was to be offered the direction of the ballets at the Paris Opéra, in succession to Gaetano Vestris who had resigned. On August 14th, 1776, de Bachaumont noted in his diary:—

"Furthermore, there has just arrived a reinforcement which can be of the greatest value to this spectacle (i.e. *the Opéra*); it is the famous Noverre. Everyone knows the talent for pantomime of this ballet master; they are trying to get him to settle in Paris but he is presently attached to the Viennese Court where he is highly successful and it would seem difficult to draw him away."[70]

82

The post of ballet master at the Paris Opéra, which was the highest to which one of his profession could aspire and one to which he had unsuccessfully laid claim two decades before, could not fail to appeal to Noverre, who abandoned all the more readily his plan to proceed to London in that his friend and patron, Garrick, had finally retired from the stage and the active management of Drury Lane in June of that year.

The Académie Royale de Musique had, because of the heavy deficits incurred during the administration of the Municipality of Paris, been placed under the direction of Papillon de la Ferté, Comptroller of the King's Pleasures, who viewed with some misgivings, which were soon to prove only too justified, the projected appointment. He addressed to the Minister responsible for the King's Household, Amelot, a memorandum setting out at length the stipulations which he felt should be laid down as a condition of Noverre's engagement if this should be finally decided upon:—

"(1) That the Sieurs Gardel and Dauberval, being the reversionaries and having even had their assistants, will enjoy the same privileges in this matter as they did as assistants to the Sieur Vestris, it being of course understood that they will nevertheless help the Sieur Noverre whenever he might so request.

(2) That, although the Sieur Noverre will have as reversionaries and assistants the said Sieurs Gardel and Dauberval, he will none the less be obliged to create the ordinary ballets attached to the works which will be given and he will not be dispensed from creating in each work at any rate the major part of the ballets.

(3) He will accept to present to the Management, when each opera is staged, a very detailed plan of all the ballets to be composed by him and by his assistants, the said plan to be agreed with the General Manager and the inspectors-general and in which he will specify the number of *premiers danseurs* and *danseuses* and of understudies and supernumeraries to be employed in each act, with their names. The Management will have to be satisfied, if and when the *Maître des Ballets* employs assistants, that he gives them the means of satisfying the public and that they comply with the regulations as to the number of dancers they may use. The Management, after receiving the report of the General Manager and of the inspectors-general on the plan, reserve the right to lay down the expenditure to be incurred without the *Maître des Ballets* or his aids being allowed to voice any opposition.

(4) That the Sieur Noverre further undertakes to stage *ballets d'action* whenever the Management consider it necessary in the interests of the Opéra, and this without the Sieur Noverre being entitled to fix either the number thereof or the time of their performance.

(5) That both with reference to the said *ballets d'action* as with the ordinary ballets he will only submit his plans after having agreed them with the General Manager of the Opéra to whom he will communicate his music, together with all information required to establish the cost thereof and, should the Management

83

consider such costs to be very heavy, the Sieur Noverre will be obliged to fall in with the orders of the Management or else to select a less expensive theme. In any case, he will comply with that which has been laid down hereabove in respect of the ordinary ballets concerning the selection and the number of dancers to be used.

(6) That by means of (*illegible*) for the larger performances of the *ballets d'action* as for ordinary performances the Sieur Noverre will be bound to supply all the music necessary to the said ballets as well as all orchestral parts, and he will submit the score to the General Manager so that he may study it and give an account of it to the Management who will be empowered not to accept such music if they consider it as unsuited to the subject of the ballet or as likely to fail to please the public, in which case the Sieur Noverre will be bound to submit fresh music, without thereby having any claim to be indemnified in any way."[71]

The controversy over the wisdom of his appointment and his chances of success spread at once to the gazettes. La Harpe, one of the most prolific writers of his day who contributed many of the literary articles to the *Mercure de France,* acclaimed the coming of "the greatest composer of ballets we have known since the Renaissance of the arts and the worthy rival of Pylades and Bathyllus in the art of speaking to the eyes with gesture and movements." De Méricourt, in his *Nouveau Spectateur,* whilst recognizing that Noverre was a man of genius, questioned whether he would find dancers capable of carrying out his ideas and even whether he was capable of succeeding in pleasing the public.[72]

On August 21st, de Bachaumont[73] could write in his diary:—

"The Sieur Noverre has finally been persuaded to join the Opéra and a bridge of gold has been made to persuade him to leave Vienna. It has been agreed to give him a salary of twenty thousand livres which is without doubt excessive."

Thus rumour-mongers were already doing their work, for in actual fact Noverre was appointed at a salary of twelve thousand livres per annum, plus a bonus of two thousand livres. The popular idea that he was an exorbitant charge on the revenues of the Opéra was exploited to the full by the established staff of the theatre who at once "ganged up" against him and saw to it that the post, which was the fulfilment of his crowning ambition, should bring him nothing but disillusionment.

Within the established hierarchy of the Opéra, the principal artists formed cliques to further their own personal ends and it became the main concern of the successive directors to prevent these from uniting against the management of the day. In Noverre, the foreigner, the little impostor from the provinces, the reformer of the dance who would want to impose his ideas and upset established and easy going traditions, the various factions found a focal point for their venom. He became at one and the same time the arch-enemy of the diehards and the hope of the all too few progressive elements. The former would try in vain to drag him into intrigues damaging to his reputation, to cast aspersions on his motives and even on his personal life.

The first blow was struck by the Gardel family. Noverre's appointment had been made without regard to the tradition that the assistant ballet master, a post shared at the time by the elder Gardel and Dauberval, should succeed to the post. Gardel's mother promptly poured out her spleen to the Marquis d'Amezaga, a wealthy Spaniard who had taken as his second wife a niece of Amelot, in a letter which makes up in spiteful anguish what it lacks in grammar:—

"I had intended having the honour of writing to pray you to solicit my entry to the amphitheatre of the Opéra and my right would have been the number of dancers I have given not least amongst which four of my children, two of whom are well playing their part.[74] At present, however, a more important matter is my preoccupation. Oh, my old friend, you who have found yourself by my side at every stage of my life, happy and unhappy, you surely do not expect to be faced with that which I am about to lay before your eyes! Who, indeed, would believe that Gardel, who in nineteen years at the Paris Opéra has achieved renown there and made himself praiseworthy by his talent, his punctilious attention to his duties, his docility, his honesty, his sacrifice of his own interests (for he has eaten up twenty thousand livres) and of countless offers of posts both lucrative and honourable; managers who have used his credit to obtain favours from the Queen would be capable of importing underhand a foreigner who has tried twenty times, in vain, to impose himself on the Opéra? The injustice was not then known of whom? The Queen's master the Court ballet master, adored by the public, beloved of his comrades, who for six years has created the most beautiful ballets in the world! His *Ernelinde*, which he created at Court, and which represented a siege, is still remembered. Madame la Comtesse de Noailles did me the honour of saying that the Marshalls of France had enquired where Gardel had learned the art of war, that Monsieur le Dauphin had discoursed of it all night and a thousand other things in the same vein as agreeable as they were gracious. He is to see himself treated as a schoolboy! They have dared to offer him the reversion of the Sieur Noverre who will be a good model for him, who will dictate melodies to him, to Gardel who is known in England and everywhere only as the *famous*, the *celebrated* Gardel. My son is good, humble, honest and it takes a charlatan to impose on him!

The said Noverre comes with one of those letters of recommendation which one delivers as one issues a consignment note; from the Empress to the Queen and which says to the contractors (*i.e. those who held the concession of the Opéra*) that she would not be sorry to see the man in question do some ballets provided this did not hurt his master; divine words worthy of the magnanimity of her soul! Her Majesty, like the Empress, may be unaware that the post of maître des ballets of the Paris Opéra is, like that of the first president, held for life and hereditary from *premier danseur* to *premier danseur*. An outsider has no right to it, except in the event of abdication as was the case with M. Dupré.

Here, however, my son has no desire to renounce his rights, from bishop to become miller, to be the subordinate of a master from the provinces and from Germany. Usually these gentlemen come to Paris to perfect themselves and not to give lessons to the great masters. The little Noverre has somewhat too much ambition and complacency. When thirty years ago he came to offer himself, he was sent back to the Fair to give his chinese ballets. The favourite had summoned him but the Sieurs Laval and Lani drew attention to their rights and the king and Madame de Pompadour admitted the justice of their claim. The little man by way of compensation went on to ruin Mademoiselle Destouches, the Prince of Wurtemberg, and to rage and fume in his ballets which only hold together by their ostentation and their colossal cost, for as to dancing there is none and this is not what is required by the enlightened public of Paris who would soon tire of these pantomimes in which art is neglected.

Forgive me, monsieur le marquis, for importuning you at such length but it relieves me. Injustice outrages me for what does my son risk? To make the most brilliant fortune at foreign courts where open arms await him. His dancing, his harp, his violin, his composition, his happy character will make him loved everywhere. You see, Sir, I am as humble as my son when justice is done to me but when I believe I am being humiliated, I rise up like a cedar tree.

What more can Gardel say to these gentlemen than: you know what I can do, try me for a year and, if I am a donkey, as you seem to think, if I fail to bring harmony and economy and if the public is not satisfied, I will give way and seek my fortune elsewhere but own that your methods cry to the heavens for vengeance. Adieu, my dear marquis, let us think on the memories of the good times of yore.

I am . . ."

Gardel remained in his post of joint-assistant ballet master and, although the intrigues of the Opéra personnel were for a time concentrated on the person of the new administrator appointed by the King, Monsieur de Vismes, who had the temerity to try and introduce an impartial regime and to put down the perpetual insurrections of the artistes, Noverre was not allowed to escape all opposition.

His first production at the Opéra, which was still housed in the Palais Royal, was a revival of *Apelles et Campaspe* given on October 1st, 1776.

"Apelles in his studio has dressed his students as Cupids and his serving women as Graces in honour of the visit of Alexander, to whose portrait he puts the final touches. A burst of martial music announces the coming of the monarch who is preceded by an escort of soldiers and ladies of his household. He is accompanied by Campaspe, heavily veiled. Apelles casts himself at the feet of the Prince, who shows him every sign of favour whilst the Graces present the portrait.

Alexander asks if the painter has no other work to show him and Apelles brings forth a painting of Venus occupied in selecting from Cupid's quiver the arrow which is to wound Adonis. The Prince, delighted with the talent of the artist, desires him to paint the portrait of Campaspe and, calling her forward, withdraws her veil. Apelles starts back in surprise and admiration.

To arouse the enthusiasm of Apelles, Alexander makes Campaspe walk and pose in different attitudes after which there is a general celebration with dances. Roxane, who has some claim to the heart of Alexander, appears and ill disguises her jealousy of Campaspe.

In the second scene, Apelles is painting Campaspe. He cannot decide how best to pose her. He draws quickly, rubs out, sketches again, now she is Minerva, now Flora, now Diana until finally he decides to paint her on a throne of flowers as the mother of the Cupids, represented by his pupils who surround her, one offering her a dove, others holding baskets, vases, perfumes, zephyrs crown her and present her flowers whilst the graces look to her toilet. Apelles flies to his canvas but the pencils slip from his fingers. He breaks his palette, dismisses his pupils and tremblingly approaches Campaspe and avows his passion. Far from taking offence, Campaspe admits her preference for the love of Apelles over the throne of Alexander. Overwhelmed with happiness, Apelles clasps her knees but Roxane who, eaten up with jealousy, has crept into the studio and been a silent but overjoyed witness of the infidelity of Campaspe runs to tell Alexander.

Alexander arrives on the scene as Apelles and Campaspe vow to each other the most tender love, and gives way to his unrestrained resentment until Campaspe falls in a faint whilst Apelles trembles, not so much for himself as for the life of his beloved. Alexander is torn by conflicting emotions of which generosity finally triumphs and, forgetting thoughts of vengeance and his own love, he pardons the two lovers.

The second act is set in the palace of Alexander with, at one end, a throne reached by several steps. Alexander, followed by a brilliant retinue, precedes the happy couple to whom he presents the nuptial cup and whom he loads with presents. He then gives his hand to Roxane and leads her to the throne, where she is crowned with every honour after which there is a general dance in which the emperor participates, for Gardel, who took the part, preferred to renounce any empire in the world rather than his *entrechats*."[75]

The indifference with which the elder Gardel performed his part was, however, compensated by the excellent rendering of *Campaspe* by Guimard, favourable to Noverre as long as her fame was likely to be enhanced by his ballets, and of Heinel, as *Roxane*, and Gaetano Vestris, as *Apelles*. The music, a new score by Rudolphe, who had changed his name to Rodolphe since leaving Wurtemberg and was now musician in ordinary to the King, was found to be brilliant and to marry well with the choreography. Despite the fact that the management, convinced that from the start they had to kill any extravagant ideas Noverre might have, withheld the necessary costumes and insisted on *pas seuls* where there should have been groups, the ballet, which was dedicated in the programme to the Queen, who honoured the performance with her presence and showed every sign of pleasure and delight, was well received.

This first triumph was, however, short lived, for the critics quickly got to work. The ballet was insufferably long, it was not as good as *Médée* as staged by the elder Vestris, and soon in an effort to placate them, Noverre, anxious to consolidate his position, modified and shortened the ballet. Instead of pardoning Apelles immediately, Alexander now had him put in chains in the first act and it was not until the second that he graciously gave his pardon which, it was at once said, destroyed the value of Alexander's sacrifice since he acted only after careful thought, and anyway the ballet would have been better concentrated into a single act.

Noverre, *Maître de Ballet de l'Académie Royale de Musique, Ancien Maître des Ballets de la Cour Impériale de Vienne, etc., etc.*, might be prepared to go so far in an effort to please his critics but he was not a man to be trifled with, neither was he at the beck and call of all and sundry. Catching sight, at the Opéra, of de Méricourt, the author of an impudent and libellous publication *Le Journal des Spectacles ou le Nouveau Spectateur* which had published an article that had annoyed him, in company with his patron and protector Crébillon, Noverre went up to the latter and enquired if he knew "a scallywag of the name of Méricourt, the author of a platitudinous rhapsody in which are collected all the mischievous tittle-tattle of the cafés". "Here he is", replied Crébillon without turning a hair. "Aho! Sir", continued Noverre quietly, "I am indeed happy to be able to tell you to your face what I think of you." "But, Sir," replied Méricourt, "You address me as if you were a Marshal of France." "No", said Noverre, "the Marshals of France carry crossed batons and I only have in my hand (showing his cane) this stick which you see here."[76]

On another occasion a Minister of the Crown sent for him, but Noverre did not come. He received a second order and still did not attend. Finally at the third request he went and excused himself on the grounds of his business and his health. "I am greatly surprised", said the Minister, "that a dancing master should have to be summoned three times before he comes to me." "Sir", said Noverre, "I am not difficult in the matter of titles; however, I could reply to you that I am as much a dancing master as Voltaire is a writing master.'[76]

On October 8th, by way of showing his gratitude and loyalty to the young Queen, Noverre organized, as part of the general festivities to celebrate the recovery from a serious illness of Monsieur, the King's brother, a great spectacle in her honour at Brunoy, the country residence of the Comte de Provence.

"Her Majesty found in the first copse knights in full armour asleep at the foot of trees on which hung their spears and shields. Their slumbers were occasioned by the absence of the beauties who had incited the Knights of Charlemagne to lofty deeds but, no sooner did Her Majesty appear than they sprang to their feet and melodious voices announced their eagerness to display their valour. They then hastened to a vast arena, decorated in the style of the ancient tournaments, where fifty dancers dressed as pages presented to the knights twenty-five superb black horses and twenty-five of a dazzling whiteness all richly caparisoned. Auguste Vestris led a party wearing the Queen's colours and Le Picq, now ballet master to the Russian Court, commanded the opposing force. There was running at the negro's head, tilting and mortal combats perfectly well imitated . . .

All fashionable Paris was ranged on the steps surrounding the arena, with the Queen attended by the Royal Family and the entire court seated beneath a high canopy. There followed in succession a play, a ballet pantomime, Les Caprices de Galathée, and a ball and the festivity was concluded by a lavish show of fireworks ending with 'Vive Louis, Vive Marie Antoinette' displayed from a prodigiously high scaffold placed on rising ground, in the midst of the dark but calm night."[77]

In September he had re-staged his *Caprices de Galathée* at Fontainebleau before the Court, and in November it was given at the Opéra where it met with considerable success and inspired Baron Grimm to send a vivid description to his master, Frederick of Prussia:—

"Galathea drives a shepherd to despair by her caprice. She accepts his gifts with every sign of pleasure soon disdainfully to cast them from her. The shepherd pretends to pay his attentions to another shepherdess and to offer her the presents destined to his beloved. Galathea, fired by jealousy, tears from the hands of her rival the gifts she has just received and adorns herself with them only to discard them once more. The shepherd is in dire distress. Cupid then comes to his aid and takes Galathea unawares and alone. She is without defence. He is a child but he has wings which she would cut off. He resists only with tears which melt her resolve. He allows himself to be chained by a lace and flies in her traces wherever she goes. He allows her to play with the arrows in his quiver but, in so doing, the young Galathea wounds herself. Her lover falls at her feet, Cupid unites them and the happiest fête celebrates his triumph.

Simple though the idea of this pantomime may be, hackneyed though the tableaux may seem, it is in its execution most pleasing and effective. One cannot imagine anything more fresh, it is a bouquet of flowers, a thought of Anacreon such as Boucher might have given it expression on canvas.

The rôle of Galathea was supremely rendered by Mademoiselle Guimard; it would be impossible to seize with greater finesse the various gradations of the same caprice, it would be impossible to marry its various shades with greater artistry or more grace.

Le Picq, as the shepherd, left nothing to be desired. A charming face, the slenderest of waists, the easiest and lightest of movements, the purest and most vivacious and yet most natural style, such are the qualities which mark the talent of this new mime. If he does not dance quite like the *Eternal Father*, to quote an expression dear to Vestris, one can at least say he dances like the King of the Sylphs. If he has not all the nobility, all the expression of Vestris, all the strength and the balance of Gardel, he has perhaps in his execution something softer and yet more brilliant. His grace and lightness triumph above all in *demi-caractère* dancing and that is the *genre* of the new ballet. . . ."[78]

Even this charming rococo work found no favour in the eyes of Noverre's critics who complained that a village was not the place for caprice and a shepherdess was hardly likely to be subject to such moods. Meanwhile, his difficulties within the Opéra itself militated increasingly against his chances of success. He needed actors and he had but dancers, he needed faces and the Opéra could offer him but legs, and his ebullient out-pouring of ideas, which he was burning to put into practice, upset or shocked those on whom he was dependent for the execution of his ballets. Vestris and the elder Gardel, who were convinced that they were destined to rule over the theatre, did not take kindly to being put back to school and Noverre, the harbinger of a new science, could not make himself heard. He was constantly distressed by the majesty and prerogatives of the *corps de ballet* and the choruses. Did he wish to place a group of supernumeraries upstage, he was met with a "Sir, we are 'old stagers' and we have the right to be in front." "But my ballet?" exclaimed the irate choreographer. "Your ballet will make do as best it can, the public must see us, it is our right."

Noverre complained and protested, he wanted everything changed at the Opéra, even to the lighting which did not lend itself to the effects he wished to produce. In desperation he was led to exclaim that he could achieve nothing unless he was given the management of the production as a whole. The powers that were thought he might succeed if he had his way but were convinced his genius would ruin the Opéra and that he was a man to whom a million for a ballet meant nothing, and they were not in a position to pay so dearly for their pleasures.

The first of his great epic tragedy-ballets to be produced in Paris, *Les Horaces,* was announced for January 21st, 1777, and the Queen was expected to be present, but the critics, like birds of evil omen, doubted whether this production would meet with the success which the Sieur Noverre promised himself and asserted that, if he did not succeed this time, he would be considered as having failed in his mission.

This gloomy forecast was justified, for although it was agreed that, taken as a whole, it was a fine spectacle mounted with some moments of great effect, and Mlle. Heinel, as Camille, the sister of the Horaces, gave a brilliant performance and rendered the imprecation scene most effectively, the subject was found unsuitable; the ballet was too long, too confused, too enigmatical and with too little dancing in it, and the décor was criticized as making Rome too modern. Certain scenes such as the famous "Qu'il mourût" tirade of the elder Horace could not, it was said, be translated into terms of dancing, and some wag was heard to remark that "before long Noverre will be making us dance the maxims of la Rochefoucault".

The second performance, on January 26th, was poorly attended so that the work could not be considered a success and yet, as de Bachaumont grudgingly remarked, "One cannot help recognizing much genius in its composer, who, as he claims in his preface, has transformed his profession into an Art, and brought back dancing to its original idea which is imitation."[79]

The management of the Opéra reverted to the hands of the Municipality and once more the intrigues gathered like a swarm of angry bees round the head of the unfortunate Noverre, but now there was no manager strong enough to uphold his rights and see that he had an opportunity to carry out his ideas. The Opéra was in fact ruled by the warring factions.

He put up in succession plans for the production of *Psyche*, *La Mort d'Hercule*, *Orphée*, *Le Jugement de Paris*, *Les Danaïdes*, *Didon*, *Les Graces*, *L'Epouse Persane*, *La Foire du Caire*, *La Joie Interrompue*, and many others, but they remained to moulder in the files. He was told that one was too gay, this too sad, the other too paltry, promises were made and never kept, and meanwhile the rumour was spread abroad that he was inactive.

He was told his ballets were too costly to produce and, unwilling to be beaten, he accepted that the supernumeraries should be dressed in rough homespun, an unheard of practice at the Opéra, and the few ballets he was allowed to produce, *Les Caprices de Galathée*, *Annette et Lubin*, *Les Ruses de l'Amour* and *Les Petits Riens* were staged with the same scenery.

Despite these constant persecutions, and the fact that these ballets were given during the off-season when the Court was away, and that they were sandwiched between excerpts so hackneyed as to deter even the most ardent of his supporters from sitting through a long and tedious programme to see them, they were not unsuccessful.

At the first performance, on March 7th, 1777, of *Les Ruses de l'Amour,* which met with particular favour, Madame Noverre was recognized in the amphitheatre and all eyes turned towards her as the audience showed their appreciation of the work they had just seen by a long burst of applause.

The following January, Noverre arranged a gay ballet in Piccini's opera, *Roland,* but his enemies promptly claimed that a ballet in the Chinese style was out of place in such a work. Noverre, still conscientiously trying to please everybody, promptly wrote a letter to the *Journal de Paris:*—

"I will refrain, Gentlemen, from entering into an argument with the public from whom I have received but kindness: I will not even argue with the few badly intentioned people who have seen fit at the performance of *Roland* to close their eyes to the fact that Angelica, Queen of Cathay, that is to say of a province of China, should have a Chinese suite and that therefore my ballet is not as foreign to the subject as they would have us believe.

Anxious as I am in so far as it lies in my power, to conciliate everybody, I will, Gentlemen, withdraw this ballet, which perhaps I will be asked for again, and I propose to spend the night creating another, but still to the music of M. Piccini, who cannot change his tunes from one moment to another as I have been able to change the movements of my dancers. I would, however, point out that a new ballet, of necessity arranged in haste, will not be as striking as that which I had thought upon at greater leisure but I will at least have the satisfaction of proving to all sections of the public my desire to please them. Assuredly it is not the fault of Quinault or of M. Marmontel, neither am I to blame, if it has pleased Aristotle to make Angelica Queen of Cathay and thereby to authorise my giving her sailors from her country."[80]

The new ballet was given the next day and this time the critics were effectively silenced.

Early in 1778 Noverre was honoured by being made a knight of the Papal Order of the Golden Spur, which had also been conferred on Gluck and on Wolfgang Mozart.[81] The latter was in Paris, composing at the house of Le Gros, the director of the Concerts Spirituels, and met with every encouragement from Noverre, who extended an open invitation to lunch at his house of which the young musician frequently availed. Noverre also arranged for him to compose for the Académie Royale de Musique, a full opera to be called *Alexandre et Roxane,* of which he would seem to have suggested the theme.

By the beginning of April the libretto of the first act had been written and Leopold Mozart was sending, from Salzburg, in his letters to his son, prolific advice on the importance of making a success of this first work by catering for French taste and heeding the counsels of his friends, Noverre and Baron Grimm. By the middle of May, Mozart awaited the finished libretto and felt sure it would be accepted by the director of the Académie Royale de Musique, Monsieur de Vismes, who owed his appointment to Noverre. He was also going to compose the music for a new ballet for Noverre.

The opera was never to be realized but the ballet, *Les Petits Riens,* had its first performance on June 11th, 1778, after Piccini's *Le Finte Gemelli* conducted by the composer himself.

The lack of success of Piccini's opera, which was found cold and tedious, is neatly summed up in a satirical poem telling the director he might as well leave the doors of his theatre closed if this was all he had to offer:—

> "Avec son opéra bouffon,
> L'ami De Vismes nous morfond;
> Si c'est ainsi qu'il se propose
> D'amuser les Parisiens,
> Mieux vaudrait rester porte close,
> Que de donner si peu de chose
> Accompagné de petits riens."

Despite the malicious pun in the last two lines, the ballet was a success. It consisted of a series of tableaux, forming three disconnected scenes in the style of Watteau and Lancret:—

Cupid caught in a net and put in a cage, danced by Guimard, the younger Vestris and a very graceful child; a game of blind man's buff, of which Dauberval was the gay protagonist, and mischievous Cupid causing two shepherdesses, danced by Mlles. Guimard and Allard, to become jealous of a third disguised as a man. The applause and the encores which greeted the *dénouement* of this last scene, in which Mlle Asselin, the shepherdess in male garb, enlightened the two jealous women by uncovering her breast, were, however, mingled with protests from a section of the audience, for, as Baron Grimm noted, "it is true that modesty still exercises on our stage a very strong hold."

The young composer was, however, far from satisfied. He considered he had composed half a ballet, and that out of friendship for Noverre, for to his twelve numbers forming the overture and the *contredanses,* had been added six pieces by others made up of "wretched old French airs". He determined to compose nothing further unless he was assured beforehand that it would be performed and knew what he would get for it. He offered to stay on in Paris for a further three months and compose an opera for Noverre on these terms, which he knew were inacceptable, for they were contrary to the practice of the Académie Royale de Musique, and so the project came to nothing.[82]

Despite all the difficulties and the intrigues which continued to assail him from every side, Noverre remained profoundly attached to his Queen. Her happy delivery of a daughter, on December 19th, 1778, was celebrated by the traditional free performances at the Opéra and the Comédie Française, known as the "rejoicings for the opening of the Queen's belly", which the redoubtable fishwives from the Paris markets attended in a body. The King offered a hundred thousand louis to provide a dowry for one hundred poor maidens, whilst the household officials promptly enjoined the priests of Paris to see that the happy recipients were not without beauty, lest their Majesties should take it into their heads to attend the wedding at Notre Dame!

All those parents of large families who were in the debtors' prison were freed and amongst them was a certain Lafosse, who claimed to be the father of twenty-five children, of whom nineteen were living. Public opinion was stirred and a subscription in his favour was opened, whilst Noverre and his colleagues at the Opéra offered such financial assistance as was in their power. Then it was discovered that the man had a mere ten children living which somewhat shook many people including the prudent Noverre, who at once wrote to the *Journal de Paris*:—

"It is when one is happy oneself that one feels the strongest urge to make others joyful. There are few sensitive souls who have not said to themselves in the excess of their happiness, I want all hearts to be happy with my joy. In the universal enthusiasm of the Nation in circumstances all the more heartfelt in that they were not unaccompanied by anxiety, one knew with regret that there were still unfortunates whom the hardships of fate withdrew from the general rejoicing. It is this precious and natural sentiment which has inspired the benevolent and human action recorded in your pages. You have initiated it, Gentlemen, and set an example to all good citizens who are fortunate enough to be able to follow it. My comrades, both of song and dance, hasten to follow in your footsteps; it is a subscription open to humanity and one cannot subscribe to it too quickly, it will assuredly soon be fully taken up.

You know from my letter of yesterday what were our intentions regarding the Sieur la Fosse. The article inserted in your paper today forces us to direct them to other channels. Not wishing to alter our designs, and desiring to bestow our small benefit on someone who really needs it, we have no alternative, if we are to avoid the risk of seeing our assistance misdirected, but to pray the Magistrates of this town to indicate to us an honest but needy family. Their active charity always has eyes open on the hardships of their citizens and it is assailing their rights to wish to relieve them but humanity is free from jealousy and is pleased to share its benefits.

We will give a dowry of thirty louis to the first poor girl to be drawn to our attention and we will bear the costs of the wedding and of the bouquet. We have, to this end, cast our eyes on the Vauxhall of the Foire St. Germain which the

'La Guimard' in her 'Bergère' costume.  Engraving by Prud'hon from the drawing
by Coeuré.  Bibliothèque du Louvre, Paris.        Photo Maurice Rigal, Paris.

*'Jason et Médée'. Print published in 1781 by John Boydell and engraved in Cheapside, London.*

*Dancing Times*

owner will lend to us with as much pleasure as disinterestedness. The newlyweds and their families will be served by the talents and the agreeable arts. We will neglect nothing to bring to this little fête the gaiety, decency and simplicity which go hand in hand with happiness.

If any honest folk (and there will doubtless be many) present themselves and wish to witness it, we will bid them deposit a louis and put their name down at M. Rouen's, notary, and the resulting sum from this benefit, which we have felt it wiseto term thus so as to avoid the crush and other drawbacks one can easily foresee, will be devoted to the care and baby food of the first child to be born of a union joined under the happiest reign and under the auspices of the Games and Laughter. Finally, Gentlemen, we will have this child held over the font and if it is a boy he shall be called Louis and, if a girl, Antoinette, for they are the patron and patroness of France. These two names, as dear to our mother-country as to humanity, never strike the ear of a Frenchman without echoing a thousand times in his heart.

The dowry will be deposited at Mlle. Guimard's, Chausée d'Antin, for we have appointed her treasurer."[83]

Alongside of the ballets proper, Noverre composed the ballets in a number of operas including Rousseau and Gluck's *Devin du Village* and Gluck's *Armide,* in which the dances found particular favour. Paris was at the time torn by the quarrel of the Gluckists and Piccinists, or those who favoured the lighter Italian style of composition in which everything was subordinated to the singer, to the musical revolution introduced by Gluck who used music and song to develop the dramatic theme.

Noverre, surprisingly enough, since Gluck was to all intents and purposes striving to bring about in music the acceptance of ideas not greatly removed from those expressed in the *Lettres sur la Danse,* would seem to have taken the part of Piccini. His feelings on the subject cannot, however, have run very high, for he had worked in intimate co-operation with both musicians and, in writings which have come down to us, warmly espouses the work of Gluck. Marie Antoinette, with whom he came into frequent contact, in his capacity of director of the fêtes at the Trianon, would, it is said, hum in Noverre's presence snatches from Gluck's *Iphigénie en Tauride,* a theme which Piccini had treated less successfully, and then, with the free and easy manner she liked to adopt at Trianon, tease him with his discomfiture.

Even in the field of opera-ballet, Noverre had to suffer from the intrigues of his colleagues. When a ballet was required to lengthen Piccini's *Iphigénie* and it was suggested that his *Annette et Lubin* should be included, the all-powerful Guimard, who headed the management committee which the artists had set up and which, although it had no

95

official authority, was the virtual ruler of the Opéra, vetoed the project and insisted on Gardel's *Chercheuse d'Esprit* being included instead.

In the same way, Gardel's *Ninette à la Cour* was coupled with Gluck's *Iphigénie en Aulide*, despite the unanimous agreement to the contrary of many of the artists of the Opéra.

This hostility of Guimard had been aggravated by the production of *Annette et Lubin* on July 9th, 1778. She had refused to dance herself and suggested disdainfully that Noverre should give the rôle of *Annette* to a young *second sujet*, Mlle. Cécile.[84] Much to the disgust of Guimard, who suddenly saw in Cécile a rival capable in Noverre's hands of menacing her popularity, the ballet was an outstanding success and caused a poet to write:—

> "Cécile, you have chosen the surest road,
> When without the assistance of art
> You follow in the steps of Guimard
> In rivalling nature.
> In Annette et Lubin, enchanting ballet,
> Thy tender and touching art disarms the critic;
> Seeing thee appear in that humble retreat,
> Where of a cherished lover you gratified the destiny,
> Every woman envied the joys of Annette
> And every man the happiness of Lubin."

In November, 1779, after an absence from the stage, Guimard made her reappearance in Gardel's *Mirza et Lindor*, which had been produced at great cost as a setting for her. The ballet was an utter failure and met with considerable criticism which the dancer believed, or feigned to believe, had been instigated by Noverre. She promptly went to the Minister of the King's Household to pour out her grievances and her "shadow cabinet" began to plot the final downfall of the ballet master.

Despite the poison which was constantly being poured into Court circles in both France and Austria, Noverre was given every outward and visible sign of the high esteem in which he was held, culminating, in December, 1779, in a brilliant marriage arranged for his daughter as a result of conversations between Marie Antoinette and the Comte de Mercy, Austrian Ambassador acting on the instructions of his sovereign, the Empress Maria Theresa.[85]

However, worn out and discouraged by the continual intrigues and realizing the impossibility of getting his ballets produced according to his own ideas, he came to an agreement with the elder Gardel and

Dauberval, embodied in a written memorandum dated November 30th, 1779, by which he agreed to resign in their favour, his post as *Maître* and composer of ballets to the Académie Royale de Musique if and when they secured the implementation of the promise made to him by the Queen that on his retirement he should be granted by the Académie a yearly pension of three thousand livres payable for the duration of his life and thereafter to his wife for so long as she might survive him. Furthermore, in accordance with the promise made to him by the Maréchal Duras, they undertook to obtain for him, at the first reversion, an academician's pension of five hundred livres.

Noverre would implement his undertaking as soon as these conditions had been complied with but, so as to give him time to settle his affairs, he would continue in office for a period of one year, during which he would draw his full emoluments. This agreement was made in confidence and each of the parties undertook on his honour never to mention or use the memorandum in any negotiations they might enter into jointly or severally.

Shortly afterwards Noverre saw the house, forming part of the buildings of the Quinze-Vingts, in which he was renting a flat at one hundred louis a month, sold over his head and was notified of the termination of his lease. Having first enquired of his successors-to-be whether they had taken any steps to implement their side of the bargain and been assured that they had done nothing further in the matter and that the project was not likely to mature for some considerable time, he took a new flat in the Rue Neuve des Petits Pères at a rent of two thousand livres and spent a thousand écus on putting it into condition. On July 14th, before he had so much as spent a night there and without his having been so much as warned by Gardel or Dauberval that they had taken any steps whatsoever, he received notification that his resignation had been accepted, a situation which left him greatly distressed, for not only was it a breach of the understanding that no final steps would be undertaken without him being advised of them, but courtesy demanded that he should in person tender to the Queen his resignation from an appointment which he had received at her hands, and at the same time express his regret and his gratitude.

Noverre addressed to Monsieur de la Ferté a seventeen page memorandum, in which he set out in dignified terms the history of his difficulties at the Opéra and of the intrigues from which he had endeavoured to hold himself aloof. He compares the personnel of the Opéra to a troupe of children building a castle with a pack of cards.

"All goes as they wish but, just as they are about to crown the edifice with the last card, a breath of air, a slight movement destroys this frail construction. Then do our urchins dance like hens on a hot girdle and wring their hands before they start afresh on some new work until a fresh accident comes to upset their projects." He points out the defects, the chaotic state of the administration of the Opéra before he goes on to destroy the criticisms which have been levelled against him and, in particular, invites an investigation into the costs of his ballets as disclosed by the books. Finally he points out that, after the first year, he has never received the bonus of two thousand livres due to him over and above his salary and he expresses the hope that the Minister will see his way to have this paid to him plus the expenses he has incurred as a result of the ignorance in which he has been kept of the negotiations for his retirement.[85]

Acceptance of Noverre's resignation was notified to M. de la Ferté by the Minister of the King's Household, Monsieur Amelot, in a letter dated July 15th, 1781. In consideration of his loyal services he was granted a pension of one thousand, five hundred livres by the Opéra, payable until his death or that of his wife should she survive him. Furthermore, the Minister would have pleasure in recommending to the King that one of the pensions of five hundred livres, provided for the dancing members of the Académie Royale de Musique, should be given to Noverre, but for the present all these were allocated. A copy of the letter was to be handed by de la Ferté to Noverre, who would continue in office until July 1st, 1781.[85]

In the meantime, to assist the general manager of the Opéra, there had been set up, in April, 1780, a committee drawn from the artists, consisting of the singer Legros who was placed in charge of lighting, Durant who was to take responsibility for stage machinery, the elder Gardel to watch over scenery and scene painting, Dauberval to look after the wardrobe and Noverre, who was given the delicate mission of watching over the finances of the theatre and seeing that royalties due under various contracts were duly paid.

Although his name does not figure on the payroll after March, 1781, when he was succeeded as *Maître de Ballet* by the elder Gardel and Dauberval, in April he still signs the payroll as one of the Committee of Management.[86]

He never received the academician's pension which he was promised. Whether or not he obtained satisfaction in respect of the bonus due to him, we do not know for certain, although a letter from Campan, the

Queen's secretary, to the Minister, Amelot, written from Versailles on November 19th, 1782, would seem to show that at that date, despite the Queen's protection, he had not been given satisfaction:—

"I have the honour, Sir, to send you herewith a memorandum from M. Noverre. The justice of his claim is too evident to fail to convince you. It seemed so much so to me that, Mr. Noverre having come to lay his deep respect at the feet of the Queen and receive her orders for London, I opposed his presenting his memorandum to Her Majesty. The profound respect due to her does not seem to permit that a just request which she has made should meet with no success.

I venture to hope, Sir, that you will not misunderstand my letter, you will not suppose me to have the audacity to solicit on behalf of the Queen, but the friendship which you are good enough to grant me authorizes my confidence in your remembering to carry out at the first opportunity the promise made to Mr. Noverre. . . ."[87]

The last works which Noverre staged for the Opéra were both revivals. Although the performance of *Jason et Médée* at the Opéra in January, 1780, was the first to be staged by Noverre himself and also the first to the original score by Rodolphe free from all embroidery, its reception had been blunted by the earlier revivals by Gaetano Vestris in 1771 and 1776 when, although it had not been improved by the additions made to it by the latter, it pleased by its very novelty.

In fact the vainglorious Vestris was later to claim for himself the authorship of the ballet and when Gardel, in a book he had written, attributed the work to Noverre, Vestris accosted him in the wings one night with: "Tell me now, where did you discover that my ballet *Médée* was given at Mannheim by Noverre; have you seen it? And your book for that matter, have you ever read it?"[88]

The following July he revived *Les Caprices de Galathée*, with Auguste Vestris in the rôle of a shepherd previously danced by Le Picq, which caused Baron Grimm to write:—

"However brilliant, however admirable, however sublime, the talent of this worthy son of the *dieu de la danse* may be, it will be no surprise that at his age he has not yet acquired in this style all the sensibility and the flowing movement which Le Picq displayed with such grace and lightness. Would not his illustrious father agree? It is not so long ago he was heard to remark, with that accent which so matches his pride, 'To here (laying his hand on his chest) there is nothing to desire for my son, but as for the upper part of the body, he still needs years of work. I have spent my entire life shortening my arms; I give him ten to learn the minuet, and it will not be too many. Ah, Sir, if I could execute today with my feet, that which I have in my head, you would see something!' . . . Dauberval, who like Vestris has lived with Mademoiselle Allard, the mother of this young prodigy, watching him a few days ago from the wings, remarked with as much chagrin as admiration: 'What talent! He is the son of Vestris and not mine! Alas! I missed him but by a quarter of an hour.' "[89]

His very last production before he left for London consisted of scenes from *Don Quichotte* created with Dauberval, on the occasion of the wedding of Princess de Rohan Guémenée and the Prince de Rohan Rochefort, in the grounds of the house of Madame de Guémenée at Montreuil, with the spectators seated in a vast amphitheatre separated from the improvised stage by a stream, a setting worthy of Noverre's great days in Vienna.

# CHAPTER VII

## Second London Period

IN the bitterness of his last months at the Paris Opéra, Noverre's thoughts turned once more to the joys of untroubled creation under the enlightened patronage of the reigning Duke Karl Eugène of Wurtemberg and wrote offering his services for four months of the year, during which he would arrange the fêtes and direct the dancing schools. He asked in return for a salary of one thousand gulden, free lodging and a carriage, and a pension of one hundred ducats. The Duke was favourably disposed towards his old ballet master but this time it was the pension which proved the insuperable difficulty.

Noverre's last letter to the Wurtemberg Minister is none the less couched in the friendliest terms and asks for details of the festivals arranged for His Serene Highness that he might mention them in the article he was editing under *Fêtes* in the *Encyclopédie*. "The monuments of the Duke's taste must be represented in the monument of the arts, intelligence and human knowledge."

His contract at the Opéra finally terminated, Noverre, having taken leave of his Queen, made his way to London and the King's Theatre where he met with a triumphant reception.

His very success, of which echoes quickly reached Paris, was, however, a thorn in the side of the management of the Opéra. Already before his departure de Bachaumont[89] had noted:—

"One of the major contributory causes of the disorder at the Opéra is the flattering promises with which the Sieur Noverre cradles the artists. Dismissed here, he is going to London to establish a show and, out of pique as much as interest, he seeks to attract the best *coryphées*."

Despite the fact that England and France were still at war, he was all too successful, for, in addition to greater possibilities of making a name, he was in a position to hold out prospects of increased remuneration.

Mlle Théodore,[90] who in Paris earned a maximum of five or six thousand louis in the year, found she could command double this in London and, instead of returning to the Opéra, wrote to M. de la Ferté and M. Amelot, the minister responsible to the administration of the theatre, to ask for eight months leave in every year or the rescission of her contract. Her request refused, she appealed to the Queen who intervened on her behalf and she was granted the annulment of her contract. She made, however, the mistake of returning to France at the end of the London season and, by way of discouraging any who might be tempted to follow her example, the director of the Opéra promptly had her clapped in gaol, on the pretext that in her letters she had dared to criticize the management of the Opéra. She was freed after eight days on the condition that she did not go near Paris for two months. Despite the clamour of the public, who wished to see her, and the entreaties of Amelot and de la Ferté, she was adamant in her determination to return to London. She also persuaded Dauberval, one of Noverre's most brilliant pupils, to follow her example.[91]

The ballets of Noverre were not unknown to the London public, although whether they gave him credit for them is open to doubt, for when Gaetano Vestris revived *Médée et Jason* and *Les Caprices de Galathée* at a performance for his own benefit on March 29th, 1781, he did so as though they were his very own work. Such was the success of the performance that the following summer, the Theatre Royal in the Haymarket produced a parody "*Medea and Jason* by Signor Novestris".[92]

The 1781-2 season opened on November 17th, 1781, with, in addition to the opera company, a brilliant ballet company directed by Noverre and including in its ranks the younger Gardel, Bournonville and Nivelon, Mlle. Théodore and Mme. Simonet, with Signor Novosielski to supply décors and costumes. The bill on the opening night included a new ballet by Noverre, *Les Amants Réunis*, "which was received by a very brilliant audience with uncommon and most universal applause."[93]

On December 11th, *Les Petits Riens* was staged before the Prince of Wales to a new score by Barthélémon,[94] the leader of the orchestra, who also provided the music for the countless *divertissements* between the acts of operas and at masked balls which Noverre turned out with seemingly inexhaustible energy.

On February 23rd, he revived, to a new score by Le Brun with décor by Novosielski, *Rinaldo et Armida,* which was acclaimed as a masterpiece by the critics and rapidly proved a major attraction. The *Public Advertiser,* commenting on the first performance, praised the light and shade and the close unity between dancing and music and concluded:—

"In short we felt it to be perfect dancing, balancing, as Prior calls it, our fear and our hope; and if there was any doubt of Mr. Locke being in the right, when in his Essay on the Understanding, he talks of 'the admirable consent between the legs of the dancing master and the fingers of the musician' after the performance of Noverre's ballet, that doubt could exist no longer."

Such was the success of the ballet that two days later the same paper commented afresh:—

"Monsieur Noverre's new ballet of Rinaldo and Armida was again received last night, as on the former evening, by a house very crowded and full of applause.

The dance is certainly a chef d'Oeuvre of the arts ingeniously planned, and admirably executed.

The duration of it as to time, is about 55 minutes, and during the whole period the performance again appeared perfect in all its parts; nothing was too much, nothing was wanting. . . ."[95]

The Prince of Wales, surrounded by the most brilliant court, attended a performance, and at the conclusion the house called for Noverre who was loath to show himself. His name was suddenly on every tongue as was that of Mlle. Théodore who, in the rôle of Armida, achieved a great personal success, ably seconded by the younger Gardel and Nivelon.

Equally great was the enthusiasm aroused by the benefit performance given for the ballet master on April 11th, when the programme included, in addition to Anfossi's opera, *Il Viaggiatori Felici,* a revival of *Medea and Jason,* this time by Noverre himself, and the first London performance of *Adela of Ponthieu,* dedicated in a thirteen line poem to the Duchess of Devonshire.

*The Public Advertiser* waxed particularly eloquent:—

"The two ballets of last night provided a kind of twofold triumph to Monsieur Noverre, and showing at once the force of his genius, and the good account to which that genius has operated, gratified equally those two innate principles, the love of profit and the love of praise. . . .

The ballet of Medea and Jason is too well known to need any particular mention; we shall only observe that the dance as it now stands *gains* some advantage over the last year's performance of it, by the introduction of Mlle. Théodore, and that there is not as much lost as we expected, from the change of the Elder Vestris to Gardel, and the Young Vestris to Nivelon. Madame Simonet was greater than usual; she out-did herself! Gluck's overture to this dance, and a great part of the Musician's Dance, cannot be too much commended.

The new ballet, at least new to us, *Adela de Ponthieu,* is like the former evidently the work of a master, and though not so sublime as Medea and Jason, is certainly not less agreeable. The Grand Chaconne, the Preparation for the Duel, the Duel itself, and the whole ceremonial of chivalry, are all to the credit of Noverre, planned in Alto Gusto, and to the credit of the performers and all executed with no less taste; Gardel, Théodore and Baccelli all deserve particular praise.

The Théodore for the first time danced to an adagio movement, which if it did nothing else, at least contributed to contrast, and by contrast, to relieve the charming allegro which followed.

For the musical composition of the air above mentioned, for several other airs in the dance, and for more than the *Ritornel* in the Grand Chaconne; for these and for the crescendo in Gardel's part of the Chaconne, and the marches, we ought to give M. Le Brun all the merit which belongs to him. The music though but appropriate to a Dance, is not inferior to many operas—it excels equally in science and in expression, and while much of it may be said to be worked up in the light, embroidered manner of *Modern Italy*, as much of it may boast a manner which may be compared *to the rich Bullion* of Corelli.

And added to this general praise of the music of its really being a fine miscellaneous concert, it yet more excels in the great requisite of *exact adaptation;* no music can have ideas more various, yet no variety can be more select and appropriate in its application.

Indeed between music and action of the dance the coalescence is the most choice and close which can be; throughout they, as it were, *groove together.* Or perhaps to indulge in a little Jeu de Mots, in the melting strains to which Baccelli dances to Florio's flute, instead of groove we may use another phrase from the same art called 'Dove Tailing'.

On the whole view of the spectacle, Monsieur Noverre is to be pronounced a genius of no mean rank; sui generis, it is true and of such *composite order,* made up of qualities such as enter the constitution of the poet, the painter and the actor."[96]

The ballets had now come to vie with the operas in the estimation of the public and such was their popularity that performances were given four times a week where previously there had been given but two.[97]

Le Picq made his first appearance in England on May 2nd, in a *divertissement* specially composed by Noverre, *Apollon et les Muses.* He was found to have:—

"more excellencies and fewer foibles than any dancer perhaps ever seen in England.

With as much expression, he has more ease than the elder Vestris; he excels the younger Vestris in everything but mere lightness of toe. In the power of exhilaration, the best power of the art, he is a formidable rival to Slingsby. And added to all this his common deportment seems to be the perfection of nature. His walk is beyond all comparison the best we know of."[98]

*Apelles et Campaspe,* given its London *première* at Le Picq's benefit performance on June 6th, was amended to omit the part of Roxane danced in Paris by Heinel. It was met with fresh outbursts of praise from the critics:—

"Count Algarotti has observed that to make the opera prosper
'we must lengthen the Dances, and at the same time shorten the dancers'

petticoats'. That this observation has in it as much truth as TURN is proved by the present circumstances of this theatre (the Opera House) which is now open four times where it used to be open but twice. . . .

The talents which Mon. Noverre has displayed in Apelles and Campaspe, more perhaps than in other ballets show him to have a degree of excellence, in that invention and taste which characterize the successful labour of a painter.

The music of Apelles and Campaspe, tho' not so good as Le Brun's Adela de Ponthieu or even his Rinaldo and Armida is still very agreeable:—the best parts of it are the Entrée of Alexander, The Pas de deux after the declaration of Apelles' love, Crespi's Chaconne, and above all, the movement following it, the passage with the Flutes, Hautboys and Bassoons, with the Violins and Tenor pizzicato, produce an effect, than which scarcely anything can be more amusing."[99]

The exceptionally long season, which closed on June 29th, had been particularly triumphant for Noverre. His ballets had been acclaimed by critics and public alike and honoured by visits of members of the Royal family. His pupil, Le Picq, had successfully made his first appearance in London and been honoured by a Command Performance. His *Letters on Dancing* had been published simultaneously in a revised French edition and in an English translation, together with the collected scenarios of his ballets, and the Prince of Wales had accepted their dedication to himself. Echoes of his triumph had crossed the Channel and perhaps his name had never stood higher in Paris.[100]

The following season opened unusually early, on November 2nd, 1782, in a theatre transformed and redecorated by Novosielski. Noverre's *Apelles et Campaspe*, revived by Le Picq, held the bill for a large number of performances at one of which, on December 2nd, Madame Rossi (Madame Le Picq) made her first appearance in London as *Apelles*, wearing "a Manteau à la reine, lately imported by our travelling milliners, and somewhat similar to that of a celebrated actress at Covent Garden, who no doubt had it from the same quarter. The body, bones and trimming are *pure*, the sleeves and the lower part of the garment are white gauze."

Noverre, prevented by ill-health and perhaps also not unaware of the financial difficulties of Mr. Taylor which were to lead to the closing of his theatre the following May, did not appear, but in 1787 he went to Lyons to produce his *Adèle de Ponthieu, Apelles et Campaspe* and *La Foire du Caire*, and the three works were given together at a performance for his benefit on March 28th.[158] In the autumn, despite the renewed tension with England, he arrived at Dover on November 20th, 1787, when an unknown correspondent sent de Bachaumont an eye-witness account of the event:—

"Never had so numerous a detachment of dancers as that which has just arrived from France, disembarked in this port. When this *light* and *sparkling* troupe with *old General Noverre* at their head, approached the banks, the ardour with which they were seen to charge from the launch towards the shore, inspired a general panic. The inhabitants who found themselves on the jetty at the time of the landing and who were still alarmed by the rumours of war current for the past month, were prepared to fly to arms. When they saw that the entire troupe, happy to be shot of sea-sickness, laughingly began to do *cabrioles, battements,* and *coupés* they realized their error and were soon reassured as to the consequences of this invasion. The citizens of Dover, enchanted by the gaiety of these agile Frenchmen, could not tear themselves away and followed them to the very door of their inn. The porters and longshoremen especially who hoped for their generosity asked for drinking money but the dancers repeated their *entrechats* and thus paid in gambols."[101]

Noverre returned once more as ballet master to the King's Theatre, now under the management of Gallini, heading a company which included Mm. Vestris, Didelot, who earned £400 for the season, Chevalier, Henry and Coulon and Mlles. Hilligsberg, Coulon, Bedini and the two Misses Simonet, with Gaetano Marinari to provide the décors and Signor Lupino to design the costumes.

The season opened on December 8th with Paisiello's opera, *Il Re Teodoro in Venezia,* and Noverre's *Les Offrandes à l'Amour,* in which Didelot made his first appearance in England.

On January 12th, 1788, the *Public Advertiser* reported:—

" The Managers have announced Monsieur Noverre as ballet master, therefore the public will be glad to see soon some ballet of his production, though six weeks are gone, and nothing has happened; however, there is one now in rehearsal, the plan of which does him honour, and 'tis needless to say more until after the performance."

The public did not have long to wait, for the new ballet, *L'Amour et Psyche,* was staged on January 29th, to music by Mazzinghi, on which occasion "The Manager of the Opera in conjunction with Mr. Noverre as Ballet Master" warned the public to keep off the stage owing to the danger of moving machinery and trap doors.

Noverre was, however, still in indifferent health and was unable to produce the dances promised for a masked ball on February 4th.

His next production, *Les Fêtes du Tempe,* was not until March 1st, followed on the 13th by a revival of *Euthyme et Eucharis* for Vestris' benefit.

Meanwhile the Manager of the Opera had a fresh trouble to deal with and, in an advertisement, hoped:—

"for the indulgence of the Public, in laying before them the great complaints which have been made to him, on account of the inconvenience in the Entertainments, arising from the enormous Caps and Bonnets, which several Ladies make it a Practice to appear in, within the Pit of the Theatre, excluding thereby that Part, which is presented from the dancing in a great degree. . . ."[102]

To which a "frequenter of the Opera" replied with a public demand as to by what authority the Manager:—

"intreats the Ladies in the Pit to diminish the height of their head-dresses till a much greater evil existing still is first of all remedied. The persons crowding the stage every night, to the great detriment of the performers, especially the dancers. . . ."[102]

On April 17th, for Noverre's benefit, there was given Sarti's opera *Giulio Sabino* with, at the end of the first act, *Les Offrandes a l'Amour* and, to conclude the evening, a revival of *Adèle de Ponthieu*. Tickets being obtainable from Monsieur Noverre at 40, Great Marlborough Street.

During the season, which ended on June 28th, there were also performed a number of ballets by Didelot, including *La Bonté du Seigneur* and Gardel's *Panurge*.

Noverre renewed his engagement for the following season, which opened on January 10th, 1789, with Martini's comic opera, *La Cosa Rara*, with ballets by Noverre assisted by his pupil Monsieur Coindre, which was followed by Didelot's *L'Embarquement pour Cythère*, which may perhaps have owed something to Noverre's ballet of the same name created in Lyons twenty-five years before. Cherubini's opera, *Iphigenia in Aulide*, was revived on the 24th, with new ballets by Noverre and Coindre and, on January 31st, Noverre created his first new independent ballet of the season, *Les Fêtes Provençales*. On March 17th, for the first appearance in England of Mlle. Saulnier, he revived *Les Jalousies du Serail*.

Mlle. Guimard, who had joined the throng of refugees, made her first appearance on April 28th, partnered by Didelot, in the Minuet from Cherubini's *Iphigenia in Aulide*, and later in the same programme danced the part of *Annette*, to Nivelon's *Lubin*, in *Annette et Lubin*.

The season came to an abrupt end when, on the evening of June 17th, 1789, the King's Theatre caught fire attracting an immense concourse of people and causing the "light fingered gentry" to be extremely diligent in their avocation.[103] The theatre was totally destroyed entailing a loss of property estimated at some seventy thousand pounds.

It was at first thought that the fire had been caused by some experiments with fireworks for a forthcoming production, but subsequently a reward of three hundred pounds was offered to anyone able to give information as to the person or persons believed maliciously to have set fire to the building.

There then began the farcical imbroglio between Mr. Taylor and Mr. O'Reilly. Mr. Taylor had transferred the name and goodwill of the destroyed King's Theatre to the Little Theatre in the Haymarket, but meanwhile a Mr. O'Reilly, who had obtained an interest in the old Opera House by the purchase of the claim of descendants of its founder, Sir John Vanbrugh, made it known that he had obtained a patent for a new opera in Leicester Square and claimed that no other patent was in existence. He succeeded in obtaining the Lord Chamberlain's licence and, in October, announced the opening of the Pantheon Theatre as an opera house soon after Christmas but, meanwhile, the reconstruction of the old King's Theatre had proceeded apace and it was ready to open its doors.

Conflicting announcements as to the plans and artists engaged by Mr. Taylor and Mr. O'Reilly filled the press. The Prince of Wales agreed to head a committee of arbitration which decided that the debts of both opera houses should be transferred to the new theatre in the Haymarket where the two companies of players, fused for the season, would alone appear. This ruling was, however, turned down by Mr. O'Reilly who, on February 9th, 1791, gave his first performance, a rehearsal for subscribers only of the opera *Armida*, with a company which included Dauberval, Didelot, d'Egville, Salvatore Vigano and his wife, Maria Medina, and Mlle. Théodore.

Mr. Taylor, not to be outdone, gave his first performance, also in private for subscribers, on February 21st, with the opera *Pyrrhus*, with Giuseppe Hayden and Federici as composers, Gaetano Vestris as ballet master and a company of dancers which included Auguste Vestris and Madame Hilligsberg.

Shortly afterwards, Mr. O'Reilly decided to change the name of the Pantheon to King's Theatre and gave his first public performance. Mr. Taylor was refused a licence for opera at the new theatre but opened, on March 26th, with entertainments of music and dancing which continued until July 19th, despite the informers sent out by Mr. O'Reilly, who threatened to have Vestris, Hilligsberg and their colleagues taken into custody under the Vagrant Act of George II. The repertoire included *La Mort d'Hercule* and *La Fête Provençale* revived by Gaetano Vestris, whilst Dauberval, at the Pantheon, gave his *La Fille Mal Gardée* on April 30th.

In September, Mr. Taylor gave up the unequal struggle and a company of actors from Drury Lane took over the theatre. Poetic justice, however, overtook Mr. O'Reilly, for the Pantheon was burnt down on January 14th, 1792. Mr. Taylor promptly applied for, and was granted, a licence for his theatre which reopened on July 26th, 1793, under the joint management of Messrs. Kelly and Storace.

Noverre meanwhile had retired to Triel, Seine et Oise. We can glimpse the disillusionment with which he is assailed in these last years of his career from a dedication, dated Clermont Ferrand, February 20th, 1790, in a manuscript *Théorie et Pratique de la Danse,* a condensed version by the Chevalier de Bernay, of the famous *Lettres:*—

"I send you my dear Fabre the ramblings of a young man of twenty-five, or the dream he then had to raise from its cradle a weak and languishing art. May you embellish it by following a career which I have lived with sorrow. May you harvest flowers where I have found but the thorns and the brambles of intrigue; may you be as happy as it is possible to be in a bawdy house where they sing of a happiness which has never been seen there, where esteem and friendship find no refuge. . . ."

His retirement was of short duration and, in 1793, he is in London for the opening of the King's Theatre, on January 26th.

The programme on the first night included, besides *Il Barbiere di Seviglia,* a new ballet by Noverre *Les Epoux du Tempe.* The critics accorded the ballet a kindly reception:—

"The charming Miss Millard, who was the most accomplished dancer at the Opéra of Paris, made her debut in England; she was received with the warmest applause, and never was applause so cordially requited. The great talent of Miss Millard is the unparalleled neatness of her motion. 'The many twinkling feet' are peculiarly applicable to her dancing—for never perhaps did the English spectator see such graceful rapidity as she possesses in the demi-caractère.

The expressive Hilligsberg lost none of her popularity by the competition. Her mocking countenance and her *naivete* secured her reiterated plaudits.

Nivelon and Favre Gardel are good dancers but not to be put forward as rivals to the female dancers. Nivelon imitates Vestris without his elastic powers and Favre Gardel his brother, without his grace.

The new divertissements are pretty and do credit to M. Noverre but they have nothing peculiarly striking."[104]

Michael Kelly had been impressed with the custom he had observed in Naples of concluding operas with a spectacular procession and tournament introducing triumphal cars drawn by horses, giants, dwarfs, leopards, lions and tigers, and he sought to introduce similar scenes in the theatre now under his control, and who better than Noverre could handle such crowd scenes?

Noverre's happiness at being once more back in the theatre and his good reception must, however, have been saddened by the sorry news from across the Channel. Everything was in confusion, money had become so scarce, as a result of the large sums sent out of the country or burned, that two-thirds of everything now had to be paid in printed notes or "assignats" and only one-third could be met in good solid silver. Louis XVI had been guillotined and the National Convention had even refused him funeral honours but had insisted that he be "buried like other citizens in the usual burying place of the Section in which he lived."[105] Noverre's beloved Queen shared his fate nine months later. On January 30th, 1793, the daily press proclaimed that France was at war with England and the Statholder of the United Provinces and, on March 11th, the Paris correspondent of the *Public Advertiser* reported that:—

"on Thursday the Mayor ordered the public places to be shut, and the rapel to be beaten as a signal to the Citizens to meet the Commissioners from the Convention in their several sections. On Friday, in concert with the Council General of the Commune, he ordered the black flag, the signal of the country being in danger to be hoisted on the towers of Notre Dame. . . ."

In Lyons, the scene of so many of Noverre's successes, Fouquet, the "mitrailleur de Lyon", presided over a "purge" in which countless citizens went to the guillotine and whole quarters of the city were destroyed by the military. "On December 30th, the Revolutionary Tribunal of Lyons ordered the Kings of Great Britain, Spain, Prussia and Sardinia, the Emperor, the Pope and Mr. Pitt, to be executed in the great square in that town. They were accordingly in effigy surrendered to the executioner and guillotined."[106]

In France, Madame Noverre, who had been unable to accompany her husband, was appealing against the sequestration of their goods and chattels and produced evidence to show that her husband had left the country in December, 1792, not with any intention of emigrating, but to pay a visit to Woodstock to get local colour for the production of a tragedy based on the legend of Rosamund. His fellow artists at the Opéra, now renamed Théâtre de la République et des Arts, came forward to testify to his work for the arts and to the fact that he was the bearer of a valid passport issued by the Republic. Madame Noverre submitted correspondence exchanged with her husband tending to

Du feu de son génie il anima la Danse;
Aux beaux jours de la Grèce il sut la rappeler;
Et recouvrant par lui leur antique eloquence
Les Gestes et les Pas aprirent à parler.

*par P. Imbert*

*Jean Georges Noverre*
engraved by B. Roger from the portrait by Guerin (probably
P. N. Guerin, 1774–1833). There is also in existence an
engraving by George Gorvel from the same portrait by Roger.
Courtesy Musée Carnavalet, Paris.

Du Feu de son Genie il anima la Danse:
Au beau jours de la Grèce il sut la rapeller.
En recouvrant par lui leur antique Eloquence.
Les gestes et les Pas aprirent à parler.

*Jean Georges Noverre*
*drawn and engraved by F. K. Sherwin.*

show his patriotism and his inability to return to France because of the war. The application was granted in February, 1795, and an order made that Mr. Noverre was not to be considered as a fugitive and his property, or the value thereof should it prove to have been sold, should be restored to him on payment of the costs of sequestration and of the sale, if sale there had been.[159]

Meanwhile, in London, Noverre, perhaps to counteract any anti-French feeling of which he might be the object, arranged a *Pas de Trois et de Quatre to the favourite air of God Save the King,* which was danced by Mlles. Millard and Hilligsberg and MM. Favre Gardel and Nivelon.

*Venus and Adonis,* given on February 26th, was acclaimed as:—

"one of the most splendid productions of Noverre: it combines the greatest effects of machinery, decoration and action, with the most exquisite dancing as far as Hilligsberg and Millard are concerned. We have had nothing comparable in point of spectacle for several years. One of the most brilliant effects of scenery we ever saw was the ascension of Cupid and Hebe and the descent of Jupiter."[107]

*Iphigenia in Aulide,* produced for the first time on April 23rd with music by Millard, achieved a phenomenal success. Noverre was recalled again and again and crowned on the stage, and the *Morning Chronicle* reported the next day:—

"The ballet of Iphigenia in Aulide, which has been for so long in preparation, was brought out last night. We cannot now from the lateness of the hour at which it continued, give any account of the performance, which in splendour of decoration exceeds everything that we ever witnessed on the British stage; nay the most brilliant period of the opera at Paris did not produce a spectacle more magnificent and more beautiful. Noverre has displayed powers of taste and imagination that give him title to the character of a poet; for the effects which he produces are magical. . . . It was received with rapturous applause and we lament only for the sake of the Theatre, that enough of their season does not remain to pay them for the enormous expense it must have cost."[108]

By the middle of May the ballet was still the main attraction and not only was the house packed night after night, but it was full by seven p.m., a most unusual occurrence since it was fashionable for society not to appear before ten although the curtain was taken up at seven-thirty.

Michael Kelly in his *Reminiscences* has recorded an amusing impression of the ballet and of Noverre:—

"The ballets were of the first class; the great Noverre was the ballet master, and there was a numerous and well-chosen corps de ballet; among others, Didelot, L'Abune, Miss Nivelon, Gardel, Aumer, D'Egville, and Mademoiselle Millau

III

H

(now Madame Gardel) and the fascinating Hillisberg. Noverre produced his magnificent ballet of *L'Iphigenie in Aulide;* the splendour of the spectacle, the scenery, the richness of the decorations and dresses, could not have been surpassed: the dancing was of the first order, and the acting of D'Egville, in Agamemnon, inimitable; the triumphal cars, with horses; the grand marches, processions, above all, the fine grouping of the corps de ballet, all was *vrai* classicality, and proved Noverre to be the greatest master of his art. But he was a passionate little fellow; he swore and tore behind the scenes, so that, at times he might really have been taken for a lunatic escaped from his keeper.

I once felt the effects of his irritability:—The horses attached to the car in which D'Egville was placed, were led by two men from Astley's, one of whom was so drunk that he could not go on the stage. I had been acting in the opera, but was so eager for the affray and so anxious that things should go on right, that I had taken off my opera dress, and put on that of a Grecian supernumerary, and, with a vizor on my face, of course was not known. I held one of the horses, and all went correctly. I was standing behind the scenes, talking to one of the men, in my supernumerary dress, and perhaps rather loudly, Noverre, who was all fire and fury came behind me and gave me a tremendous kick. 'Taisez-vous, bête',[109] exclaimed he; but when I took off my vizor, and Noverre found he had been kicking his manager, he made every possible apology, which I of course accepted, and laughed at the incident; at the same time begging him not to give me another such *striking* proof of his personal attention to the concern. By the way, the carpenters seemed, by their looks, to say, that the kicking was better bestowed on *me*, than on one of themselves; however, I can assure the reader it was the manager's *last* kick."

The 1794 season opened on January 11th with Cimarosa's opera, *Il Matrimonio Segreto,* with dances by Noverre who also produced a new ballet, *Adelaide ou la Bèrgere des Alpes,* with a caste which included Mlles. Miller and Hilligsberg and MM. Aumer and Gentile. On March 1st, Gazaniga's opera *Don Giovanni Tenorio Il Convitato di Piedra* was produced, with a ballet by Noverre in which a funeral procession of over one hundred persons, attired in Spanish period costumes, had to cross the stage but, on the first night, the press of uninvited mourners was such that the artists could barely move and, at subsequent performances, the ban on members of the audience coming on to the stage had to be enforced with renewed strictness.

Noverre, now an accepted favourite with the public, found himself at times called upon to meet the most unexpected calls. On one occasion, after a performance of Bianchi's opera, *Semiramide,* the audience called for the famous singer, Mme. Banti, who had retired to her dressing-room. The prompter made a dozen awkward attempts to make himself heard but the clamour from the auditorium merely grew in violence until Noverre came forward and announced: "Madame

Banti va arriver ce moment", which she did shortly afterwards, in her petticoat, to sing an encore.

On June 23rd a great gala display was staged, to celebrate Lord Howe's victory over the French Republican fleet off the coast of Brest on June 1st, in the course of which there was given an allegorical ballet by Noverre.

Noverre's last production for the stage would seem to have been an allegorical ballet to conclude Paisiello's opera, *La Vittoria*, given at the King's Theatre on July 2nd, 1794. The 1795 season opened on December 6th, 1794, with Mlle. Hilligsberg, Aumer and d'Egville, but Noverre's name does not appear. For a time ballets continued to be given at the King's Theatre and in 1797 the ballet company under Louis d'Egville gave *L'Amour et Psyche* at Covent Garden for a special benefit for the widows and orphans of the men who fell in action at Cape St. Vincent under Sir John Jervis.

# CHAPTER VIII

## *Last Years*

NOVERRE returned to Paris soon afterwards, broken in health, his savings lost in the Revolution, his pension stopped because of his association with the old régime and the lack of funds at the Opéra, and his son dispossessed of his post.

He had no option but to plead with the new authorities for some employment or at least some payment in recognition of his past services. Even though his fame was legendary, he had to wrestle with a bureaucracy handicapped by lost files and the general confusion of the times. He is promised payments which are never made and the post of ballet master at the school attached to the Opéra, previously held by Deshayes, which he never gets. The few letters preserved in the old Archives of the Paris Opéra tell the story of a struggle which must have been particularly galling to the great dancer's proud spirit:—

"23 germinal an 5 (*April 9th*, 1797)
The Citoyen Guinguéné
Ministry of the Interior, 5th division.
Directorate of National Fêtes and Theatres.
To the Administrators of the Théâtre de la République et des Arts.

You will find enclosed, Citoyen, a letter from the Temporary Director General of the liquidation concerning the Citoyen Noverre. Please take note of it and return it to me as soon as possible with such information as will enable one to suggest to the Minister a reply which will leave nothing to be desired concerning the services of this recommendable artist.

Salut et Fraternité."[110]

The letter is endorsed: "The Citoyen Noverre will send us for reforwarding such testimonials as he can obtain from his contemporaries", and round the edge of the paper is written the following answer:—

"22 Floreal, an 5 (*May 11, 1797*)
The Administrators of the Théâtre de la République et des Arts
To the Citoyen Guinguéné
General Directorate of the Home Office
Office of the National Fêtes and Theatres.

Citoyen,
    The Temporary Director of the liquidation has asked the Minister for definite information concerning the numerous and lengthy services of the Citoyen

Noverre and you requested us to undertake all necessary enquiries in the matter.

We enclose, Citoyen, with a letter from Citoyen de Normandie, two testimonials from contemporaries of the Citoyen Noverre, the only documents we have been able to obtain. These statements confirm that in the year 1742 this famous artist was already known and that in 1755 there were in existence several ballets of his composition. There is, however, no information on the year 1738 given as the year of his début or on the date of his retirement from the Opéra. We must point out that this last point can only be confirmed by an extract from the old records which are all in your offices and that absolutely no theatre archives are in our hands.

Salut et Fraternité."[110]

In the meantime the Minister himself intervened:—

"27 germinal an 5 (*April 13 1797*)
The Minister of the Interior to
The Administrators of the Théâtre de la République et des Arts.

It was not without sorrow that I learnt the Citoyen Noverre, whose talents are universally known and have been so valuable to the Théâtre de la République et des Arts, has not yet received the two hundred francs a month which I authorized you to pay to him until the School of Dancing recommences. His colleague Vestris who has had performances for his benefit has none the less drawn a provisional salary. Noverre has at least an equal right since it is the only resource of his advanced years. I therefore pray you, citoyens, to pay here and now, to the Citoyen Noverre, the months of his provisional salary which have fallen due. If the cash resources of the Théâtre do not enable you to pay the whole, you should at least give him the largest possible amount on account. I have no doubt you will do everything in your power to give satisfaction to an artist whose very name should be a sufficient recommendation to an enlightened administration.

Salut et Fraternité."[110]

The months went by, however, and nothing happened, and this time it is Noverre who writes:—

"29 Floreal an 6 (*May 18th, 1798*)                     Paris, 6 Rue du Mail.
The Citoyen Noverre to
The Administrator Théâtre de la République et des Arts.

Citoyen Administrateur,
Permit me to send you my regards and to ask you not to forget me when you send a report to the Minister of the Interior. He assured me he would let me know my fate and that he would give me the position previously held by Deshayes together with the emoluments attached to it when you had assured him that I was fit to fill it.

Salut et Fraternité<br>Noverre."[110]

The letter is endorsed: "the report has been sent".

It is not until 1800 that some final settlement is in sight to judge from a letter from:—

"The Citoyen Noverre, Artist,
To the Minister of the Interior (*Lucien Bonaparte, brother of Napoleon*)
17 Frimaire, an 9 (*December 8th, 1800*)

Citoyen Minister,

I have the honour to inform you that the Citoyen Comptroller has paid me six hundred francs on account of the three thousand due to me according to the attached liquidation signed and certified by him.

Whilst asking you, Citoyen Minister, to accept this expression of my gratitude, I have the honour to suggest that this instalment is absolutely inadequate to lift me out of the sorry situation in which I find myself.

I beg you, Citoyen Minister, to take into consideration my plea not to forget an artist who would have lost all had he ceased to hope in your justice and your kindness.

Salut et Respect

Noverre."

There is attached a statement showing as still due to Noverre:—

| Year 5 | 1400 francs |
|:---:|:---:|
| 6 | 800 |
| 7 | 400 |
| 8 | 400 |
| | In all   3000 francs[110] |

Noverre retired with his wife to the peaceful little town of St. Germain en Laye where he lived at No. 1, Rue de la Surintendance, a stone's throw from the old castle and the hunting lodge in which Louis XIV was born. Not far away Madame Genet Campan, reader and confidante of Marie Antoinette to the day of her death, had opened a school for young ladies of noble birth, to which the Empress Josephine extended her patronage.

Perhaps it is from Madame Campan that he received the dress worn by Marie Antoinette which now hangs in the Castle Museum in Norwich. It is not impossible that the unhappy Queen may have remembered her old dancing master in the hours of her tribulation and have desired him to be given some personal souvenir.[111]

His time is divided between tending the flowers in his garden and rapidly glancing through the daily papers, "for the most part annals of falsehood of which the authors destroy tomorrow what they say today in long phrases descriptive of little things", in which he reads "the follies and extravagances of the day".

When he tires of these he takes his compass and ruler and builds castles in the air, or designs English gardens and Chinese bridges. If the hours should seem to pass slowly there are always good books to turn to, but novels he does not read, for life itself provides a complete romance.

When he goes to Paris, it is to enjoy the society of a few talented artists and men of letters or men whose taste and knowledge he admires.

His ardent spirit, however, cannot rest. He still goes to the Opéra where he follows the progress of the newcomers. He attends rehearsals where he gives his advice to young dancers and deplores that no male dancers are being formed, with the result that the *danseuses* now exceed the *danseurs* in numbers.

He is sorrowed by the deadly monotony which he sees creeping into the spectacles of the Opéra and above all by the manner in which Vestris is forgetting all principles and wasting his great talent in successions of pirouettes.

For the coronation of Napoleon at the end of 1804, he draws up and has printed a first outline of a plan for a gigantic horse-ballet of four *quadrilles,* each made up of sixteen horses preceded and followed by chariots and costumed cavalry, to be staged by torchlight beneath the walls of the Tuileries Palace. This he suggests, should be followed by a firework display and a dinner ballet.[160]

His ballets continue to be revived; *Jason et Médée* is re-staged in 1804, by the younger Gardel and Vestris, and in Russia by his pupil Le Picq, together with *Adèle de Ponthieu,* and *L'Amour et Psyche.*

Fresh editions and translations of his *Lettres sur la Danse et sur les Ballets* are published in Amsterdam in 1787, and Copenhagen and St. Petersburg in 1803.

He publishes in 1807, under the title of *Lettres sur les Arts Imitateurs en général et sur la Danse en Particulier* two volumes dedicated to the Empress Josephine, containing, in addition to the *Lettres sur la Danse et sur les Ballets,* revised, augmented and addressed to his pupil Dauberval, his letters to Voltaire on Garrick, *Letters on the Opéra to a German Princess,* which are a survey of the history of the Opéra since 1740, a series of letters on the organization of public festivals and *Letters on the construction of a new Opera House.* In this latter series of essays he brings his deep knowledge of the stage to bear on the problems facing the architect of a new theatre; passing in review acoustics, lines of sight and the provision of adequate wings. Above all he is concerned with reducing the fire risk which he has seen take such a terrible toll of life and property during his career. He advocates the introduction of a safety curtain, satisfactory gangways and good fire drill measures which are taken for granted now but were unheard of at the time. He favours also replacement of footlights by indirect lighting from the pillars of the proscenium arch which would be hollowed out and furnished with reflectors.

His death at 3 p.m. on October 19th leaves unfinished an article to replace that by Cahusac in the Encyclopædia and a Dictionary of the Dance on which he was working. His wife followed him a month later.

# CHAPTER IX

# *The Ballet d'Action before Noverre*

THE extent and the nature of the contribution of the Chevalier Noverre towards the development of his art must be measured against the low ebb to which the ballet had sunk since the glorious days of the Court Ballet at Versailles in the early years of the reign of Louis XIV.

The decline had set in long before the monarch made his last personal appearance in a court spectacle in 1669 or 1670,[112] as witness the Abbé Michel de Pure's lament in his *Idée des Spectacles Anciens et Nouveaux*, published in 1668:—

"What a relief would it not be . . . if they (*i.e. the dancing masters*) met with persons capable of carrying out their ideas, and of executing correctly a *pas* which they had taught. However able, however ingenious they may be, they are sadly embarrassed by the stupidity of most of the great nobles and persons of quality. Ordinarily they are quite incapable, and thus compel the most dexterous and the most knowledgeable masters to subtract from the form of the *pas* and the sharpness of the movement, and the other graces of the dancing, so as not to kill an *entrée* by the difference between their *pas* and their acting.

The *entrées* of old were made up of but few people . . . and they were, in the ordinary way, careful to trace only four figures, one downstage when dancing facing the audience, one on either side and the fourth and last before returning to the machine or other place whence they had issued. Thus were the dancers appraised and examined from every direction. One saw the defects of the steps, of agility, of expression and, in a word, of all that could be appreciated by the senses. However, luxury having prevailed over intelligence, greater stress was laid on expense than on perfection, on showiness than on solidity and on accessories than on the principal. Little regard now came to be had for the various talents of the dancers, the originality of the steps was despised and, worst of all, it was desired to please the Court and the Ladies, who are the two rocks on which common sense is wrecked and are the evil destinies of fine works. The scene was packed with people of quality who were shamelessly sought out that a part of the expense might be unloaded on them and who accepted out of vanity. All that the intelligent professionals, who found themselves burdened not only with this large number of people of quality, but also with their clumsy, presumptuous and therefore incorrigible efforts, were able to do was to complicate the *entrées* by a large number of figures and mask as best they could by these various changes the faults of these great nobles, who were either badly made or poor dancers. This I believe to be the source of this habit of multiplying and varying at every turn the number of figures."

He goes on to point out that the result was badly made figures which were too short to take in their real character and that the failure of the performers to study the manner in which they should proceed from one figure to another resulted in general confusion.[113]

The decline in the number of good dancers, which forced Molière in 1661 to separate the various entrées of *Les Fâcheux* and to insert them in the intervals of the comedy, so that the dancers might have time to change their costumes, caused the court ballet to merge insensibly into opera with Jean Baptiste Lully.

Jean Baptiste Lully, one of the leading violinists in eighteenth-century Europe, was a composer of genius as well as a good dancer and a sound theatrical craftsman. Whilst his operas, evolved from the Italian opera which had failed to gain any real popularity in France and from the Court Ballet, gave pride of place to the musical score, they were well constructed and contained a large element of dancing expressive of a mood or mass characterization, as witness the "baneful dreams" in *Atys* (1676), or the "trembleurs" in *Isis* (1677). His music, whilst retaining the traditional dance rhythms, the gigues, canaries and passepieds, had clarity of form and, just as Bérain, who designed the décors and costumes for most of his productions, refined the exuberant baroque of Parigi and Torelli, so Lully developed a classical stylization in keeping with the theme in place of the Italian bravura.

In the comedy-ballets of Molière as in the operas of Lully there was a theatrical coherence, resulting from the close co-operation of one librettist, Molière and later Quinault, one musician, Lully, one choreographer, Beauchamp, and one designer, Bérain,[114] which was lacking in the later ballets.

The adoption of a raised stage, separated from the audience by the proscenium arch, caused the stage-spectacle to be seen from in front instead of from above, and this gave added importance to the vertical plane where hitherto the accent had been essentially on the horizontal choreographic pattern.

At the same time, the impetus given to the development of technique by the work of the School of Dancing, added to the Royal Academy of Music in 1672, and the emergence of the professional *danseuse*[115] opened the door wide for the virtuoso.

The cynical comment made by Campra, on whose shoulders had descended Lully's mantle of principal purveyor of ballet music, that "the only way to popularize opera-ballet is to lengthen the dances and shorten the dancers' skirts" was soon realized, for, in 1730, Camargo shortened her skirt by several inches to just above the instep, the better to beat her *entrechats.*

The serious operas of Lully gave way to the *opéra-divertissements* of A. Houdar de la Motte, which were no more than a number of separate *divertissements* loosely united by a common theme. By the middle of the century, any pretence even of a coherent theme had been abandoned and the earlier *Fêtes de* . . . and *Amours de* . . ., which served as a generic title, had been replaced by the more appropriate *Fragments de* . . ., a hotch-potch of ten or twelve scenes from various operas and ballets which the public no longer looked on as a dramatic entertainment but as an excuse to display the virtuosity of their favourite star attired in the costume of her choice.

As late as 1774, F. A. de Chevrier could write in *Les Ridicules du Siècle:*—

"The ballets of the last century constituted a *divertissement* inspired by reason and governed by good taste, the décors were governed by verisimilitude and the dancers expressed but pleasure; the harmonious music, facile and tender was made to charm the ears. . . .

Our ballets conceived without genius, devised without any plan, executed without taste, are but a shapeless warehouse of notes, of paintings, of dances, of woods, of monsters and of women. Mythology, which reigns over our lyric theatres, has been the cause of some of the vexations we have come to tolerate. Did not men suffice to produce extravaganzas, was it necessary to associate gods further to depart from realism?

A ballet divided into three or four *entrées* forms four different themes or, to be more precise, provides four occasions to introduce machines and dances divided between pleasure and suffering which proclaim by exactly the same figures love or the death of a hero."[116]

An English writer, Angelo, in his *Reminiscences* published in 1830, has left us a description indicative of the extent to which the stage was dominated by the dancer in vogue:—

"To return to Fierville, when he made his entrée in the ballet sérieux, the figurantes retired to the further end of the stage, and you beheld a figure with a cap on and an enormous high plume of ostrich feathers, a very long waist and a hoop extending on each side above a foot, the petticoat hanging as low as the knee; when sinking like a lady's curtsey, and rising gradually till he stood in an erect position, he was seen standing on the points of his toes. In a very few strides, he seemed to move in the air, till he approached almost to the orchestra and after a few *entrechats,* he lights on the extremity of one of his feet and then, in a most graceful attitude, he balances himself and remains stationary some seconds— which used to elicit abundance of applause."[117]

The reaction came in the first instance not from the dancing masters, but from the philosophers and the æsthetes who seized afresh on the idea of rediscovering the theatre of the ancient Greeks and Romans, an idea which, since the fall of Constantinople to Mahomet II in 1452, had sent Greek men of letters flying to the West to kindle the Renaissance and the discovery, at St. Gal in 1414, of Vitruvius' *De Architectura*, which was to govern theatrical architecture for nearly three hundred years, had obsessed poets, dramatists, musicians and dancing masters responsible for the creation of court entertainments.[118]

The Abbé de Pure's *Idée des Spectacles Anciens et Nouveaux* (1669) is a passionate plea for the reform of the ballet which he defines as:—

"a dumb show in which gesture and movement express that which would be conveyed in words. By this it is easy to see the defects of those ballets in which one knows nothing except by the recitative sung therein, by the programmes which are distributed and by the verse which is inserted to unravel the subject and to display the idea, the substance and the link between them. For this entertainment is designed almost for the eyes alone. The ears are only entitled to secondary pleasures and all that which the spectator cannot see in the *pas*, in the characters and in the other play of the spectacle, all that, I say, is not subject matter for a ballet and can but uneasily be put into a reasonable form.

It must therefore be a performance both spiritual and sensible, of which the design must be ingenious, the substance even and artistic and the execution full of strength and relief. . . . Thus tragedy and ballet are two kinds of painting. . . . Provided that it can dispense with words and yet make its silence intelligible . . . it speaks but with feet and hands, and that its gestures and its movements decipher and develop all the mysteries of the drawing, it has satisfied all its requirements. For the ballet is after all but a dumb fable, in which the Ancients were so well versed that, without any need of an interpreter they caused to be read in their acting and their dance, their designs and their thoughts, as though they had used voice and words."

He then proceeds to stress the importance of the choice of a suitable subject capable of expression in terms of the ballet without the need of cumbersome accessories; the necessity of subordinating the part to the whole and the importance of composition and design; the advisability of division to make for clearer understanding, whilst seeing that the various *entrées* spring naturally from the subject matter and maintain balanced proportions to each other.

"The *pas* does not consist merely of subtle movements of the feet or varied agitation of the body. It is made up of both of these and embraces all that a well-trained body may be capable of in the way of gestures and acting to express something without words . . . the principal and most important rule is to make the *pas* expressive, that the head, the shoulders, the arms, the hands may convey that which the dancer does not say. In the time of Nero a mime was prized by a barbaric king above all other gifts which he might hope to receive from the Emperor, because of the great talent he possessed of speaking with his hands whilst dancing and of representing by his gestures all that which might have emanated from his words. It is easy to see thereby that dancing did not consist in dexterity of the feet alone or in the precision of the rhythm (for he would do without all the instruments current in his time) but in a certain converted manner taken from natural movements, which escape from the body following on the disturbances and various agitations of the soul which betray despite our wishes the interior movements which we try to conceal and keep secret. Therein lies the skill of the dancing master, in attuning this movement of the dance with his idea, with the rhythm of the tune, and in so managing that he runs counter to neither the one nor the other: to observe in a furious person a hasty, choleric *pas* that, by broken measures or broken *coupés*, one may realize the confusion and frenzy of the character. . . ."

The music, he suggests, should be suited to the characters to be represented, majestic tunes for kings, sad airs for grief, etc. and he deplores the lack of interest of the poet-librettists in the music and the dance, with the consequent failure to co-ordinate the whole. The dancers do not consider the recitative in any way necessary to the ballet and the singers are convinced a ballet is imperfect if music and recitative are lacking. The recitative, which is usually sung by a single voice or at the most by a very small chorus, he regards as a useful complement to the ballet but far from essential and he would have it express the action of the dancer.

Masks, provided they are well made, he considers as a help in identifying the character represented in the eyes of the spectators, but he deplores the failure to suit the costumes worn to the period and the personage portrayed. Regardless of the desire of the dancers to please the ladies or themselves, they should be made to wear costumes suitably designed for the part.[113]

After the Abbé de Pure the Dutch philologist, Isaac Vossius (1618–1689), in his *De Poematum cantu et viribus Rythmi,* published at Oxford in 1673, deplored the lack of expression in the danced spectacles of his time which, despite their lavish presentation, were devoid of anything more than form designed to please the eye and he opposed to the meaningless gestures of the dancers the eloquent pantomime of the ancients.

In 1710, Pierre Jean Burette, physician and musician, published his *Treize Mémoires sur la Gymnastique des Anciens* followed, in 1713, by Niccolo Calliachi's *De Ludis Scenicis Mimorum et Pantomimium* and the Abbé Jean Baptiste du Bos' *Réflexions sur la Poésie et sur la Peinture,* published in 1719 and reissued in 1723 in an augmented edition. The essence of their thinking was based on the concepts of Plato, Aristotle and Plutarch. They visualized the danced spectacle as an animated and living painting and advocated the exteriorization of the human passions by rhythmic imitation of the actions which they naturally engendered.

Du Bos, a noted archæologist and historian, unlike his coll eagu, was not only conscious of the gulf which separated the dancing choruses in the Greek tragedies from the ballets of his time but able to see in the operas of Lully an attempt, conscious or unconscious, to realize an expressive form of dancing. He had witnessed too, at the fourteenth *Grande Nuit de Sceaux* in 1708, an experimental attempt engendered by the seeking after novelty of the Duchess de Maine rather than by any desire for reform, by Françoise Prévost and Balon[120] to render in mime the last scene of the fourth act of Corneille's *Les Horaces* set to music by Jean Joseph Mouret.

In 1746, therefore, after Noverre had made his stage début, there appeared *Les Beaux Arts réduits à un Même Principe,* by the Abbé Batteux, in which the function of the arts was defined as:—

"to transport the lines and features which are in Nature and to present them in objects to which they are not natural. . . . The arts, in that which is pure art, are but imitations, resemblances which are not Nature, but seem so to be; and the substance of the fine arts is not the real but only the verisimilar. . . . In a word an imitation wherein one sees Nature, not as she is in herself, but as she can be, and one can conceive her in spirit. . . . A distillation of nature, not a copy of a living character but a collection of all the characteristic features of such people."

Like his predecessors, Batteux justified his theories by reference to the Ancients and especially to Aristotle. He commented on the fact that music used to embrace the dance and declamation and put forth the dictum that all music and all dance must have a meaning and made a plea for unity of conception to be found in the imitation of the same subject in nature. His knowledge of dancing was, however, rudimentary and he conceived the composition of the ballet very largely by analogy with musical theory:—

"All is calculated by the measure which regulates the duration of each tone and each gesture; secondly by the tempo which hastens or retards this same time without increasing or diminishing the number of tones or gestures, or changing their quality; thirdly by the melody which unites these tones and gestures to form a suite and fourthly by the harmony which regulates the chords where several different parts unite to form a whole. . . .

. . . the measure is in the steps; the tempo in the deliberation or the speed; the melody in the development or continuity of the steps, and the harmony in the agreement of all the parts with the accompanying instrument and especially in the other dancers, for in the dance there are solos, duos, choruses, refrains, meeting points and repeats which follow the same rules as in music."

Rémond de Saint-Mard, in his *Réflexions sur l'Opéra* in 1741, and Jean Jacques Rousseau, in his *Nouvelle Héloise* and his *Dictionnaire de la Musique*, added their voices to the call for more expression in the arts.

Louis de Cahusac brought the focus down from the arts in general to the dance in particular with his *Danse Ancienne et Moderne, ou Trait historique de la Danse*, published in 1754, in which, embracing the æsthetics of du Bos and Batteux, he deplored the dance of his day and forecast the coming of the *ballet d'action*. He saw this expression, however, as something which would be attained by embroidering gestures on to the traditional dance forms.

Diderot, in his *Troisième Entretien sur le Fils Naturel* in 1757, wrote:—

"Above all, forget the sensational; seek for pictures; get close to real life and first of all leave room for the exercise of pantomime to the fullest extent. . . . I really believe that neither the poets, musicians, décor artists, nor dancers, have as yet a true conception of their theatre. Is it not prostituting philosophy, poetry, music, painting and dancing to busy them with an obscurity? Each of those arts in particular has for aim the imitation of nature. . . .

The dance awaits still a man of genius; it is everywhere bad because it is barely suspected that it is an imitative art. The dance is to pantomime as poetry is to prose, or rather as natural declamation is to song. It is a measured pantomime.

I would like to be told what is the meaning of all these dances such as the minuet, the passe-pied, the rigaudon, the allemande, the sarabande, in which one follows a predetermined pattern. . . .

A dance is a poem. That poem should therefore have its separate performance. It is an imitation in movement which supposes the assistance of the poet, of the painter, of the musician and of the mime. It has its subject; that subject can be broken down into acts and scenes. The scene has its recitative and its arietta."

He thought of the ballet as a spectacle in which everything was subordinated to the theme, but that theme and the co-ordination of the work of the musician, the scenic artist and the ballet master were to be dictated by the poet-librettist, the rôle of the ballet master being confined to the devising of the steps and gestures to fit the music.

All these advocates of reform, with the possible exception of Cahusac who, whilst he could write with authority on the history of dancing, was unacquainted with its technique, had, however, no real practical experience of the stage, and the only attempts by men of the theatre before Noverre to put these ideas into practice remained outside the main stream of the art of ballet.

John Weaver, a Shrewsbury dancing master, in his *Essay towards a History of Dancing* written in 1712, pointed out that:—

"stage dancing was at first designed for *Imitation;* to explain Things conceiv'd in the Mind, by the *Gestures* and *Motions* of the *Body,* and plainly and intelligibly representing *Actions, Manners* and *Passions;* so that the Spectator might perfectly understand the *Performer* by these his *Motions,* tho' he say not a Word. . . . Scenical *Dancing* is a faint imitation of the Roman *Pantomimes*" and "explains whole *Stories* by *Action.*"

He had in fact created at Drury Lane as early as 1702, an entertainment of "Dancing, action and motion only", *The Cheats of Scapin or the Tavern Bilkers,* followed by *The Loves of Mars and Venus, Perseus and Andromeda* and *The Rape of Columbine* in 1716, *Orpheus and Eurydice* and *Cupid and Bacchus* in 1717. We know little about these productions which, together with those of John Rich at Lincoln's Inn Fields, led to the development of the English pantomime, but they would seem to have exercised little or no influence on the art of ballet on the Continent, unless it be indirectly through Dupré, who appeared in the *Loves of Mars and Venus,* and Marie Sallé. Noverre himself would seem to have been but little impressed by the English pantomime as it was when he came to London in 1755.

In Vienna, Franz Hilverding, to judge from the titles of his ballets and the claims put forward by his pupil Angiolini, and his apostle Stefano Arteaga, would appear to have created a form of *ballet d'action* on which we are ill informed but which would seem to have taken the form of loosely linked sequences of character dances. His work remained little known in France, although it may have exercised greater influence in Russia where the ballet was still at a very early stage of development. Noverre did not meet Hilverding until the close of the latter's career, and seven years after the publication of the *Lettres sur la Danse,* and would not seem to have had any opportunity of studying his work at first hand although he had probably heard accounts of it from Eva Weigel or Violetti who, before her marriage to Garrick, had been a pupil of Hilverding in Vienna.

# CHAPTER X

# *The Writings of Noverre*

NOVERRE's æsthetic theory, as expressed in his *Lettres sur la Danse et sur les Ballets*, published in 1760, and which he refines perhaps but does not alter in his *Lettres sur les Arts Imitateurs* in 1807, is that held by the enlightened æsthetes of his century, with whose work he was certainly acquainted, but he differs from them in that his approach is essentially that of a practical man of the theatre. He brings to bear an intimate knowledge, gained on the stage, of the problems of creation and production of spectacles of dancing, from which his theories are built up step by step.

His *Lettres sur la Danse* are, in his eyes, but a "frontispiece to the monument" he proposed to erect to the action-dance, and his real contribution is to be his ballets created on the living stage and the pupils he will form and who will in turn add to and pass on his teaching by example and precept, and it is as much by his ballets as by his writings that we must appraise his work.

His writings are, to all intents and purposes, grouped together in the two volumes of his *Lettres sur les Arts Imitateurs en général et sur la Danse en Particulier*, published in Paris in 1807. The whole of the first volume and the first three chapters of the second may be said to embody, in the form of letters addressed to his pupil Dauberval, his ideas on the teaching of dancing and the creation and production of ballets as originally set out in his *Lettres sur la Danse et sur les Ballets*, published in Lyons and Stuttgart in 1760, revised in 1783, and enlarged upon in the prefaces to the various ballets included in the *Recueil des Programmes de Ballets*, published in Vienna in 1776. Chapters four to thirteen of the second volume, letters addressed to a German princess, form a history of the Paris Opéra, its administration and the dancers and ballet masters who have appeared or are appearing there and, whilst they are of the greatest interest historically, add little to our knowledge of his art. Neither can we learn anything from chapters fourteen and fifteen, containing the correspondence with Voltaire, or from chapter sixteen, outlining his suggestions for the construction of a new opera house, unless it is to note once again his extraordinarily catholic knowledge. Chapters seventeen to twenty-one are a criticism of government-sponsored fêtes and chapter twenty-two is largely an account of the theatre arts at the beginning of the nineteenth century. We are left, then, with the first volume and the first three chapters of the *Lettres sur les Arts Imitateurs* and the scenarios contained in the last chapter of the second volume together with those published in Vienna and London.

In the *Lettres sur les Arts Imitateurs*, the vivid imagery and forceful style of the 1760 *Lettres sur la Danse*, from which lengthy passages are incorporated with little or no alteration, has been retained, but there is some attempt at a more logical classification of the subject matter and the vitriolic outbursts of the young ballet master striving to make himself heard have been tempered where they are likely to wound. The ideas expressed are sometimes enlarged upon but remain fundamentally unaltered except that, whereas in 1760 he thought, like his contemporaries, to recreate the Græco-Roman theatre, by 1807 further research into the past has convinced him that the pantomime of the Ancients was an art of gesture, governed doubtless by rhythm and measure but not a danced spectacle, with which comparison was rendered impossible by the progress in stage and dancing technique over the centuries.

The essence of his æsthetic philosophy is that "Poetry, painting and dancing are, or should be, no more than a faithful likeness of beautiful Nature". For him there is "but one rule common to all the arts and which we may depart from only at the risk of being misled, and that is the imitation of beautiful Nature", imitation denoting creative synthesis rather than servile copy.[122]

All the hitherto accepted conventions and rules of his art are measured afresh and retained only insofar as they can contribute to the imitation of nature. The "five positions" are "good to know but better still to forget"; in other words they are the ABC which should become so automatic as not to intrude on the consciousness of artist or audience. He bids his dancers "renounce over-complicated steps" and would have them "give less attention to their legs and more to their arms; abandon *cabrioles* in favour of gestures; perform fewer difficult steps but put more expression into their faces; devote less strength to their execution but invest it with greater meaning; gracefully set aside the narrow rules of the classroom to follow the impression of nature and to give to dancing the soul and the action required to arouse interest". He is at pains to stress that action does not mean a "bustling activity" but "the art of impressing, by truly significant movements, gesture and facial expression, our feelings on the minds of the audience". In the dancer, "each gesture, each *port de bras* must have a different expression for true pantomime in any style follows nature in its every shade".[123] Gesture must be spontaneous expression underlining the feelings; artificial gestures are meaningless and pantomime must not be construed as movements of the arms alone or as the conventional mime devised by the Abbé de l'Epée.[124] The entire body of the dancer must be expressive, including his eyes and his hands. "The expression of the head, the action of the arms, attitudes . . . that is what speaks in dancing . . . Dancers must speak and express their thoughts through the medium of gestures and physiognomy; all their movements, their every action, their repose even, must have a meaning, be eloquent . . ."[125]

"Whilst recognizing that there are a multitude of things which pantomime cannot convey, in the passions there is a degree of expression which words cannot attain. That is where the action-dance triumphs. A step, a gesture, a movement, an attitude say that which no words can express; the more the sentiments to be painted are violent, the fewer the words to convey them. Exclamations which are as the ultimate terms to which the language of the passions can rise become inadequate and they are then replaced by gesture."[124] By this means the ballet will rise above the spoken drama for "with a play, the impression received by each member of the audience will vary accordingly as he is possessed of a greater or lesser propensity to be moved so that, from the least sensitive to the most sensitive spectator, there are a multitude of shades each of which is proper to each one of the spectators". It follows that "the dialogue of the author will be pitched above or below the degree of sensitivity of the greater majority of the audience. The cold and unemotional man will nearly always find it exaggerated whilst he who is easily exalted will the more often find it weak . . . Pantomime has not this drawback. It does but indicate by steps, gestures, movements and the expression, the physiognomy, the situation and the feelings of each character and it leaves it to each spectator to give to it a dialogue which will be all the more fitting in that it will always be in just proportion to the emotional impulse received".[126]

The choreographer will, therefore, not confine himself to the art of "arranging with grace, precision and facility steps to a given air", any more than the musician confines himself to "combining sounds and modulations calculated agreeably to flatter the ear", but he will "study the character and accent of the passions and transmute them into his compositions" by "seeking the movements and gestures which characterize them". All that exists in the universe can serve as his model and he should, therefore, examine everything. "How many varied pictures will he not find amongst workmen and artisans! Each has different attitudes born of the positions and movements which his work imposes. This stance, this deportment, this way of moving, always common to his trade and always pleasing, must be suggested by the choreographer for it is all the easier to imitate in that it is inherent in the people of a given trade even when they have made a fortune and given up their profession, for it is the result of habit acquired in the course of the years and strengthened by toil and hardship."

"How many quaint and curious pictures will he not find in the crowd of pleasing idlers made up of those petty fops who ape and caricature in the most ridiculous manner those on whom age, rank and fortune seem to confer the privilege of being frivolous inconsequent and fatuous."

"Crowded streets, public walks, pleasure gardens, rural pastimes and occupations, a village wedding, hunting, fishing, harvesting and the vintage, the rustic manner of watering a flower, of plucking it and offering it to one's beloved, of bird-nesting and playing a reed pipe, all will provide him picturesque and varied pictures different in colour and character . . ."[127]

Mime, however, is not in his eyes a substitute for dancing. He makes this clear, in his *Lettres sur la Danse*, when he writes:—

"A *Maître de Ballets* who is not perfectly acquainted with the Dance can be but a mediocre choreographer. I understand by Dance, the classical dance which is the fundamental basis of the ballet . . . I compare the classical dance with a mother-tongue; the mixed and corrupt styles derived therefrom are as those barely intelligible jargons which vary in ratio to the distance away from the Capital where the pure tongue is spoken."[128]

Lest his contemporaries should be under any misapprehension on the subject, he is later at pains to reiterate the principle, in the preface to *Euthyme et Eucharis:*—"I will try to put action into my ballets without, however, renouncing dancing which must be the basis and foundation", and in the *Lettres sur les Arts Imitateurs:*—"A ballet without dancing cannot exist . . . A ballet is but a great dancing composition and pantomime is the soul of the dance and vivifies the ballet . . . I have decided to reunite action with dancing; to accord it some expression and purpose . . ."[129]

A ballet, as he conceived it, was "a picture, or rather a series of pictures connected one with the other by the plot which provides the theme of the ballet; the stage is, as it were, the canvas on which the choreographer, who is the painter, expresses his ideas; the mechanical movements of the dancers are his colours, their physiognomy is the brush and the *ensemble* and variety of the scenes, the choice of music, the décor and the costumes are the tones."[121]

In selecting the theme it must be borne in mind that "there are limits to any art which the wise choreographer will not transgress" and, in particular, that mime can only express the present but not the past or the future unless recourse be had to conventional mime which he discards.

"It is impossible for the dancer happily to dialogue" and mime "cannot express all that which is related to cold reasoning. In a ballet there must be a good deal of spectacle and of action to replace speech, much passion and feeling to take the place of discourse and, even so, the passion must be strongly expressed in order to create great effects. Pantomime must always paint broadly and use the strongest colours and the boldest strokes because half-tints throw but an obscure and indefinite half light on the nature of this or that person . . ."[130]

He advocates "less of the fairy tale, less of the marvellous, more truth and more realism . . . A comet, the signs of the zodiac, the hours and so on" cannot be expressed except by conventional figures, and he pleads for the appearance of "ordinary mortals" on the stage for, "it is certain the tears of Andromache, the love of Junia and Britannicus, the passion of Merope for Aegisthus, the submission of Iphigenia and the eternal love of Clytemnestra will arouse our feelings much more than all the magic of our Opéra."[131]

He breaks with contemporary practice in the French theatre and, following Shakespeare and the British school of dramatists, decrees that a ballet need not necessarily be bound by Aristotle's unities of time, place and action, but it "must be divided into scenes and acts and each scene, like each act, should have a beginning, a central portion and a conclusion" or, in other words, an introduction, plot and climax . . . but it must not be "stretched out to five acts if it will fill but three."

"A skilful *maître de ballet* should be able to see at a glance the general effect of the entire scene and never sacrifice the whole to the part. It is only by forgetting for a while the principals in the ballet that he will be able to concentrate on the company as a body. If he confine his attention to the leading dancers, the development of the theme will be halted and the progress of the scenes slowed down when the execution will fail to achieve its effect . . ."

"There is no room for the superfluous in the theatre and, therefore, the stage should be stripped of anything likely to retard the action, and only the exact number of artists necessary to the execution of the play should be introduced . . ."

"The ballet-pantomime should always be concerned with action and the *corps de ballet* should only take the place of the artist who leaves the scene, in order to fill it in turn not merely with symmetrical figures and formal steps, but with a lively and animated expression calculated to hold the interest of the audience in the subject developed by the preceding artists . . ."[132]

"Make the members of your *corps de ballet* dance, but let them express whilst dancing something that will contribute to the picture; let them be mimes constantly transformed in appearance by the passions with which they are imbued. If their gestures and features are ever in harmony with their souls, the resulting expression will convey their feelings and strengthen your work. Never go to a rehearsal with a head stuffed with figures but devoid of common sense, but be imbued with your subject and an imagination of the theme you wish to depict will provide you with the means of translating it into form and colour. Your composition will be full of life and will ring true. Raise the love of your art to the pitch of enthusiasm. One succeeds in theatrical composition only insofar as the heart is stirred, the soul is moved, the imagination is kindled, the passions thunder and genius flashes."

"If on the contrary you are tepid, your blood is sluggish in your veins, your heart is of ice and your soul insensitive, then give up the theatre; renounce an art that is not for you and turn to a profession in which imagination is secondary to muscular effort and where genius is of less import than manual dexterity."[133]

The size of the *corps de ballet* will be determined by the size of the stage, but usually twenty-four plus eight *coryphées* will be found adequate.[134]

The *coryphées* head the *corps de ballet*, determine the alignment and lead in tracing the figures. They play a definite part in the unfolding of the theme.[135]

"A ballet must not be painted in miniature but with bold strokes of the brush and the *corps de ballet* should pronounce and articulate strongly and clearly all their movements . . . They should not be given steps too complicated for them to execute."[134]

"Music must take into account that legs cannot move as quickly as fingers . . . Rameau set an example which was followed by Gossec, Floquet and Sacchini, when composing for the dance and took into account the ability of the dancers."[134]

"Music is to dancing what words are to music . . . The *maître des ballets* who is ignorant of music will ill-phrase his melodies and will fail to understand their spirit and their character. Unless he be endowed with that sensitive ear which is more often the gift of nature than the result of art and which surpasses that which may be acquired by study and practice, he will not fit the danced movement to the measure of the music with the requisite precision and fine musicality . . ."

"The selection of suitable music is as essential to the dance as is the choice of words and the turn of phrase to eloquence. It is the tempo and melodic line of the music which fix and determine the movements of the dance . . ."

"From the intimate affinity between music and dancing, there is no doubt that a *maître des ballets* will derive definite advantages from a practical knowledge of that art. He will be able to communicate his ideas to the composer and, should he unite taste to knowledge, he may compose the music himself or indicate to the composer the principal themes which should inspire his work . . . Good music should paint, should speak, and the dance, in imitating these sounds, will be the echo which repeats everything it articulates. If, on the contrary, it be mute and give the dancer nothing, he cannot reply to it and then all feeling and all expression is banished from the execution."[136]

"A dancer without an ear is the picture of a madman who talks ceaselessly and who articulates disconnected words devoid of common sense. Speech serves him but to show reasonable people his madness and his extravagance. The dancer without ear, like the madman, executes ill-combined steps, is always astray in his execution, ever chasing after time and never catching up with it. He feels nothing and everything is wrong in him, his dancing has neither reason nor expression and the music which should govern his movements, order his steps and determine his rhythm, but underlines his failings and his imperfections."[137]

"A composer should have a knowledge of dancing, or at least be familiar with the steps and the possibilities of the movements proper to each style and each character . . ."

He goes on to plead for closer collaboration between choreographer and composer and the abandonment of the traditional dance forms in favour of compositions better suited to modern dancing technique. "It is not sufficient to arrange notes according to conventional rules; the harmonic progression of the tones must in this case imitate those of nature and the judicious inflexion of the sounds suggest the dialogue."[137]

Any recitative is unnecessary and words which "chill and weaken the interest" are superfluous if the dancing is expressive.

"Ballets are . . . not subject to unity of time, place and action but demand absolute unity of design so that all the scenes may converge to the same end."[138]

"The combination of colours, their gradation and their effect under stage lighting should also claim the attention of the choreographer . . . Any décor is a giant picture ready for the insertion of figures. The actors, actresses and dancers are the characters who are to grace and embellish it but, if the picture is to please and not offend the sight, just proportions must be observed in all its different parts . . The colours of the draperies and costumes must stand out against the décor which I compare to a beautiful background which if it be not restful and harmonious, or if the colours be too bright or gleaming, will destroy the harmony of the picture. It will destroy the relief which the figures should enjoy and nothing will stand out because nothing will be ordained with artistry and the garishness resulting from the unhappy association of colours, will offer but a panel of cut-outs illuminated without taste or intelligence . . .

"In scenes of chaste beauty, carried out with few colours, rich and striking costumes can be introduced as well as those slashed with brilliant primary colours. In fanciful and exotic scenes, such as a Chinese palace or a public square in Constantinople decorated for a festival, which are subject to no strict rules and therefore leave greater latitude to the painter whose originality in conception will determine the success of the décor, in such scenes, high in colour, hung with fabrics, enriched with gold and silver, draped costumes, in a simple style in hues entirely contrasted with those prominent in the décor, are desirable. Unless this rule is observed, the whole effect will be lost for lack of shade and contrast. All must be harmonious on the stage and, when the décor is made for the costumes and the costumes for the décor, the charm of the performance will be complete."[139]

He pleads for the abolition of *tonnelets, panniers* and full-bottomed wigs, and to appreciate the urgency of this reform it may not be amiss to consider the costumes currently worn by dancers at the time.

The accepted costume of the classical *danseur* was based on that of contemporary representations of that of a Roman officer, and consisted of a plumed and jewelled headdress, a tight fitting coat (in imitation of the *cuirasse*) ending in a short skirt or *tonnelet* stretched over an iron or whalebone frame with sleeves puffed from shoulder to elbow and then tight-fitting to the wrist, breeches and buskins or stockings and shoes. The costume might be embroidered in silver on blue caddis with breeches of red caddis or pink and blue taffeta, likewise embroidered. The coat might have a *tonnelet* of black damask. As a shepherd, a dancer might wear white caddis with a headdress of white with two plumes; as a warrior the colour scheme might be of silver squares on black and red caddis; as a magician grey linen embroidered with red woollen bullion . . .

For the female dancer, the classical costume was an adaptation of the contemporary court dress with hair drawn back flat over the head and ornamented with jewels or, more often, flowers. The dress consisted of a bodice, cut low at the breasts, tightly laced and terminating in a point with puffed sleeves ending at the elbow, so as to leave the lower arm bare with ribbon at the wrist; the skirt was stretched over a *pannier* or "hen-coop", a hooped petticoat which varied in shape, as fashions changed, from being funnel shaped to becoming elliptical as it was flattened front and back; later still it grew in circumference and small pads, high enough to rest the elbow on, were added at the sides. The skirt proper was made up of an over-skirt and an under-skirt, falling to just above the instep.

The embroidered skirt might be of blue caddis with a bodice and over-skirt of red taffeta with blue sleeves, or a white satin skirt embroidered in gold with bodice and over-skirt of green taffeta trimmed with braid and fringe, or bodice and skirt of one piece in white taffeta ornamented with blue and poppy red and embroidered down the front. For character parts the only changes made were in the degree and motive of the trimmings. The shoes invariably had a heel.

Instead he wished "to banish all symmetry in the costumes" and preferred to see "light and simple draperies of contrasting colours worn in such a manner as to reveal the dancers' figure . . . light but without stinting material, beautiful folds, beautiful masses with the ends of the draperies fluttering and producing ever changing forms and, as the dance becomes more lively and animated, gaining in lightness". He praised the efforts made by Mlle. Clairon, M. Chassé and M. le Kain towards a greater degree of realism and historical accuracy in costume and regretted that Boquet had not been allowed to carry his reforms at the Opéra as far as he would have wished. Finally he urged the abolition of masks which made any visual expression impossible and gave to the dancer a stereotyped appearance out of keeping with the introduction of a greater element of mime into his dancing. "Would it not be possible, by abolishing masks, to induce the dancers to make up their faces in a more picturesque and realistic manner? Could they not make good the toning down of distance and, with the aid of light colours and lines artistically applied with a brush, give to their faces the particular character desired?"[140]

There must be graduation in the heights of the dancers, even to the point of introducing children to respect perspective where figures were required to be seen in the distant background.

Lighting too is passed in review. It is not "a large number of lamps distributed haphazard or symmetrically arranged that adequately light a stage or set off the scene to advantage; the art lies in knowing how to distribute the lights in uneven groups so as to bring out the parts which require full lighting and to leave in shadow or darkness, as may be required, the other parts. The scenic artist, being obliged to put varying shades and tones into his décor to give it perspective, should be consulted by the person responsible for the lighting so that the same highlights and shadows may be respected. Nothing would be worse than a décor painted in the same tone of colour and the same hue, for there would be neither distance nor perspective. In the same way, if the various parts which make up a décor are lighted uniformly, there will be no harmony, no grouping and no contrast and the scene will be ineffective."[141]

The opera-ballet presents a different problem, which he solves by using it, much as did Norton and Somerville in *Gorboduc*, in 1561, or Molière in *Les Fâcheux*, to point the moral of the previous act and to link it with the following act.

"So long as ballets in opera are not intimately linked to the theme and do not contribute to its introduction, plot and climax, they will seem cold and tedious. Each ballet should, to my mind, present a scene which links and binds the first act intimately to the second, the second to the third and so on. These scenes, which would be essential to the unfolding of the theme, would be lively and animated. The dancers, to interpret them realistically and precisely, would have to abandon their posturing and take unto themselves a soul; they would have, as it were, to forget their legs and feet and to think of their facial expression and their gestures. Each ballet would be a poem suited to the act and these poems, based on the very essence of the theme, could be written by the librettist . . ."[141]

These principles he rounds off with a list of the subjects with which a choreographer must be well acquainted, even though he cannot be expected to be master of all of them. In addition to a profound knowledge of every aspect of the dance, based on long practice, and a good musical background sufficient to guide him in the choice of music and the phrasing of danced movements in harmony with the score, he will find some knowledge of geometry useful in the construction of his figures. He should be sufficiently acquainted with stage machines to be able to make his own working model, explain just what he requires and relate his requirements to the theatre he is in. He should know enough of the painter's arts to make the most of drapery, *chiaroscuro*, the blending of colours, etc. The laws of drawing and composition should have no secrets for him. The observation of people in different walks of life should have provided him with an intimate knowledge of their type of movement and their behaviour in given circumstances. The study of the masterpieces of drama should have instructed him in dramatic construction, and the reading of history and mythology and the frequentation of other artists should have refined his taste and widened his horizon. He must be capable of demonstrating to his dancers just what he requires of them and must personally sketch out the steps and action until they have been mastered and this he cannot do sitting in a chair. He must be able to enter into the age, sex and feelings of each character in each situation and finally he must be endowed with taste and imagination.

"A *premier danseur*, however sublime he may be, should not give himself up to choreography until he has ceased to dance himself. At the age of forty-five or fifty, the brilliance of his execution will begin to tarnish, his strength and energy to wane and his powers to decline; his facial appearance shows the ravages of time and the muscles which gave them nobility lose their elasticity and under such conditions the features lose their eloquence . . . A choreographer should never appear in his own ballets."[142]

His views on the training of the dancer are of necessity governed by his conception of the ballet. Granted that the would-be dancer is suited by nature to his profession, the first duty of the teacher is to study his physical conformation and his temperament and to instruct him accordingly. "There may be only one right principle to be taught, but is there only one way of demonstrating it and of imparting it to the students one undertakes to teach, and must one not of necessity lead them to the same end by different ways? I admit that in order to do so one must have real knowledge, for without thought and study it is impossible to apply given principles varied to suit different types of physical conformation and varying degrees of aptitude, for one cannot see at a glance what is convenient to one and cannot suit another, and one cannot vary one's classes in proportion to the variations which nature and habit, often more rebellious than nature, offer and present us."

"It is, therefore, left to the teacher to train each student in the style to which he is suited. It is not sufficient to possess a thorough knowledge of the art; it is also necessary to guard against vain pride which inclines each one to believe that his manner of execution is the one and only one which can please, for a teacher who always puts himself forward as a model of perfection and who endeavours but to make of his students a copy of which he himself is the good or bad original, will succeed in making tolerable dancers only when he meets with subjects gifted with the same disposition, height, conformation and intelligence as himself."[143]

He then proceeds to analyse the anatomy of various types of dancers and to draw conclusions as to how they should be trained and the style they should adopt. He points out that "in my youth, I studied osteology which I have found of great advantage in my teaching, both to allay the tediousness of the lessons and to throw more light on the demonstration of principles. This art has taught me to see the causes which oppose themselves to the execution of this or that movement and, knowing the bony structure of man and the levers and hinges which govern its play, I did not require from my pupils that which nature did not allow and I directed their classes after a deep analysis of the conformation of each one of them."[144] He studies the mechanics of the various movements in relation to the muscular and bony structure and is at pains to stress the importance of a position turned out from the hip and attained, not by the various mechanical aids current at the time but by suitable exercises.

He lays down the basic principles which form the hard core of the art of dancing, but he makes it clear that these are but the alphabet and "the teacher, having taught his pupil the steps, the manner of combining them one with another, the opposition of the arms, the *effacements* of the body and the positions of the head, should then show him how to give value and expression to them by the help of the features. To do so, he would need but to devise for him *entrées* in which he would have to interpret varied passions. It is not, however, sufficient to have him paint the passions in all their strength, he should also be taught the succession of their moods, their degrees of light and shade and the effects which they produce on the features. Such lessons would cause the dance to speak and the dancers to reason . . ."[145]

Finally he stresses that technique will be of little avail to the dancer, if he has not a general education such as will enable him to study and understand the very spirit of his art.

These principles, which form the basis of his written work, may perhaps be debated on minor points which are a matter of opinion, but fundamentally they are as true today as when they were written nearly two centuries ago and they form, perhaps, the most complete survey of the choreographer's art ever published.

# CHAPTER XI

# The Ballets of Noverre

It has been sometimes assumed that the principles outlined in Noverre's writings were not put into practice by their author, but a deep study of his ballets suggests that this conclusion is based on too hasty a survey of the evidence which has come down to us and that, in fact, his writings are a synthesis of the experience gained in the production of his works.

His early ballets, such as *Les Métamorphoses Chinoises* or *La Fontaine de Jouvence*, are not mere suites of disconnected dances but entertainments complete in themselves. The costumes and décor, if we can relate the designs by Boquet in the Musée de l'Opéra or the painting by Boucher in the Musée de Besançon to *Les Métamorphoses Chinoises*, show a degree of realism and a sense of style surprising for the time. Above all, it is the "prodigious number of new and perfectly designed attitudes which form and dissolve with the greatest of ease", "the variegated and novel tableaux", the lack of confusion and turmoil, which impress contemporary critics.

As early as 1755, in *Les Réjouissances Flamandes*, the customary mythological sources are abandoned in favour of a theme drawn from the life of the country people which shows an acute sense of observation and perhaps too some study of the Dutch school of painting.

Noverre was then already a craftsman capable of a choreographic invention which drew forth the praises of contemporary critics. He had seen the court of Berlin, where he had met the great Voltaire, and travelled widely in France. He was technically proficient in every aspect of his art and well acquainted with the drama of his day. During his stay at the Opéra Comique, he had been brought into contact with Marie Sallé and had observed her sensitive mime and he had found in Rameau a pioneer in the field of musical reform. He had had ample opportunity to study the work of Favart, the virtual founder of the opéra-comique style and one of the ablest dramatists of his day, and we may perhaps see in some of his later works, such as *La Rosière de Salency* and *Annette et Lubin*, something of Favart's influence.

It is, however, his contact with David Garrick which acts as a catalyst to Noverre's genius. He finds in Garrick, a style of acting which gives him the clue to the form of expression for which he is groping. Garrick is "so natural, his expression has so much truth in it, his gestures, his facial expression, his very glance, are so eloquent, so persuasive, that even those who understand not a word of English comprehend without difficulty the scene enacted before them. He is touching in the pathetic style, whilst in the tragic he makes one feel the successive movements of the most violent passions, he lacerates the vitals of the spectator and tears at his heart strings, pierces his soul and makes him shed tears of blood. In comedy, he captivates and enchants and in farce he is diverting and amusing. His make-up is so artistically contrived that he is often unrecognized by people living with him . . ."[140]

Noverre's keen sense of observation is trained on the great English actor, his gestures, his characterization, his costume, his adaptation of existing plays. Even Garrick's library is combed, the better to understand. Throughout his life, Garrick remains his model and, twelve years later, his impressions are still so fresh that he can write two lengthy essays on the subject for Voltaire.

On his return from his second visit to London, in 1757, he proceeds to put his ideas to the test with the staging of *La Toilette de Vénus ou les Ruses de l'Amour* which creates a sensation such that he is encouraged "finally to forsake the traditional style in favour of the more expressive *danse d'action*, painting in a broader and less over-refined manner calculated to appeal to the mind instead of pleasing the eyes alone."

By 1760, Noverre's ideas have crystallized sufficiently to enable him to put down on paper some basic principles in his *Lettres sur la Danse et sur les Ballets* and he has created a number of *ballets d'action* of which, although no musical score has survived, from the vivid descriptions in the *Lettres,* we can form a good idea of the structure and a better opinion of the movement used than is possible from the more succinct scenarios of his later works. Thus we can break down *Les Fêtes ou les Jalousies du Serail* (see page 51) into:—

Scene I    Introductory mime scene: the harem—the eunuchs present sherbet and other delicacies to the women. One of them asks for a mirror and proceeds to strike attitudes and generally prepare herself for the coming of the Sultan. The other women imitate her. (This device of using the *corps de ballet* to echo the movements of a principal is one to which Noverre frequently has recourse; compare the Nymphs imitating Venus in *La Toilette de Venus* (Appendix A).) Solos and ensemble dances.

Scene II    The soft music and murmur of the water, the fountains of the first
scene, gives place to a "proud and well-marked air" for the danced
*entrée* of the mutes, black eunuchs and white eunuchs who herald the
coming of the Sultan.

Entry of the Sultan followed by his retinue. Exit of the retinue
leaving the Sultan alone with his women.

Pantomime scene in which the Sultan finally bestows his favours on
Zaïre.

Lyrical *pas de deux* for the Sultan and Zaïre ending with their exit.

Scene III    *Pas seul* of despair for Zaïde ending in her attempted suicide.

Mime scene in which she is disarmed.

Return of Zaïre and mimed combat scene between the two women in
which the *corps de ballet* is used in two groups to separate the
antagonists and drag them apart—opposition of the dramatic movements of the principals with the mass movements of the *corps de ballet*.
Return of the Sultan and dramatic melting of the confusion into calm.

Scene IV    Festivities:—*Pas de deux* of reconciliation for Zaïre and Zaïde.

*Pas de trois* for Zaïre, Zaïde and the Sultan.

*Contredanse noble* for the company (Compare this with the final
Chaconne in *La Toilette de Vénus*).

Scene V    Apotheosis—Tableau.

Whereas in *Les Métamorphoses Chinoises* and *Les Réjouissances
Flamandes,* Noverre was content to paint a living tableau, we have here
a definite dramatic plot, even though it be not very original and bears
a certain resemblance to the *divertissement* added by Marie Sallé to the
5th *entrée* of La Motte and Campra's *L'Europe Galante* on June 14th,
1736. Of greater interest than the plot, is the fact that the characters
are of real flesh and blood, torn by human passions, and cardboard
characters on Noverre's stage will become increasingly rare and
finally disappear altogether as he completes his transition from the
rococo to the classical style.

The general structure of his ballets at this time already forecasts
that of Petipa and Ivanov, in *Swan Lake* for instance, without seeking
after any such virtuoso effects as the thirty-two *fouettés*. The first act
is virtually a prologue to set the scene, the second act creates a situation
which leads to the dramatic crisis of the third act, the fourth brings the
dramatic plot to a conclusion, and the fifth is but an apotheosis.

The plot is sometimes resolved, in the manner of the early opera-
ballets, by the introduction of the *Deus ex Machina* as in *L'Amour
Corsaire ou l'Embarquement pour Cythère* (Appendix A):—

The climax, when Constance lies at the mercy of the High Priest,
who stands over her with knife upraised, is built up to by successive
scenes in which hope alternates with despair in the shipwreck, the

various phases of the struggle between Clairville and Dorval with the Mysoginians and the assassination of the Sacrificer, by Constance herself, on the steps of the altar. Every dramatic device is used from the transformation scene, in the raising of the new altar and the trees, to the very gestures of the dancers where rolling eyes and flashing daggers, deathly pallor and bristling hair are introduced. The plot is resolved by the coming of Cupid on his ship, when the elements subside and the turbulent and struggle-strewn scene is suddenly frozen into immobility.

We have, in the *Lettres*, not only the plot of another ballet, *Les Jaloux sans Rival*, but also its derivation:—

*Scene I*  inspired from the game of backgammon incident in Diderot's *Père de Famille*, Scene I.
Clitandre, a French coxcomb, and Beatrix, his lover, quarrel violently over a game of chess. Inez, lover of Fernando, tries in vain to reconcile them. Beatrix goes out followed by the despairing Clitandre, leaving Inez alone on the stage.

*Scene II*  of Noverre's own composition.
Clitandre begs Inez to help him. He falls to his knees and kisses her hand in gratitude for her promised aid but, at this moment, Fernando enters and, jumping to the conclusion that Clitandre is trying to take Inez from him, attacks him dagger in hand. Beatrix arrives in time to stay his arm and Clitandre flees.

*Scene III*  Fernando, in a paroxysm of jealousy, turns on Inez and raises his arm to strike her but her reproachful look causes him to let the dagger fall from his hand.
This scene is taken from the passage in Voltaire's *Mahomet*, in which "Ines", whom Mahomet is about to stab, says:

> "Ton bras est suspendu! Qui t'arrête? Ose tout;
> "Dans un coeur tout à toi laisse tomber le coup."
> (Thy arm is stayed! Who stops thee? Dare all;
> Let the blow fall on a heart thine entirely.)

*Scene IV*  Taken from Molière's *Le Dépit Amoureux*, Act IV Scene 4. Inez, despairing of overcoming the suspicions of Fernando, lets herself fall into a chair; Fernando, jealous but ashamed of his violent outburst, casts himself into another chair. Inez draws from her bosom her lover's portrait and Fernando takes from his pocket that of Inez. They gaze at these portraits and then, with a mixture of contempt and sorrow, throw them away.

*Scene V*  after Molière's *Le Tartuffe*, Act II Scene 4. Beatrix reconciles the two lovers.

*Scene VI*  Due entirely to Noverre.
Fernando expresses his gratitude to Beatrix by taking her hand but Inez surprises them at this moment and, seeking sweet revenge, feigns jealousy. She pretends to stab herself and falls into the arms of her attendants.

*Scene VII* modelled on the rages of Orestes in Racine's *Andromaque*. Fernando, believing his beloved dead, gives himself up to despair and attempts to take his own life.

*Scene VIII* inspired from Crébillon's *Rhadomiste* and *Zenobie*. Inez, in turn, is in despair. She flies to take her prostrate lover in her arms and this leads to the final reconciliation.

*Conclusion, Pas seuls* for each of the four protagonists and general *contredanse*.

Noverre's work as a librettist lay, in this case, in linking together the various scenes and his aim would seem to have been to prove that tragedy could be expressed in terms of dancing and yet retain the favour of the public. That he was successful is shown by the fact that the work had been in the repertoire for ten months at the time he put the finishing touches to his *Lettres*. Despite petty criticisms of the realism of certain scenes, such as the introduction of a game of chess, the work as a whole met with public approval even to the third scene, part of which was played seated.

How closely he modelled his work on that of the dramatist who inspired him is clearly shown from an analysis of scene IV:—

| Noverre, *"Jaloux Sans Rival"*, *Sc. IV* | Molière, *"Le Tartuffe"*, Act II, Sc. 4 |
|---|---|
| Beatrix, witnessing the quarrel of Fernando and Inez, seeks to reconcile them. | Dorine, witnessing the quarrel of Valère and Mariane, endeavours to reconcile them. |
| Inez takes flight. | Valère leaves the scene. |
| Beatrix stays her. | Dorine recalls him. |
| Fernando, seeing his mistress wishes to avoid him, flees in turn. | Mariane makes as if to go. |
| Beatrix perseveres in her efforts to reconcile them. | Dorine continues her endeavours to reunite them. |
| She makes them take each other's hand. | Dorine: "You are mad both of you. There, your hand, each of you." (To Valère): "Come, yours!" |
| Each has to be pressed but she finally succeeds in bringing them close to each other, and in reuniting them. | Valère (giving Dorine his hand): "Of what use is my hand?" Dorine (To Mariane): "How now! yours!" Mariane (giving her hand to Dorine): "Of what use is all this?" Dorine: "My god! Quick, come! You love each other more than you think." |

She regards them with a mischievous smile. The two lovers, still not daring to look at each other despite their desire to do so, stand back to back.

Valère and Mariane hold hands for a time, without looking at each other.

Imperceptibly they turn round. Inez in a glance assures Fernando of his forgiveness. He rapturously kisses her hand and all three withdraw full of unbounded joy.

Valère (turning towards Mariane): "Oh, do not make things so hard, and look just a little on folk without hate." Mariane smilingly turns to Valère. They are fully reconciled.

We have an interesting testimony from an unusual source, a book for the guidance of students of textile design published in 1764, of the impression made by Noverre's work at this period on his contemporaries:—

"I could wish that every designer could see and see again the Ballets Pantomimes which M. Noverre had given at Lyons. This celebrated man has raised this type of performance as high perhaps as the Romans. His *Ballet Chinois*, his *Caprices de Galathée*, his *Toilette de Venus*, the *Ballet du Serail* and others which he has composed or had performed in that city are as many masterpieces in this style which should be for ever engraved in the memory of an artist. What fire, what genius in his compositions; what variety in his subject; what nobility and majesty in his principal characters; what grace and ease in the attitudes of his women; what expression in his characters in general; what spectacle more agreeable than his pastoral dances; with what artistry he shows us suddenly a thousand different objects with the aid of wreaths or garlands of flowers of which the shepherds and shepherdesses make in turn trellisses, cradles, summerhouses, palaces, parterres, etc.? Finally what beautiful harmony in all his tableaux, what fine execution in the *ensemble!* One could wish that every designer might be familiar with all the productions which this able man has given to the public and thus could assuredly sometimes use his ideas and profiting by his talents combine the agreeable and the useful."[153]

The novelty of these works lay not only in their dramatic coherence, which was lacking in his earlier work as in that of his contemporaries, but also in the construction and the handling of the various groups.

The *corps de ballet* throughout make a definite contribution to the action built up of a number of carefully studied minor rôles. Noverre himself tells us how, in his ballet *Alceste*, he inserted in the first act, as part of the celebrations which Admetus gives for Hercules and Iscomède, a *pas* of twenty-four wrestlers in which he "renounced all symmetry of figures, movement, position, attitudes and groups" and "to give the accent of truth, composed separately twelve different *pas de deux* which took several days and then, when all the *pas de deux*

145

were arranged and partly learned by the executants" he "brought them together to form one large ensemble".[148]

The dances are linked by mime scenes and *pas seuls, pas de deux, de trois et de quatre* are introduced in the manner of soliloquies, duets and trios. They are in the nature of *pas d'action* expressive of love, jealousy, despair and so on, rather than formal dances devoid of meaning.

We will find this same method of composition in all of his later works and, in January 1771, Baron Grimm notes:—

". . . in the ballets of Noverre, dancing and rhythmical walking are quite distinct. There is dancing but in the great movements of the passions, in the decisive moments, in the scenes, there is walking, in time it is true but without dancing. The transition from rhythmic walking to dancing, and from the dance to the rhythmic walk, is as necessary in this spectacle as is the transition from recitative to song and song to recitative in opera, but dancing for the sake of dancing cannot occur until the danced play is over."[146]

To the contemporary spectator, who had come to expect a ballet to be a colourless series of minuets, *loures* or *passepieds,* expressed in conventional steps and attitudes, movement based on an imitation of nature, or as we would say in modern parlance, a heightened realism, must have seemed highly dramatic. Reading Noverre's scenarios today it may even sound melodramatic but it is good theatre, of a stronger flavour perhaps than we are accustomed to of recent years, when realism has been the order of the day and declamation and dramatic gesture have, by the whim of fashion, been banished from the stage. We can see here the influence of Garrick in the first flush of Noverre's enthusiasm for his art. In later works it will possibly become more subdued, but it will never vanish completely from his palette.

The costumes, designed by Boquet, for *L'Amour Corsaire,* are of particular interest by their departure from contemporary court dress

"The Nymphs wear elegant dresses with bodices not unlike those of amazons. The savages are dressed in unusual costumes carried out in primary colours with part of the chest and legs and arms of flesh colour. Cupid is dressed in the style of a Brigantine Corsair and is recognizable only by his wings. The Games and Pleasures are attired in the costumes of the sailors of a Brigantine Privateer except that they are more elegant. The troupe of children look like porcelain figures from Saxony of the type one stands on the mantelpiece. Clairville, Constance and Dorville were attired in good taste and, suitably, a happy disorder was the keynote to their dress."

The costumes for *La Toilette de Vénus,* to judge from Noverre's description, showed an equal desire to break with the conventional:—

"The Fauns were without *tonnelets* and the Nymphs, Venus and the Graces without panniers. I had proscribed masks which would have been opposed to all expression. . . . A kind of laced shoe, in imitation of the bark of a tree had seemed to me preferable to dancing shoes; neither white stockings nor gloves for I had selected a colour to correspond to the flesh of these forest inhabitants. A plain tiger skin drapery covered part of the body and all the rest appeared nude and, so that the costume should not appear too hard and should not offer too great a contrast with the elegant attire of the Nymphs, I had caused the drapery to be edged with a garland of leaves mixed with flowers."

The tradition which required that the Games and Pleasures should dance to a *passe-pied*, Cupid be given a gavotte and Greek Warriors enter to a chaconne, clashed inevitably with the introduction of characters drawn from life, just as the substitution, for highly stylized dance forms, of expressive movement based on a close study of the natural exteriorization of the emotions and, above all, the replacement of loosely connected suites of dances by closely knit dramatic productions, could not be reconciled with the work of musicians who composed "*passe-pieds* because Mlle. Prévost tripped them with elegance, *musettes* because Mlle. Sallé and Monsieur Dumoulin danced them with grace and voluptuousness, *tambourins* because that was the style in which Mlle. Camargo excelled . . ."[147]

The realization of Noverre's ideas demanded the complete subordination of the music to dramatic requirements and therefore the co-operation of musicians prepared to abandon traditional dance forms and to restrain their own inclination to develop a particular musical theme once it has ceased to strengthen the action.

Noverre has told us how he set to work:—

"Before selecting tunes to which steps could be adapted, before studying *pas* to form what was then termed a ballet, I sought either in a fable, or in history or finally in my imagination, for a subject which not only offered opportunities for inserting dances, fêtes, etc., but which furthermore, offered in their development a graduated interest and action. My poem once conceived, I considered all the gestures, all the movements and all the expressions which could translate the passions and the sentiments to which my subject gave birth. It is only once this work was done that I called music to my aid. Putting before the musician all the various details of the tableaux I had just sketched, I then asked him for a piece of music adapted to each situation. Instead of arranging *pas* to existing tunes, as one fits lyrics to a known air, I composed, if I may so express myself, the dialogue of my ballet, and I had the music made for each sentence and each idea.

It was thus that I dictated to Gluck the characteristic air of the Ballet of the Savages in *Iphigénie en Tauride*. The steps, the gestures, the attitudes, the expressions of the various characters which I drew for him, gave to this famous composer the character of the composition of this beautiful piece of music."[148]

Thus, having conceived his ballet and sketched out the dramatic skeleton, he builds up each scene group by group and dance by dance, working closely with the musician whom he requires to compose music to fit his needs, matching the duration of the movements of the dancers and the pattern of the choreography.

Leaving aside his work with Gluck, Piccini and the young Mozart, which forms a relatively small and unimportant part of his output, he was fortunate in securing the co-operation of a number of competent musical craftsmen who, although almost unknown today, enjoyed considerable popularity in their lifetime. They served Noverre's purpose better than would have a great musical genius in that they were more ready to mould their work to his desires and such of their scores as have come down to us bear the unmistakable imprint of his mind.

The first of his musical collaborators known to us is the cellist François Granier (1717-1779), who was accompanist to the Concert de Lyon and none of whose ballet scores have, alas, survived. According to the actor Marignan, who was at Lyons at the time, he had but a vague idea of composition and was content to write to the dictation of Noverre who traced for him both the spirit and the character. On the other hand, Granier has left six pieces for violoncello, published in 1754, which are both agreeable and competent and from which it would seem that he must have been possessed of greater ability than Marignan gave him credit for.[150]

That Noverre himself thought highly of his compositions is evident from his *Lettres:*—

"An expressive, harmonious and varied music such as that to which I have lately worked suggests to me a thousand ideas, a thousand little touches; it transports, exalts and inflames me and I owe to the different impressions it has made me experience and which have entered my very soul, the harmony, the *ensemble*, the striking and unusual characters which impartial judges have thought to see in my ballets. These are the material effects of music on dancing and of dancing on music when two artists work in harmony and when their Arts blend and mutually exchange graces to captivate and to please. . . . There are few musicians as capable as he of setting a composition to all *genres* of ballets and of moving the genius of men of fine feelings and of knowledge."[151]

And referring to his music for *L'Amour Corsaire:*—

"It imitated the accents of nature: without being a uniform song it was harmonious. In a word, he had expressed the action in music; each line was an expression which lent strength and energy to the movements of the dance and animated its every picture."[152]

In Stuttgart, his principal musical collaborators are Florian Deller (1729-1773), violinist and court composer to the Duke, and Johann Joseph Rudolph, or Rodolphe as he later styled himself (1730-1812). I have only been able to study one of Deller's scores but, from the writings of eminent German musical critics who made a study of his work before the war destroyed so much of the wealth of the museums in Berlin and Darmstadt, it would seem that his melody was essentially Viennese with a happy use of folk tunes. His score for *Orfeo ed Euridyce,* which has been particularly praised, is programmatic in character and in a free form.

Rodolphe, the greatest French-horn player of his time, who studied composition under Traetta and Jomelli and, later, taught at the Paris Conservatoire, has left a number of opera and ballet scores and horn concertos. His ballet scores are more richly orchestrated than those of Deller but perhaps less graphic.

Throughout his career, Noverre continues to seek the scenarios for his more important works in the drama but, when he has the resources of a large company of dancers and a big stage at his disposal, he turns for his inspiration to the Greek classical tragedies and to legends of knight errantry. At Stuttgart he is limited in his choice of subject matter and the extent to which he can develop it, by the essential subordination to the operas of Jomelli, but in Vienna and Milan he creates great epic ballets in four and five acts in the style of Racine and Corneille.

In Vienna he works with Franz Aspelmayer (1721?-1786), who has left incidental music for *Macbeth* and *Der Sturm* (a play after *The Tempest*) as well as a number of symphonies, and Carlo Giuseppe Toeschi (1724-1788), the leader of the Mannheim court orchestra. His greatest collaborator is, however, Josef Starzer (1726-1787)[155], leader of the Vienna court orchestra and of the orchestra at the French Theatre and, for a time, a member of the court orchestra at St. Petersburg. He had written music for Hilverding but, according to Lisbeth Braun and other German critics who have made a special study of his work, his earlier scores lack the dramatic concentration of his work for Noverre.

The published scenarios of these, his greatest works, have sometimes been held to show a lack of real dramatic sense but it must be borne in mind that they were primarily intended to be danced, not declaimed, and in reading them, we must imagine the pageantry inherent in their production. Where they fail is, perhaps, in their adherence to a literary and dramatic formula which may sometimes have led Noverre to attempt to stretch his medium beyond the limitations inherent in mimeo-drama. This is perhaps implied in his statement that, after fifty years of work and research, he had taken but a few steps forward and has stopped before seemingly impassable barriers. It is also borne out by the poet, M. J. Chénier, when, in his *Essai sur les Principes des Arts*, written *circa* 1818, he writes:—

> "I do not like to see the children of Jason,
>> Strangled whilst dancing by their dancing mother,
>> Under rhythmic blows expire in measure.
>> If chance has caused the three Roman brothers,
>> To enter the lists against the three Alban brothers,
>> Is it meet that in concluding this fratricide struggle,
>> Of the fate of Alba and of Rome an *entrechat* decides?
>> No, respect taste; as does Gardel.
>> Noverre, of an art which he thought universal,
>> On the most august tone indoctrinating Europe,
>> Would have caused *Joad*, *Phèdre* and the *Misanthrope* to dance.
>> Oh! How much better is it, far from your great aims,
>> To limit pantomime to amiable themes. . . ."

If these later scenarios are less detailed, we have a compensation in the shape of a number of musical scores which have survived in whole or in part (although many were destroyed during the war), and of criticisms by such enlightened commentators as Baron Grimm. The ballets are no longer welded quite as closely to the literary source from which they are inspired. The theme is, as it were, recreated in a form better suited to choreographic interpretation, the dramatic joinery has gained in craftsmanship and the situations are stronger.

Thus if we compare Noverre's *Les Horaces*[154] with Corneille's great tragedy, we find that the plot has been simplified by the elimination of Sabina, the Alban wife of Horatius, and of Valère, Roman suitor to Camilla, who in the play provided a subsidiary interest incompatible with the direct approach inherent in a purely visual presentation. In this, Noverre is following Livy (I-XXIV-i-5) who, in his account, from which Corneille derived his inspiration, is content to state that the sister of Horatius had been promised to one of the Curiatii and makes no mention of Sabina. Fulvia, daughter of Proculus who, a Roman soldier in the play, has become a senator in the ballet, is introduced as the betrothed of Horatius.

Noverre, realizing that it would be impossible to maintain without the aid of speech, the growing tension as the news slowly filters through

of the truce in the war between Rome and Alba, the decision to settle
the issue by a single combat between the three warriors from either side
and, finally, the choice of the three Horatii and the three Curiatii as the
champions of their respective countries, starts his ballet at act two,
scene three of the play. When the curtain is taken up, at the conclusion
of the rousing sixty bar introduction in C in 3/4 time, which leads
without a break into the first act, we see Camilla, already acquainted
with the cruel decision which will oppose her lover and her brothers in
mortal combat, her distress clearly heard in soft broken passages on
the oboe and violins.

The introduction at this point of the scarf which Camilla has
worked with her own hands for Curiatius, her betrothed, is a touch of
genius which gives added poignancy to the first act and, by making
the cause of Camilla's distress clear to the audience, intensifies the
emotional climax of the third. As Camilla gives the scarf to Julia,
her attendant, to deliver to Curiatius, he comes to bid her farewell.
Her conflicting emotions, as she is torn between love of her country
and for her beloved, are expressed in a slow chaconne in F.

A burst of martial music recalls Curiatius to his duty and rekindles
his martial ardour. In vain, Camilla wishes to follow him and, to a
halting diminuendo passage for strings, she staggers and collapses in a
chair, wholly given up to grief and despair. Her brothers come, in their
turn, to bid her adieu. Running to each she bedews their cheeks with
fast flowing tears and here there is an intimate and gracious oboe solo
in B flat, we may presume for a *pas seul* for Camilla.

The elder Horiatius now comes with Proculus and Fulvia to exhort
his sons to conquer or die for Rome. A short passage in A minor
follows as Camilla's agitation is increased by these patriotic effusions.

To a proud mæstoso movement in B flat, the three brothers depart
for battle, followed by their father and Proculus. Fulvia catches the
fainting Camilla in her arms as the music changes to a faltering figure
and the act ends swiftly on a hesitating phrase in A minor.

The combat, which in the play takes place out of sight of the
audience, provides in the ballet a second act full of martial pageantry.
After a short, tranquil *entracte,* the act opens on a fanfare in C. The
Roman and Alban armies, led by their respective kings, Tullus and
Mettius, are drawn up with colours flying on either side of an altar
surrounded by priests and acolytes.

At a word of command, arms are laid down and the soldiers
prostrate themselves as, to a solemn prayer in F minor, the priests make

libations and burn incense. There is a thrice repeated burst of the horns, trumpets, oboe and drums, followed by a pause as, in silence, the two kings advance to the foot of the altar and take an oath to bind themselves by the outcome of the combat, a scene which would appear to have been particularly impressive.

A long roll on the drums introduces the battle scene which provides some virile dances for the six men. Two of the Horatii are soon stretched in the dust whilst only one of the Curiatii is wounded and the Alban troops make the air ring with their bucklers and their cries of joy. Then, one of the Curiatii is killed. Horatius feigns flight and then, suddenly turns on his pursuer and runs him through with his sword. The last of the Curiatii, already wounded, is no match for Horatius who offers his life to the spirits of his brothers as the Romans shout their cries of triumph and gratitude. The entire scene, so packed with action, is of but two minutes duration to a lively and inventive music which provides a good climax to the act.

The full orchestra breaks into a vigorous passage with well-marked rhythms as Tullus crowns the conquering Horatius in the presence of the Roman army whilst the Albans carry off their dead.

To a slow gavotte in G, Horatius throws himself on the bodies of his brothers in lament at the price of victory. To a second and more lively gavotte in B flat, the elder Horatius comes running to embrace his son in a transport of joy and the act concludes with a march in C major as Horatius is borne off in triumph to the Capitol.

To pursue this analysis through the whole five acts would be tedious. Taken as a whole, the score is closely written to intense emotional mime scenes and it is clear that Noverre's insistence on deep characterization has had to be observed. For instance, Camilla's sobs are clearly heard during the playing of a very masculine chaconne, which one imagines was a man's dance. There are a great many changes of tempo and interpolations of new figures and Starzer[155] has used adventurous changes of key. The dances are as arias set amongst the mime scenes at the emotional climaxes. The situations are concise and theatrically effective. The characters are drawn in a style strongly reminiscent of Corneille and one gets the impression of an attempt to make them live.

Of Noverre's work in Milan, where his musical collaborators were Louis de Baillou, leader of the orchestra at the Scala and a companion of his Stuttgart days, and Etienne Joseph Floquet (1750-1785), a pupil of Padre Martini, Baillou's *La Prima Eta dell'Innocenza ossia la Roasia di*

*Salency* is of particular interest as, together with Starzer's *Adèle de Pon-thieu*, it marks the dawn of the Romantic movement. The lofty themes dealing with man's domination of his passions, the subordination of the emotions to duty and the inevitable and terrible punishment of evil, which formed the theme of the ballets of his middle period, and were intended, to judge from the *Letters*, to cause vice to be detested and punished and virtue to be cherished and rewarded, now give place to the love of a simple maiden triumphing over intrigue and the machinations of a corrupt ruling class. *La Rosaia di Salency* recalls *La Fille Mal Gardée* created by Noverre's pupil, Dauberval, in 1786, and the earliest ballet performed to this day and in consequence regarded as the first "modern" ballet.

The scene depicts the festival, still current at the time, in the village of Salency, at which the most virtuous maiden is to be crowned as *rosière*. The crown is bestowed upon Julie by the steward of the lord of the manor. The steward, in love with Julie who will not marry him for her heart has been given to Colin, reproaches her with ingratitude as he alone is responsible for the honour bestowed upon her. He plots her downfall and bribes a number of village maidens, each of whom imagines she will be the new *rosière*, to state that Julie is not virtuous and he draws up a formal statement of their testimonies. Colin leaves for his home in a storm and his little boat is wrecked. The steward again tries to force himself on Julie but she will not admit him to her cottage, and he is about formally to elect a new *rosière* when the lord of the manor arrives on the scene. He quickly sums up the situation, confirms Julie as *rosière* and but for her merciful intervention, would imprison the steward.[144]

After reading the libretto of *La Rosaia di Salency* or the accounts of the earlier *Les Caprices de Galathée* which was inspired from Boileau's

"Un baiser cueilli sur les lèvres d'Iris,
"Qui mollement résiste, et par un doux caprice
"Quelquefois le refuse, afin qu'on le ravisse,"

one may wonder whether these works unhampered by any literary formula, which Noverre may have regarded as mere trifles, would not, could they be re-created, give us greater pleasure than the four- and five-act tragical ballets which he believed to be his masterpieces.

At the Paris Opéra, Noverre no longer enjoyed the same freedom as in Lyons and Stuttgart to carry out his ideas in the staging of his ballets. The wearing of masks was, it is true, abolished after an incident in

1772, when Gaetano Vestris, who was to have danced the part of Apollo in the fifth act of Rameau's *Castor et Pollux* wearing a full bottomed wig, a mask and a huge breastplate representing the sun, was prevented by a sudden indisposition from dancing; Gardel, asked to replace him, would consent only on the condition that he be allowed to appear in his own fair hair, without wig, mask or brass attributes. The public applauded the innovation, and thereafter the use of a mask was retained only for "winds and furies" and the *corps de ballet* in certain circumstances. Here, however, the reform of costume stopped short for a time and, although Noverre lived to see the old hidebound traditions of the Opéra swept away by the Revolution and even strongly to disapprove of the "immodest" costumes of gauze with skirts split up the leg in the fashion of the *merveilleuses*, in 1777, protest as he might, "the Horatii were bedecked with gold and the Curatii with silver and they could wear no helmets but must have five white powdered curls on either side and a great raised toupet, whilst Camilla was dressed as elegantly as Cleopatra stepping out of a gilded barge".

Similarly, in John Boydell's engraving of a scene from *Jason et Médée*, published in 1781, the dramatic attitudes of the dancers contrast strangely with the costumes altogether out of keeping with the theme.

The score composed by Rodolphe for the Paris production of *Apelles et Campaspe*, although we do not know how much it owes to the original score created in Vienna by Aspelmayer, lacks the graphic imagination of the Vienna scores although it may be better music. Noverre may have been restricted even as to the music he was allowed to use.

Mozart's score for *Les Petits Riens*, to which, to his disgust, were added numbers by other musicians, whilst it is very charming, lacks the characterization and programmatic style of Starzer and Rodolphe and was intended for what must have been little more than a suite of dances with a very slender theme.

We have no indication as to the reasons which impelled Noverre to re-stage a number of his ballets in London to completely new scores. Was it that the earlier music no longer satisfied him, or that the Vienna and Paris theatres would not part with the scores they held, or that these were rendered inaccessible as a result of the Revolution?

Of the ballet scores of Noverre's London period, those of Louis Sebastien LeBrun (1764-1829), who was to become chapel-master to Napoleon I, and of Camillo Federici (1749-1802), have eluded me. François Hippolyte Barthélémon (1741-1808) wrote some compositions for the violin and a number of operas, but his score for the *Prince of Wales Minuet* is but a trifle with simple harmonies and well-marked rhythms.

Joseph Mazzinghi (1765-1844), a pupil of J. S. Bach and Sacchini, composer and conductor to the King's Theatre and music master to the Princess of Wales, later Queen Caroline, has left a number of operas, a mass and many glees and arias, but we can only judge his ballets for Noverre from piano excerpts, probably greatly simplified that young ladies might play them with ease. They would seem to have consisted of a succession of pleasant but uninspiring chaconnes, gavottes and other traditional dance forms and to have ended with a final coda.

Of greater interest is the score of Miller or Millard's *Iphigenia in Aulide*, which contains a number of gracious dance passages and many precise notes as to the dancers by whom they were to be executed.

That these London scores do not approach those of Starzer in conciseness and dramatic structure is not perhaps surprising when it is remembered that Noverre was by then an exile ruined by the Revolution, in indifferent health and bowed down by the years, who had to please the public in order to live and was in no position to dictate to his management.

Taking such of Noverre's scores as I have been able to examine as a whole, whilst they may not be great music they are the work of competent craftsmen, programmatic in character with a pleasant melody. The orchestration is usually for strings with two oboes, flutes, bassoons, horns, trumpets and occasionally kettledrums. The oboe solo is used for pathetic passages whilst the trumpets and drums are usually introduced for effects and martial music.

The earlier ballets include a sung or spoken recitative in accordance with the custom of the time, and a rondo for song and dance from *La Fontaine de Jouvence* was preserved in Berlin until the 1939 war. The later ballets dispense with any spoken commentary, an innovation possibly due to Noverre, but a chorus from the wings is sometimes used for effects such as the cries of the dying in the massacre scene and the murmuring of the crowd in the execution scene in *Les Danaïdes* (Acts 4 and 5).

There is little use of counterpoint but dance forms such as the gavotte, and especially long chaconnes which often provide a finale, are frequently introduced. From the careful phrasing, the considerable variations of tempi and indications such as "loud, soft, proudly held" and definite indications of action such as "brings a letter", it is obvious

155

that at least in the scores of his last period the music has been welded to the movement rather than the movement fitted to the score.

It may well be that not the least of Noverre's contributions to the ballet, was his influence on the evolution of the score. What is certain is that the music he used denotes a dramatic coherence which suggests that his ballets were constructed and executed in accordance with the principles set out in his writings.

# Epilogue

To claim that any one person was the creator of the *ballet d'action* would be a gross exaggeration inasmuch as progress is by evolution rather than by revolution, but the part played by the Chevalier Noverre in the development of the ballet as we know it today compels our deepest respect.

The basic principles of the style and technique of the art of dancing had been laid down by Beauchamp, Rameau and others before him, but he brought teachers of dancing back to the importance of placing their work on a sound anatomical basis and of studying the specific problems of each individual dancer.

His reforms of costume were called for by a number of his contemporaries in the theatre and he saw them adopted in the ballet to a large extent, even though they were to be swept away in later years by new conventions in the form of stereotyped tutus and pink satin shoes.

His views on the reform of the opera-ballet and of music, as set out in his *Lettres sur la Danse et sur les Ballets* in 1760, precede Gluck's *Orfeo* by two years but were the logical development of the ideas of Rameau, Jean Jacques Rousseau and Batteux.

His real merit lies above all in having taken the æsthetic ideas of the élite of his time and known how to put them into practice in the face of rabid opposition. We cannot re-create his ballets as they were, but we know that they were performed again and again in the greatest cities in Europe and his output—we know of over eighty ballets, twenty-four opera-ballets and eleven *divertissements* in addition to countless ridottos, fêtes and children's ballets—is astounding even by present-day standards.

Pupils trained in his methods of composition and teaching passed on his principles to succeeding generations down to the present day and included, amongst their numbers, most of the "fathers" of modern choreography. The ballets of Dauberval, Didelot and Vigano show the unmistakable impress of Noverre's ideas and the annotations in Perrot's hand on a copy of the *Lettres sur la Danse et sur les Ballets* in the Bibliothèque de l'Opéra in Paris, are there to prove his indebtedness.

His successors adopted the form of his work, the ballet as an entertainment complete unto itself, both the one-act expressive of a theme or tableau and the five-act episodic ballet. They gradually lost sight, however, of his plea for greater expression in movement and for a genuine study of the movement-reaction exteriorizing an impulse springing from an emotional state. They did not go out and study the artisan in his workshop, the smith in his forge and the labourer in his field, but were content further to explore the highly stylized geometry of what has come to be called the classical ballet without comprehending or seeking to understand the wider principles of movement of which the virtuosity of the Italian school and the grace of the French school were but one manifestation.

They lost sight too of his insistence on unity of conception and choreographer, musician and designer all too frequently went their own sweet way with little reference to each other. We may even question whether by subordinating the musician to the choreographer, whereas in the days of Lully and Molière the spectacle as a whole was the work of the poet-librettist or of the musician, Noverre did not to some extent pave the way for the indifferent ballet scores composed, for close on a century, by hack musicians to the direction of ballet-masters who lacked his understanding of the necessary and intimate relationship between music and dance.

What is certain is that his ideas did not begin fully to be understood until, nearly a century after his death, they were discovered intuitively by Isadora Duncan and analytically by Michel Fokine and Rudolf von Laban.

No plate marks the building in which Noverre died, even his tomb has disappeared under the present market place. The only record of his passing is an entry in the dusty records of the Municipal Archives:—

"20th October 1810, nine o'clock in the morning, death certificate of the Sieur Jean Georges Noverre, native of Paris the 29th April 1727, aged 83 years and a half, State pensioner, husband of Marguerite Louise Sauveur, deceased yesterday at three in the afternoon at his domicile, rue de la Surintendance No. 1, on the declarations of Mr. Etienne Louis François Malet, parish priest domiciled rue Au Pain, and François Petrau, cook, rue de la Selle No. 28, who have signed as witnesses after hearing read this certificate, of which we, mayor, acting as public officer, have duly taken note according to the law.

(Signed)    Mallet, Priest    François Petreau."

Amiable and witty in his social contacts, constant in his loyalty to his friends, conscientious in the extreme where the interests of his employers were concerned, conscious of his merit as an artist, dignified in his dealings with the great, admired and beloved of his pupils, all these aspects of the man were eclipsed by his love of his art.

Above all else he loved the dance, the pure dance, stripped of all mannerisms, of all false graces and mumbo-jumbo. He loved and lived and fought for the dance born of natural movement, expressive of the passions and heightened to meet the requirements of the stage, but still the dance and not pantomime devoid of rhythm and design. In defence of his ideals he was unsparing of himself and of others, against all opposition, striving, creating, pouring out ideas in a ceaseless ebullient stream.

A revolutionary denied a stage in the land of his birth, he was forced to seek in exile an opportunity to put his ideas into practice and yet he lived to see his reforms, in production, in movement, in costume, in teaching, gradually adopted and even refined and surpassed by the best of his pupils.

If, subsequently, his ideas were sometimes obscured by the dictates of contemporary fashion and the failure of lesser minds to appreciate their full significance, yet they were never wholly lost and, to this day, greater than any monument of stone or brass, his work lives in every dancer in classroom or theatre, in every choreographer and every producer the world over, a living and eternal tribute to a great artist and a great thinker.

*Some descriptions of ballets translated from J. G. Noverre,*
*"Lettres sur la Danse et sur les Ballets", 1760*

*"La Toilette de Venus ou les Ruses de l'Amour"*

The stage represents a voluptuous *salon*. Venus, clad in the most elegant *déshabillé* is at her toilet. The Games and Pleasures vie with each other in proffering everything which can serve for her adornment. The Graces dress her hair, Cupid laces one of her sandals, young nymphs are engaged in fashioning garlands, others in preparing a helmet for Cupid, yet others in placing flowers on the costume and the cloak which will adorn his mother. The toilet concluded, Venus turns towards her son and seems to consult him. The little god applauds her beauty and throws himself rapturously into her arms. This first scene offers all that is most captivating in voluptuousness, coquetry and feminine grace.

The second scene is devoted entirely to the dressing of Venus. The Graces take charge of her attire, some of the nymphs occupy themselves in tidying the dressing table whilst others bring to the Graces the necessary accessories. The Games and Pleasures, no less eager to serve the goddess, hold the one the rouge box, others the patch box, the bouquet, the necklace, the bracelets, etc.

Cupid, with an elegant attitude, seizes the mirror and flits constantly round the nymphs who, to revenge themselves on his levity, wrest from him his quiver and bandeau. He pursues them but is stopped short by three of these same Nymphs who present him with his helmet and a mirror. He puts on the former and admires himself in the latter. He flies into his mother's arms and sighing, meditates the idea of wreaking revenge for the kind of affront he has suffered. He prays and begs Venus to help him in his enterprise by disposing their (*i.e. the nymphs'*) minds to tenderness by painting all the most touching aspects of voluptuousness.

Venus then displays all her graces, her attitudes, her glances and the very picture of the pleasures of love itself. The Nymphs, affected beyond measure, endeavour to imitate her and to grasp all the shades she uses to captivate them. Cupid, witnessing the impression made on them, takes the opportunity to deal the final blow and, in a general *entrée*, makes them portray all the passions he inspires. Their confusion grows and increases unceasingly and from tenderness they pass to jealousy, from jealousy to fury, from fury to despondency, from despondency to inconstancy; in fine they experience in succession all those varied feelings by which the heart can be moved and Cupid even recalls them to that of happiness. This god, satisfied and content with his victory, wishes to leave them; he flies and they follow him eagerly but he escapes and disappears with his mother and the Graces whilst the Nymphs run in hot pursuit of the pleasure fleeing from them.

This scene, Sir, loses everything in the reading. You see neither the goddess nor the god, nor their following. You distinguish nothing and, faced as I am with the impossibility of rendering that which the features, the countenance, the looks and the movements of the Nymphs expressed so well, you have and I can only give you but the most imperfect and feeble idea of the most live and varied action.

The following scene sets the plot. Cupid appears alone. With a gesture and a glance he brings nature to life. The scene changes and represents a vast and gloomy forest. The Nymphs who have not lost sight of the god enter precipitately on the scene: but how great is their fear! They see neither Venus nor the Graces. The darkness of the forest and the silence which reigns there makes their blood run cold. They retire trembling but Cupid at once reassures them and invites them to follow him. The Nymphs give themselves up to him. He seems to challenge them by his fleetness of foot. They run after him but profiting by a number of feints he always eludes them and, at the moment when he seems to be in the greatest difficulty and when the Nymphs think to stop him, he disappears in a flash and is promptly replaced by a dozen Fauns.

This sudden, and unforeseen, transformation makes all the greater impression in that nothing is so striking as the contrast resulting from the situation of the Nymphs and the Fauns. The Nymphs are the picture of charm and innocence, the Fauns that of strength and ferocity. The attitudes of the latter are full of pride and vigour. The positions of the former express only the fear born of danger. The Fauns pursue the Nymphs, who flee before them but are soon captured. Some of the Nymphs, taking advantage of a moment of confusion into which the excitement of victory has thrown the Fauns, take to flight and escape, so that there are only six left amongst the twelve Fauns who begin to quarrel over their conquest. None of them will agree to a decision and, jealousy soon giving place to fury, they struggle and fight. The Nymphs, trembling and frightened, constantly pass from the hands of one to the hands of another, as each in turn becomes victor and vanquished. However, at the moment when the combatants seem occupied only with the defeat of their rivals, the Nymphs attempt to escape. Six Fauns dart after them but cannot stay them because they are in turn held back by their adversaries who pursue them. Their anger rises more and more. Each runs to the forest trees and they furiously tear down branches with which they deal each other terrible blows but being equally skilful at warding them off, they cast far away these useless instruments of their rage and vengeance and, impetuously darting at each other, they struggle with the frenzy of despair; they grip one another, throw themselves down, lift one another from the ground, crush, stifle, squeeze and hit each other and there is not a single moment of this combat that is not a painting. At last, six of the Fauns are victorious. They trample their fallen enemies with one foot, with arm upraised to deal the final blow, when six Nymphs, led by Cupid, stay them and present them with a wreath of flowers. Their companions, feeling the shame and dejection of the vanquished, let fall at their feet the wreaths which were destined for them. The vanquished, in an attitude which portrays all that is most terrible in sorrow and prostration, remain immobile; their heads are bent and their eyes fixed on the ground. Venus and the Graces, moved by their troubles, urge Cupid to favour them. That god hovers around them and, with a light breath, revives them and brings them back to life. They are imperceptibly seen to raise their dying arms in invocation to the son of Venus who, by his attitudes and his glances gives them, as it were, a new existence. They hardly enjoy it when they perceive their enemies preoccupied with their happiness and frolicking with the Nymphs. A new resentment takes hold of them and their eyes flash fire. They attack, combat and triumph in their turn. Ill-pleased with their victory unless they carry off the spoils, they tear from them the wreaths of flowers in which they gloried but, by a spell cast by Cupid, these wreaths divide into two. This event restores peace and tranquillity amongst them; the new victors and the newly vanquished each secure the reward of victory; the Nymphs offer their hand to those who have just succumbed and Cupid unites at last the Nymphs to the Fauns.

Now the symmetrical ballet begins; the mechanical beauties of the art are unfolded in a *Grande Chaconne* in which Cupid, Venus, the Graces and the Pleasures dance the principal variations. Here I was afraid the action might be slowed but I seized the moment when Venus, having bound Cupid with flowers, holds him in leash to prevent him from following one of the Graces, for whom he has formed an attachment, and, during this expressive *pas*, the Graces and Pleasures lure the Nymphs into the forest. The Fauns follow them eagerly and, to safeguard the proprieties and so as not to render too obvious the comments which Cupid causes his mother to pass in regard to their disappearance, I bring back a moment later these same Nymphs and Fauns. The expression of the former and the satisfied air of the latter paint, in restrained colours in a suitably expressed passage of the Chaconne, pictures of voluptuousness tempered by sensibility and modesty.

This ballet, Sir, has an animated plot in which all the executants participate throughout.

I had also imagined pauses in the music and these silences produced the most flattering effect. The spectator's ear suddenly ceasing to be struck by the harmony, his eyes embraced with all the more attention every detail of the pictures, the position and design of the groups, the expression of the heads and of the various parts of the *ensemble;* nothing escaped his glance. These pauses in the music and in the movements of the body diffuse a sense of repose and light; they give increased fire to the passages that follow. They are shading which, used sparingly and with art and distributed with taste, give a new and enhanced value to every part of the composition, but the skill consists in using them with economy. They would become as fatal to dancing as they are sometimes to painting when one abuses them.

### "*L'Amour Corsaire ou l'Embarquement pour Cythère*"

The scene is set on the seashore of the Isle of Mysogeny. A number of trees unknown in our climate embellish the land. On one side of the stage is an altar in the style of the ancients erected to the divinity worshipped by the inhabitants and surmounted by a statue representing a man plunging a dagger into a woman's breast. The inhabitants of the isle are cruel and barbarous and it is their custom to sacrifice to their god all the women who have the misfortune to be cast up on this shore. They impose this same law on all men who escape the fury of the waves.

The first scene deals with the initiation of a stranger saved from shipwreck. This stranger is led to the altar on which lean two high priests. A number of the inhabitants are disposed round the altar holding in their hands clubs with which they exercise themselves whilst other Islanders celebrate in a mysterious dance the coming of the new proselyte. The latter finds himself forced to promise solemnly to sacrifice with the knife with which he is about to be armed, the first woman whom a too cruel destiny brings to the Island. Hardly has be begun to utter the terrible oath, at which he himself shudders even though deep in his heart he vows to disobey the new god whose worship he embraces, than the ceremony is interrupted by piercing shouts, at the sight of a long-boat tossed by a terrible storm, and by a lively dance expressive of the savage joy born of the hope of the sight of new victims being struck down. In this boat can be seen a woman and a man who raise their hands to Heaven and implore help. As the boat gets near Dorval, for that is the stranger's name, thinks he recognizes his sister and her friend. He looks attentively and his heart is filled with pleasure and with anxiety; at last he sees them out of danger and gives way to an excess of irrepressible satisfaction but the satisfaction and the joy derived therefrom is of short duration and soon steadied by the recollection of the terrible place he inhabits and this sudden thought plunges him into the most profound dejection and grief.

The eagerness which he displayed at first has deceived and impressed the Mysoginians; they thought to see in him a zeal and an inviolable devotion to their law. Meanwhile Clairville and Constance (these are the names of the two lovers) reach land. Death is painted in their features, they can barely open their eyes and their bristling hair reveals their terror. A deathly pallor tells the horror of the fate they faced a thousand times and which they still dread but what is not their surprise when they find themselves warmly embraced! They recognize Dorval, they throw themselves into his arms and can hardly believe their eyes. All three cannot tear themselves apart and the extent of their happiness is shown by all the outward signs of the purest joy; they drown each other in copious tears and these tears are the undoubted signs of the different feelings by which they are swayed. Then the situation changes. A savage presents Dorval with the knife which is to pierce the heart of Constance and bids him plunge it into her breast. Dorval, indignant at so barbarous an order, seizes the dagger and would strike the savage but Constance, freeing herself from her lover's arms, arrests the blow which her brother was about to deal. The savage makes the most of his opportunity, disarms Dorval, and would pierce the breast of the woman who has just saved his life. Clairville stays the traitor's arm and tears the dagger from him. Dorval and Clairville, equally sickened by the ferocious inhumanity of the islanders, rally to the side of Constance whom they clasp tightly in their arms so that their bodies form a rampart against the barbarity of their enemies and their ardent eyes, flashing with anger, seem to defy the irate Mysoginians. The latter, furious at the resistance, order those of the savages who have clubs to tear the victim from the arms of the two foreigners and drag her to the altar. Dorval and Clairville, stimulated by danger, disarm two of these cruel people and fight with fury and bold ardour, ever rallying round Constance whom they never lose sight of for an instant. The latter, trembling and distraught, fearing to lose two beings equally dear to her, gives way to despair. The sacrificers, aided by several savages, throw themselves on her and drag her to the altar. At this moment, summoning all her courage, she struggles with them and seizing the dagger of one of the sacrificers, stabs him with it. Freed for a moment, she flings herself into the arms of her lover and her brother only to be torn cruelly from them. She frees herself again and flies to them once more. However, Dorval and Clairville, overcome by numbers and at the point of death are bound with chains. Constance is dragged to the foot of that altar which is the seat of barbarism. An arm is upraised, the blow is about to fall when a god, who is a protector of lovers, stays the arm of the sacrificer and casts a spell over the island which renders every inhabitant motionless. This transition from the most active motion to immobility creates an astonishing effect. Constance, fainting at the feet of the high priest, and Dorval and Clairville, almost blinded, have fallen back into the arms of a number of savages.

The day improves, the waves subside, calm succeeds the storm, several Tritons and Naiads disport themselves in the water and a richly adorned boat appears on the sea. It is commanded by Cupid in the shape of a corsair. Games and Pleasures form the crew and a troupe of Nymphs dressed as Amazons are the soldiers who serve on this vessel; everything is elegant and announces the presence of the child of Cytherea.

The vessel comes alongside; Cupid has the anchor dropped and comes ashore followed by the Nymphs, the Games and the Pleasures and, whilst awaiting the god's orders, this gay company forms into battle array. The Mysoginians recover from the ecstasy and the immobility into which Cupid had plunged them.

A glance from the god restores Constance to life; Dorval and Clairville, now assured that their liberator is a god, prostrate themselves at his feet. The savages, enraged at this profanation of their beliefs all raise their clubs to massacre both the worshippers and the followers of the son of Cytherea; they even turn their rage and fury against him but how can mortals prevail when Cupid decrees? A single glance from him stays the armed hands of the Mysoginians. He commands that their altar be overturned and their infamous divinity destroyed. The Games and Pleasures execute his bidding; the altar subsides under their blows, the statue crumbles and pieces break away. A new altar appears and replaces that which has just been destroyed. It is of white marble and garlands of roses, jasmine and myrtle add to its elegance. Columns spring up from the ground to adorn this altar and a richly decorated canopy, borne by a group of cupids, descends from the skies; the ends borne by Zephyrs who rest them on the four columns surrounding the altar. The ancient trees of the Island disappear and are replaced by myrtles, orange trees and groves of roses and jasmine.

The Mysoginians, at the sight of their divinity overturned and their faith profaned, become enraged, but Cupid only permits their anger to break out at intervals and he stops them each time they are about to strike or to seek revenge. The moments when the spell immobilizes them offer an infinite number of tableaux and groups which differ from each other by their position, distribution and composition, but which nevertheless express all that is most awful in fury. The pictures offered by the Nymphs are a complete contrast in taste and colouring. They stave off the blows which the Mysoginians would deal them with graces and glances imbued with voluptuousness and tenderness. However, Cupid bids them combat and vanquish the savages and they attack them with the arms of sentiment and the savages offer but a feeble resistance. If they have the strength to raise their clubs to deal a blow, they lack the courage to deliver it. Finally they let go their clubs which fall from their hands. Vanquished and defenceless, they throw themselves at the knees of their victors who, tender by nature, grant them mercy and bind them with garlands of flowers.

Cupid, satisfied, unites Clairville to Constance and the Mysoginians to the Nymphs and bestows on Dorval, Zénéide a young nymph whom the god has carefully shaped. A triumphal march constitutes the conclusion of this ballet; the Nymphs lead the vanquished in leash; Cupid orders festivities and the general *divertissement* begins. The god, Clairville and Constance, Dorval and Zénéide, the Games and Pleasures dance the principal passages. The *Contredanse noble* of the ballet is faded out gradually in pairs as the company take their place in turn on the boat. Little benches arranged in different directions and on various levels serve as it were as a pedestal to this amorous troupe and present to the eye a group elegantly distributed. The anchor is raised, the Zephyrs and the lovers' sighs fill the sails and the vessel gets under way and, impelled by favourable winds, voyages towards Cytherea.

# The Known Productions of Jean Georges Noverre

LES FETES CHINOISES (Les Métamorphoses Chinoises, The Chinese Festival)
First performed 1751 or earlier, possibly at Marseilles or Strasbourg.
Revived Opéra Lyons, season 1751–2.
Revived Opéra Comique, Paris, July 1st, 1754. Costumes Boquet. Décor Guillet et Moulin and possibly Leuse, possibly after designs by Boquet or F. Boucher.
Revived Drury Lane, London, November 8th, 1755, with costumes and décor by Boquet.

CYTHERE ASSIEGEE
Created Opéra Comi que, Paris, 12.8.1754, as part of Favart's vaudeville of that name.

LA FONTAINE DE JOUVENCE
Opéra Comique, Paris, 17.9.1754.

LES REJOUISSANCES FLAMANDES
Opéra Comique, Paris, 11.8.1755.

LA PROVENCALE
Divertissement, Drury Lane, London, November, 1755 (before the 4th).

THE LILLIPUTIAN SAILORS
Divertissement, Drury Lane, London, 6.11.1755, with Miss Noverre, Mr. Lauchéry, Balettijr.

LA TOILETTE DE VENUS OU LES RUSES DE L'AMOUR
Created Opéra, Lyons, before 1760, probably before September, 1758. Music F. Granier.
Revived Opéra, Paris, 6.3.1777.
Revived King's Theatre, London, 1.4.1794, with MM. Aumer, d'Egville and F. Gardel.

L'AMOUR CORSAIRE OU L'EMBARQUEMENT POUR CYTHERE
Opéra, Lyons, season 1758–9. Music F. Granier. Costumes Boquet.

L'IMPROMPTU DU SENTIMENT
Opéra, Lyons, 11.9.1758. Music attributed F. Granier.

LES JALOUSIES OU LES FETES DU SERAIL
Opéra, Lyons, September 21st, 1758. Music attributed F. Granier.
2nd version—Teatro Regio Ducal, Milan, 17.10.1771, to music by Mozart.
Inserted between the two acts of Mozart's festival play Ascanio in Alba (libretto Parini) given for the wedding of Archduke Ferdinand of Austria and Princess Maria Ricciarda Beatrice of Modena. MS. notes of piano score in Mozarteum, Salzburg.
Revived, King's Theatre, London, 17.3.1789. Relationship of this revival to two previous productions unknown.

LES JALOUX SAN RIVAL
Spanish ballet in one act.
Opéra, Lyons, early 1759, probably to music by F. Granier.

LES CAPRICES DE GALATHEE
Pastoral ballet. Created before 1760. Probably Opéra, Lyons, early 1758, to music by F. Granier.
Revived 11.2.1761, Stuttgart, between acts 1 and 2 of Jomelli's opera, L'Olimpiade, as Capricii di Galatea, music Rodolphe or Deller.
Revived 30.9.1776 before French Court at Fontainebleau. 8.10 1776 at Brunoy.

Revived 11.'76, Opéra, Paris, after opera *Euthyme et Arveris*, with Guimard as Galathée, Mlles. Allard and Peslin as her Companions and M. Le Picq as A. Shepherd.

Revived Opéra, Paris –.8.1780, with A. Vestris as A Shepherd.

Revived 29.3.1781, King's Theatre, London, by G. Vestris as his own work, with costumes and décor by Novosielski. Mlle. Baccelli as Galathée.

Revived, King's Theatre, London, 7.5.1789, with Guimard as Galathée.

*LES RECRUES PRUSSIENNES*
    Comic ballet. Created before 1760, probably Opéra, Lyons.

*LES FETES DU VAUXHALL*
    Comic ballet. Created before 1760, probably Opéra, Lyons.

*RENAUD ET ARMIDE*
    Heroic pantomime ballet based on Tasso's *Jerusalem Delivered*.
    Created before 1760, probably Opéra, Lyons.
    Revived as *Rinaldo ed Armida* in two scenes with chorus to music by Rodolphe, between acts 2 and 3 of Jomelli's *L'Olimpiade,* at Stuttgart, 11.2.1761, with G. Vestris as Renaud.    Presumed scenery by Colomba and costumes by Boquet.
    Revived, Stuttgart, 23.2.1763, with G. Vestris (Renaud), Léger (Ubaldo), Le Picq (Chevalier Danois), Mlle. Nency (Armide), Mlle. Salomoni (Volupté) and Balletti (A Fury—rôle created by Mlle. Lolly who was ill).
    Revived by Le Picq, Teatro San Carlo, Naples, July, 1773.
    Revived in a third version dedicated to Archduchess Maria Beatrice d'Este, Princess of Modena, Teatro Regio Ducal, Milan, 1775 (probably June), with Mr. Gallé (Renaud), Mme. Dupré (Armide) and Mmes. Franchi, Terrades and Villeneuve.
    Revived in a fourth version to music by Le Brun with décor by Novosielski, King's Theatre, London, 23.2.1782, with Gardel, jr., Nivelon, Mlle. Théodore (Armide) and Mlle. Simonnet.

*LA DESCENTE D'ORPHEE AUX ENFERS*
    Serious ballet, created before 1760, probably Opéra, Lyons.

*LE JUGEMENT DE PARIS*
    Heroic pantomime ballet in two acts and an epilogue. Created Marseilles *c.* 1755.
    Revived at Stuttgart or Ludwigsburg between 1760 and 1766 (probably after 1761).
    Revived as *Das Urteil des Paris*, Burgtheater, Vienna, with Mlle. Delphine, summer of 1771.
    Revived Castle of Prince Esterhazy, near Vienna, 12.6.1772, with Mlle. Delphine

*LA MORT D'AJAX*
    Serious ballet. Created before 1760, probably Opéra, Lyons.

*LE BAL PARE*
    Comedy ballet. Created before 1760, probably Opéra, Lyons.

*LA MARIEE DU VILLAGE*
    Comedy ballet. Created before 1760, probably Opéra, Lyons.

*ADMETE ET ALCESTE*
    Tragic ballet. Created Stuttgart, 11.2.1761, at conclusion of Jomelli's *L'Olimpiade,* with G. Vestris (Admete), music Rodolphe or Deller.
    Revived, King's Theatre, London, 31.3.1789, as *Admete* to music by Mazzinghi. Score in B.M. b.52.9.

*AMORS SIEG UBER DIE KALTSINNIGKEIT*
    Created Ludwigsburg, 4.11.1761, and interpolated in Jomelli's *Isola disabitatta.*

*DIE UNVERHOFFTE ZUSAMMENKUNFT*
    Created Ludwigsburg, 4.11.1761, and interpolated in Jomelli's *Isola disabitatta.*

*LA MORT D'HERCULE*
    Created Stuttgart, 11.2.1762, between acts 2 and 3 of Jomelli's *Semiramide,* Music Rodolphe, Décor Colomba, Costumes Boquet, with G. Vestris (Hercules).

Revived Stuttgart, 13.2.1763, with G. Vestris (Hercules), Lépi (Hylus, son of Hercules), Angiolo Vestris (Philoctète), Mlle. Toscanini (Déjanise), Mlle. Nency (Iclé) and MM. Balletti, Léger, Le Picq and d'Auvigni (Wrestlers).
Revived Taylor's Opera House, Haymarket, London, by G. Vestris, 2.6.1791.
Revived St. Petersburg by Le Picq between 1777 and 1796.

PSYCHE ET L'AMOUR
Created Stuttgart, Feb. 11th, 1762, between acts 1 and 2 of Jomelli's Semiramide, Music Rodolphe, Décor Colomba, Costumes Boquet.
Revived 13.2.1763 Stuttgart with Mlle. Nency (Psyche), Mlle. Toscanini (Venus), M. Balletti (Tysiphone).
Revived in a new version, King's Theatre, London, 29.1.1788, Music Mazzinghi (Score B.M. London), Décor G. Marinari or Bellanger, Costumes Lupino, with Mlles. Hilligsberg (Psyche), Coulon (Venus) and MM. Chevalier (L'Hymen), Vestris (l'Amour), Didelot (Adonis), Coulon (Mercure). Dedicated to the Prince of Wales.
Revived by Le Picq, St. Petersburg, between 1777 and 1796—in the repertoire 1796-1801 with décor by P. Gonzago.
Revived by C. L. Didelot, St. Petersburg, 1802. (This may be an original work by Didelot and not after Noverre.)

A PERSIAN BALLET (?"Les Fêtes Persanes" or "L'Epouse Persane")
Created Stuttgart at the conclusion of Jomelli's Semiramide, 11.2.1762. Music Rodolphe or Deller. Revived 13.2.1762.

MEDEA ET JASON
Created Stuttgart, February 11th, 1763, after act 1 of Jomelli's Didone Abbandonata, Music Rodolphe (Score B.M. London), Décor Colomba, Costumes Boquet, with Mlles. Nency (Médée), Toscanini (Créuse), MM. G. Vestris (Jason), Angiolo Vestris (Créon), Lépi (Fire), Balletti (Vengeance), Delaître (Steel), Le Picq (Hate), Léger (Poison) and d'Auvigni (Jealousy). Repeated, Stuttgart, 21.2.1763.
Revived Burgtheater, Vienna, 25.2.1767, by G. Vestris.
Revived 1767-8, Warsaw, by G. Vestris.
Revived Opéra, Paris, 11.12.1770, by G. Vestris to a new score by de la Borde, with G. Vestris (Jason), Guimard (Créuse) and Allard (Médée).
Revived Opéra, Paris, 31.12.1775, to score by Rodolphe with additional airs by Berton, with G. Vestris (Jason), Guimard (Créuse) and Heinel (Médée).
Revived Opéra, Paris, 30.1.1780, to original score by Rodolphe, with Dauberval as Créon. Given six times that year.
Revived King's Theatre, London, 29.3.1781, by G. Vestris as his own work, décors Novosielski, with Sga. Baccelli (Créuse).
Revived King's Theatre, London, 11.4.1782, with décors by Novosielski.
Revived late 18th century, St. Petersburg, by Le Picq.
Revived Opéra, Paris, 1804, by Gardel, jr., and Vestris with Vestris (Jason), Milon (Créon), Aumer (Despair) and Mme. Gardel (Créuse), for five performances.

ORPHEUS UND EURYDICE
Created Stuttgart, February 11th, 1763, between acts 2 and 3 of Jomelli's Didone Abbandonata, Music Deller (Score B.M. London), Décor Colomba, Costumes Boquet, with MM. Lépi and G. Vestris (alternating as Orpheus), Angiolo Vestris with 12 attendants (Pluton), Baletti (Tisyphone), Mlle. Toscanini (Eurydice).

DER SIEG DES NEPTUN
Created Stuttgart after Jomelli's Didone Abbandonata, February 11th, 1763, Book J. Uriot, Music Deller, Décor Colomba, Costumes Boquet, with G. Vestris as Neptune. Repeated Stuttgart, 21.2.1763.

LE TRIOMPHE DE L'AMOUR
Created Palais de la Magnificence, Ludwigsburg, February 17th, 1763. Pastorale by Jomelli with Ballets by Noverre. Presumed Décor Colomba, Costumes Boquet. Repeated Stuttgart, 23.2.1763.

*HYPERMNESTRA*
Mythological tragedy in 1 act. Created Stuttgart, with Jomelli's *Demofoonte*, February 11th, 1764, Music Rodolphe or Deller, Presumed Décor Colomba, Costumes Boquet.
Revived Ludwigsburg, 11.2.1765.

*DER TOD DES LYKOMEDES*
Mythological ballet in 9 scenes.
Created Stuttgart after act 1 of Jomelli's *Demofoonte*, February 11th, 1764, Music Deller(?), Décor presumed Colomba, Costumes Boquet.
Revived Ludwigsburg, 11.2.1765.

*DAS FEST DES HYMENAUS*
Created Ludwigsburg with Jomelli's *Il Vologeso*, February 11th, 1766.

*DER RAUB DER PROSERPINE*
Created Ludwigsburg with Jomelli's *Il Vologeso*, February 11th, 1766.

*DIANE ET ENDYMION*
Created Stuttgart or Ludwigsburg 1760–1765 (probably after 1761).
Revived 1770 Neustadt.
Revived in revised version Vienna Burgtheater, 1772, Music Starzer.
(Score Archiv der Musikfreunde, Vienna.)
Revived Paris Opéra, Nov. 1765, seemingly without consent of Noverre, possibly by Vestris.

*ANTOINE ET CLEOPATRE*
Created Stuttgart or Ludwigsburg 1760–66 (probably after 1761).

*LES AMOURS D'HENRY IV*
Created Stuttgart or Ludwigsburg 1760–66 (probably after 1761).

*LES DANAIDES*
Created Stuttgart or Ludwigsburg 1760–66 (probably after 1761) with G. Vestris as Danaüs.

*ALEXANDRE*
Created Stuttgart between 1760 and 1766 (probably after 1761).

*L'APOTHEOSE D'HERCULE*
Created Vienna Burgtheater or Kärnthnertor Theater, September 10th, 1767 for betrothal of Erzherzogin Maria Josefa to King of Naples.

*DONCHISCHOTT*
Comedy ballet in 1 act. Created Vienna 1768, Music Starzer, Choreography presumed Noverre. Score Kl. A. Univ. Bib. Jena.

*ACIS ET GALATEE*
3 acts. Created Vienna, 1772, Music Aspelmayer, based on Ovide Metam. 13.
Revived St. Petersburg 1777–1796 by Le Picq

*ROGER ET BRADAMANTE*
Created Milan, Teatro Regio Ducal, October 17th, 1771, for betrothal of Archduke Ferdinand and Princess Maria Beatrice of Modena.
Revived Vienna Burgtheater, 1772, Music Starzer, based on Aristotle's *Orlando Furioso*.

*DER GERÄCHTE AGAMEMNON*
Tragic ballet, 5 acts. Created Vienna, Kärnthnertor Theater, 1772, Music Aspelmayer.

*DIE FÜNF SULTANINEN*
Created Vienna Burgtheater, 1772, Music Starzer.

*DIE WÄSCHERINNEN VON CYTHERE*
Created Vienna 1772.

*DIE MATELOTTEN*
Created Vienna 1772.

*DIE QUELLE DER SCHÖNHEIT UND DER HÄSSLICHKEIT*
Created Vienna, 1772.

*IPHIGENIE EN TAURIDE*
(A sequel to *Der Gerächte Agamemnon*, in 4 acts.)
Created Vienna, 1772–3. Music Aspelmayer.

*ADELE DE PONTHIEU*
5 acts. Created Vienna, probably Burgtheater, 1733. Music Starzer (Score Nationalbibliothek, Vienna and Univ. Bib. Jena).
Revived 1774, San Carlo Theatre, Naples, by Le Picq
Revived March, 1787, Lyons, Opéra.
Revived 11.4.1782, King's Theatre, London, to new score by Le Brun, Décor Novosielski, dedicated to Duchess of Devonshire.
Revived 17.4.1788, King's Theatre, London.
Revived between 1777 and 1796, St. Petersburg, by Le Picq.

*SEMIRAMIS*
Created Vienna, Burgtheater or Kärnthnertor, between 1768 and 1773.

*LES AMOURS D'ENEE ET DIDON OU DIDON ABANDONNEE*
Heroic ballet in 5 acts, created Vienna 1768–1773.
Revived Lyons, 12.6.1781, to music Starzer, Décor Chevalier Moretti (3 scenes only, stock scenery used for remaining scenes), costumes l'Espérance.

*LES GRACES*
Anacreontic ballet drawn from C. M. Willand's poem. Created Vienna, 1768–73.

*GLI ORAZI EGLI CURIAZI*
Tragic ballet after Corneille in 5 acts. Created 6.1.1774, Kärnthnertor, Vienna Music Starzer (score Paris, Bib. Op.; 2 acts only—Vienna Nationalbiblisthek).
Revived 1776 (Carnival) in Venice, by Franchy; Naples, by Le Picq; Vienna, by Gallet; and Milan, by Noverre.
Revived 21.10.1777, Opéra, Paris, with Mlle. Heinel as Camille.

*APELLES ET CAMPASPE* or *Alexandre et Campaspe de Larisse* or *Le Triomphe d'Alexandre sur soi-même*
Heroic ballet in 2 acts. Created Vienna, 1774. Music Aspelmayer.
Revived 1.10.1776, Opéra, Paris, to revised score by Rodolphe, with G. Vestris (Apelles), Guimard (Campaspe), Heinel (Roxane), and Gardel ainé (Alexandre).
Revived 9.11.1776, Opéra, Paris, in shortened version (score by Rodolphe Bib. Opéra, Paris).
Revived 1776, Fontainebleau, 1777, Lyons, March, 1787, Lyons.
Revived 5.6.1782, King's Theatre, London, possibly to new score by Le Brun, in version omitting part of Roxane.
Revived 2.11.1782, King's Theatre, London, by Le Picq.

*FLORA*
Created 1766–1774, Vienna. Music Aspelmayer.

*DIE SCHINDLER*
Created Vienna, 1768–74. Music Starzer. May have been by Angiolini.

*BALLO DEL AMORE*
Created Vienna, 1768–74. Music Starzer (Score Univ. Bib. Jena). Ballet attributed to Noverre.

*BALLO OLANDESE*
Created Vienna, 1768–74, and attributed to Noverre. Possibly a children's ballet. Music Starzer.

*LA STATUA ANIMATA*
Created Vienna, 1768–74, and attributed to Noverre. Music Starzer.

*DAS STRASSBURGISCHE FEST*
Folk ballet. Created Vienna, 1768–74, and attributed to Noverre. Music Starzer.

*GLI AMORI DI VENERE OSSIA LA VENDETTA DI VULCANO*
Ballo episodico. Created Milan, 1775. Music E. J. Floquet.

*EUTHYME ET EUCHARIS*
Heroic ballet in 3 scenes. Created Vienna or Milan before 1776.
Revived 13.3.1788, King's Theatre, London. Costumes Lupino. Décor Marinari, with Vestris (Euthyme), Hilligsberg (Eucharis), Henry (L'Ombre), Coulon (Bellone), and Didelot (Mars).

*LA PRIMA ETA' DELL' INNOCENZA OSIA LA ROSAIA DI SALENCY*
13 scenes. Created Milan, 1775. Music Baillou, with Villeneuve (Rosaia) and Franchi (Cola).
Revived 19.3.1782, King's Theatre, London, with Gardel jr., Nivelon, Baccelli, Théodore, Simonet, and Bournonville.
Revived 29.7.1783, Opéra, Paris, by M. Gardel, with Guimard and Vestris (Some doubt as to whether a new ballet by Gardel).

*LA FOIRE DU CAIRE*
(?)Created Lyons, March, 1787. May have been first given Vienna or Milan, 1768–1775.

*GALEAS DUC DE MILAN*
Created Milan, 1771 or 1775.

*RITIGER ET WENDA*
Created Milan, 1771 or 1775.

*HYMENEE ET CRYSEUS*
Created Milan, 1771 or 1775.

*BELTON ET ELIZA*
Created Milan, 1771 or 1775.

*LES PETITS RIENS*
3 scenes. Created 11.6.1778, Opéra, Paris, with Piccini's opera *Le finte Gemelle*. Music Mozart (12 pieces) et al. (6 pieces)—score Bib. Op. Paris.
Revived 11.12.1781, King's Theatre, London, to score by Barthélémon (possibly Mozart's own with fresh orchestration or additional airs), Décor Novosielski.

*ANNETTE ET LUBIN*
After poem by Marmontel. Created 9.7.1778, Opéra, Paris, with Cécile (Annette).
Revived 28.4.1789, King's Theatre, London, to score by Federíci with Guimard (Annette).
Revived 1778–96, St. Petersburg, by Le Picq.

*DON QUICHOTTE* (scenes from)
Created August 1780, Gardens of Mme. de Guéménée, Montreuil, for wedding of Princesse de Rohan Guéménée with Prince de Rohan Rochefort. Choreography Noverre and Dauberval with dancers from Paris Opéra.

*PRINCE OF WALES MINUET*
Divertissement. Created 13.12.1781 for masked ball at King's Theatre, London. Added to repertoire 26.1.1782. Music Le Brun (score BM.G.442.F.1 and BM.B.51.F.3). Dance was later incorporated in Le Brun's *Armide* the same year. There may have been another score by Barthélémon (BM.b.51).

*LES AMANS REUNIS*
Tragic ballet. Created 5.1.1782, King's Theatre, London. Décor Novosielski.

*LE TRIOMPHE DE L'AMOUR CONJUGAL*
Divertissement. Created 10.1.1782, King's Theatre, London. Décor Novosielski. May be variant of pastoral by Jomelli—see 1763 above.

*THE EMPEROR'S COSSACK*
Divertissement. Created 29.1.1782, King's Theatre, London, for Nivelon and Théodore.

*LE TEMPLE DE L'AMOUR*
Divertissement. Created 25.4.1782, King's Theatre, London.

*APOLLON ET LES MUSES*
  Divertissement. Created 2.5.1782, for Le Picq's first appearance in England, King's Theatre, London.

*LES OFFRANDES A L'AMOUR*
  Created 8.12.1787, King's Theatre, London. Costumes Lupino, Décor Marinari, music Mazzinghi (score BM.b.51), to which may later have been added a finale by Haydn, with Vestris and Hilligsberg.

*LES FETES DU TEMPE*
  Created 1.3.1788, King's Theatre, London, Décor Marinari, costumes Lupino, score Mazzinghi (BM.b.52.8).

*A BALLET*
  Created 8.4.1788, King's Theatre, London (score B.M.b.51).

*LES FETES PROVENCALES*
  Created 31.1.1789, King's Theatre, London.
  Revived 22.6.1791 by Vestris, Mr. Taylor's Opera House, London.

*LES FOLIES D'ESPAGNE*
  *Pas de Trois.* Presumed created 15.6.1789 (but may be the *divertissement* in a Spanish style given on 18.3.1794), King's Theatre, London, with Guimard and Didelot.

*LES EPOUX DU TEMPE*
  Created 26.1.1793, King's Theatre, London.

*PAS DE TROIS ET DE QUATRE*
  Created to the air of God Save the King, 19.2.1793, King's Theatre, London, with Millard, Hilligsberg, F. Gardel and Nivelon.

*VENUS AND ADONIS*
  Heroic ballet. Created King's Theatre, London, 26.2.1793 with Hilligsberg (Hebe), Millard (Venus), F. Gardel (Adonis), d'Egville (Jupiter) and Gentili (Mercury). Costumes Settini, Décors Marinari.

*LE FAUNE INFIDEL*
  *Divertissement.* Created 6 4.1793, King's Theatre, London.

*IPHIGENIA IN AULIDE OR THE SACRIFICE OF IPHIGENIA*
  Music Millard, Décor Johnstone, costumes Settini, King's Theatre, London, 27.4.1793, with Hilligsberg (Iphigenia), Millard (Clytemnestra), d'Egville (Agamemnon), F. Gardel (Egith).

*LES NOCES DE THETIS*
  Created 1793, King's Theatre, London.

*ADELAIDE OU LA BERGERE DES ALPES*
  Created 11.1.1794, King's Theatre, London. Music presumed Miller.

*L'UNION DES BERGERES*
  *Divertissement.* Created 4.3.1794, King's Theatre, London.

*LA SERVA PADRONE*
  Allegorical ballet. Created 19.6.1794, King's Theatre, London.

*LA BATAILLE DE FONTENOY*
  Historical ballet. MS. scenario in Bibliothèque Nationale, Paris. If this work was produced it would seem to have been one of Noverre's earliest ballets.

*Opera Ballets and Operas in which Noverre may have directed the movement*

*L'OLIMPIADE,* Stuttgart, 11.2.1761, libretto Metastasio, music Jomelli. See also *Admete ed Alceste* above.

*L'ISOLA DISABITATTA,* Ludwigsburg, 4.11.1761, music Jomelli. See also *Amors Sieg über die Kaltsihnigkeit* and *Die unverhoffte Zusammenkunft* above.

*SEMIRAMIDE*, Stuttgart, 11.2.1762, libretto Metastasio, music Jomelli, revival of a work previously given at Turin. See also *La mort d'Hercule, Psyche et l'Amour*, and *A Persian Ballet* above.

*DIDONE ABBANDONATA*, Stuttgart, 11.2.1763, libretto Metastasio, music Jomelli. See also *Medea et Jason, Orpheus und Eurydice* and *Der Sieg des Neptun*, above.

*LE TRIOMPHE DE L'AMOUR*, Ludwigsburg, 17.2.1763. Pastorale by Jomelli with songs by Tagliazucchi. See also above.

*DEMOFOONTE*, Stuttgart, 11.2.1764, libretto Metastasio, music Jomelli. See also *Hypermnestra* and *Der Tod des Lykomedes* above. Revived 11.2.1765.

*IL VOLOGESO*, Ludwigsburg, 11.2.1766, libretto Verazzi, music Jomelli. See also *Das Fest des Hymenaüs* and *Der Raub der Proserpine* above.

*IL MATRIMONIO PER CONCORSO*, Ludwigsburg, 4.11.1766. Opéra-buffa, libretto G. Martinelli, music Jomelli, ballets Noverre.

*ALCESTE*, Burgtheater, Vienna, 26.12.1767. Libretto R. de' Calzabigi, music Gluck, concluded by ballet in grotesque style by Noverre. Revived in Italian, Vienna 21.9.1770 with Delphine dancing in ballet.

*PARIDE E ELENA*, Burgtheater, Vienna, 3.11.1770, text R. de' Calzabigi, music Gluck, ballets Noverre.

*ASCANIO IN ALBA*, Teatro Regio Ducal, Milan, 17.10.1771, libretto G. Parini, music Mozart, ballet Noverre. See also *Roger et Bradamante* above.

*LA FRASCATANA*, text F. Livigni, music Paisiello. First created Teatro San Samuele, Venice, and revived Vienna 29.4.1775 and Trieste May 1775, but we have no evidence as to who created the ballets if any. Revived Teatro Regio Ducal, Milan, autumn 1775 with ballets by Noverre.

*ADELE DE PONTHIEU*, Opéra, Paris, 21.1.1777, music Starzer (score Bib. de l'Opéra, Paris), ballets by Noverre. Revived again 1779–80. See above ballet of the same name by Starzer–Noverre.

*LE DEVIN DU VILLAGE*, text and music J. J. Rousseau, created Fontainebleau 18.10.1752 and frequently revived. Noverre is said to have created the ballets in April 1777(?).

*ARMIDE*, Opéra, Paris, 23.9.1777, text Quinault, music Gluck, ballets Noverre. Vestris, Gardel, Guimard and Allard appeared at first performance.

*ORFEO ED EURIDICE*, text R. de Calzabigi, music Gluck. Created Burgtheater Vienna, 5.10.1762 with ballets by Angiolini. At a later date possibly at the Paris Opéra, the ballets were composed by Noverre.

*ROLAND*, Opéra, Paris, 27.1.1778, text Quinault–Marmontel, music Piccini, ballet by Noverre (revised 31.1.1778).

*IPHIGENIE EN TAURIDE*, Opéra, Paris, 18.5.1779, text N. F. Guillard, music Gluck, ballet (? to music by Gossec) possibly by Noverre.

*IPHIGENIA IN AULIDE*, King's Theatre, London, 25.5.1782, text F. Moretti, music Cherubini, dances by Noverre. Revived 24.1.1789 with dances by Noverre and Coindre.

*LA LOCANDIERA*, King's Theatre, London, 15.1.1788, comic opera by Cimarosa with dances by Chevalier and Vestris and a *pas de deux* by Noverre for Didelot and Mlle. Coulon. N.B. This may be Salieri's opera (created Vienna 8.6.1773, with additions by Cimarosa).

*L'OLIMPIADE*, text Metastasio, music Cimarosa, created Vicenza 10.7.1784 and revived King's Theatre, London, 8.5.1788 with ballet by Noverre.

*LA COSA RARA*, text L. da Ponte, music Martin y Soler, created Vienna 17.11.1786 and revived with ballet by Noverre and Coindre, King's Theatre, London 10.1.1789 (? with additions by Cherubini).

*IL DISERTORE*, King's Theatre, London, 28.2.1789, opera by Tarchi with ballets by Noverre and Coindre.

*LA VILLANA RICONSCIUTA*, opera by Cimarosa, King's Theatre, London, 24.3.1789, with dances by Noverre and Coindre.

*I ZINGARI IN FIERA*, text G. Palomba, music Paisiello, created Naples 21.11.1789, revived King's Theatre, London, 14.5.1793 with ballets by Noverre.

*LA VITTORIA*, King's Theatre, London, 2.7.1794, opera by Paisiello with allegorical ballet by Noverre.

*IL MATRIMONIO SEGRETO*, text G. Bertati, music Cimarosa, created Vienna 7.2.1792. Revived with ballet by Noverre, King's Theatre, London, 11.1.1794.

*DON GIOVANNI TENORIO*, text G. Bertati, music Gazzaniga, created Venice, 5.2.1787. Revived King's Theatre, London, 1.3.1794, in revised version with additional airs by Sarti, Federici and Guglielmi and dances by Noverre to music by Millard.

*I CONTADINI BIZZARRI*, King's Theatre, London, 4.3.1794, music Sarti or Paisiello with ballet by Noverre.

*LA BELLA PESCATRICE*, text S. Zini, music P. Guglielmi, created Naples, 1789. Revived King's Theatre, London, 18.3.1794, with a Spanish ballet by Noverre.

*LA SERVA PADRONA*, text G. A. Federico, music Paisiello, created St. Petersburg, 10.9.1781. Revived King's Theatre, London, 29.5.1794, with allegorical ballet by Noverre, possibly to additional music by Millard.

# FOOTNOTES

¹ J. G. Noverre, *Lettres sur les Arts Imitateurs*, 51.

² According to an extract★ from the register of baptisms of the Church of Lausanne, Jean Louys, son of Jean Nicolas Noverre, Grand Forester and Citizen of Lausanne, and of Honeste Magdeleine Bon Vepre, his wife, was baptized on August 11th, 1690.

From an excerpt★ from the Lausanne register of marriages it appears that Jean Louys Noverre was married on February 10th, 1722, by the Rev. F. C. Dartis, a priest of the Church of England and chaplain to Sir Robert Sutton, British Minister in Paris, in the chapel of the latter, to Marie Anne de la Grange, of Mesnil St. Firmin, Picardy, daughter of Pierre de la Grange and of Marguerite Habourg.

According to a manuscript note on a list of pensioners of the Paris Opéra (Arch. Nat.624), Jean Georges Noverre was baptized in the Chapel of the Dutch Ambassador on April 29th, 1727.

In the 17th and 18th centuries the Dutch ambassadors were protestant and had the right to maintain their own place of worship. Their official residence in Paris was the Hotel des Ambassadeurs de Hollande, a beautiful mansion built in 1638 by the architect Cottard at No. 47 Rue Vieille du Temple, where it may be seen to this day although the chapel is now used as a kitchen (see Paul Brenot, *Un vieux Hotel du Marais du XV au XX siècle*, 1939). From 1717 to 1727, however, the .Dutch ambassador, Viscount Boreel, had his apartments at the Palais Royal and his private chapel nearby in the Rue St. Honoré whilst Marcus Guitton, chaplain to the Dutch Embassy, lived at the Hotel des Ambassadeurs but preached in both chapels. It is possible that the Adjutant Noverre may have been quartered in the Palais Royal in the service of Monsieur, the King's brother, whose residence it was.

According to an entry recording the death of Jean Georges Noverre in the municipal archives of St. Germain en Laye, he was born on April 29th, 1727, and this date is also given by his great-great-nephew, C. E. Noverre, *The Life and Works of the Chevalier Noverre*. André Levinson, preface to *Les Lettres sur la Danse et sur les Ballets*, Duchartre & van Buggenhoudt, Paris, 1927, and C. W. Beaumont, preface to *Letters on Dancing and Ballets*, 1930, however, both give the date as April 27th, 1727, without stating the source.

According to an extract★ from the record of baptisms in the Chapel of Monseigneur van Hoey, Dutch Ambassador in Paris, Augustin Noverre, son of Jean Louys Noverre and of Marie Anne de la Grange, was born on May 3rd, 1729, and presented the next day by Augustin Noverre, a citizen of Lausanne, and Marie Thérèse Courtois, bourgeoise of Paris, for baptism by M. Dumont, chaplain.

Jean Georges Noverre was therefore born of a Swiss father and a French mother and baptized in the protestant faith.

★Records in the possession of Mrs. M. Farebrother, a descendant of AugustinNoverre.

³ *Lettres sur la Danse et sur les Ballets*, XII. Jean Denis Dupré (1706-1782), known as "le petit Dupré" to distinguish him from Louis Dupré, appeared at the Opéra in secondary rôles until 1757 when he retired on a pension. Louis Dupré, known as "le grand Dupré" (circa 1697-1774), was dancing at the Opéra, where he arranged a number of ballets, until 1751.

⁴ Letter VIII:—"The advantage which would have accrued, not only to the Dance, but also to the other arts which contribute to the charm and perfection of opera, could the celebrated Rameau, without offending the Nestors of this century and that mass of people who can see nothing beyond Lully, have set to music the masterpieces of the father and creator of lyric poetry, is undoubted. This man of vast and sublime genius embraced everything at one and the same time in his works; his compositions are, or could easily be, the triumph of the arts. All in his works is beautiful, grand and harmonious. . . ."

"It is to the varied and harmonious compositions of M. Rameau, to the brilliant melody and the lively expression that inspire his tunes, that the dance owes all its progress. It was awakened and drawn forth from the lethargy into which it was plunged from the moment when this creator of a music which whilst being learned was always agreeable and voluptuous appeared on the scene. What might he not have achieved if the practice of mutual collaboration had been in force at the Opéra. . . ."

Letter VIII:—". . . but we have M. Lany, whose superiority excites our admiration and raises him above anything I could say of him.

. . . they wish to copy the precision, the gaiety and the beautiful arrangement of M. Lany's *enchaînements*. . . ."

Letter XII:—". . . Mlle. Camargo and M. Lany enjoy that precious touch and that fine precision which give to dancing a sparkling gaiety and a vivacity which one does not find in dancers endowed with less sensitiveness and delicacy of hearing. . . ."

Letter VIII:—". . . Mlle. Lany has effaced all those who shone by the beauty, the precision and strength of their execution. She is the first dancer in the universe but we have not forgotten Mlle. Sallé's artless expression, her graces are always in our thoughts. . . ."

*Lettres sur les Arts Imitateurs·*—"Mlle. Sallé . . . replaced this tinsel glitter by simple and touching graces. Her physiognomy was noble, sensitive and expressive. Her voluptuous dancing was written with as much *finesse* as lightness; it was not by leaps and frolics that she went to your heart."

N.B.—J. B. Lany (1718-1786) danced at the Opéra 1748-61 and was ballet-master until 1767.

L. M. Lany (*circa* 1733-1777), sister of J. B. Lany, at the Opéra 1743-65.

Marie Sallé (1707-8-1752?) at the Opéra 1727-32 and 1735-39. For a detailed account of her life see Emile Dacier *Marie Sallé*, and Deryck Lynham *Ballet Then and Now*, pp. 40 *et seq*.

⁵ *Lettres sur les Arts Imitateurs*, p. 87.

Noverre dates this incident in the spring of 1740 but he was writing some sixty years after the event and it would seem his memory may have been at fault as there is nothing to suggest that Monnet took any interest in the stage prior to 1743 and, in fact, he spent a good part of 1741 in Fort l'Evêque prison as a result of writings deemed libellous.

It may perhaps be not unreasonable to date this incident about the time of Noverre's appearance before the Court at Fontainebleau. C. E. Noverre (*The Life and Works of the Chevalier Noverre*) and most historians since have given the date of this appearance at Fontainebleau as August, 1743, but the *Nouvelle Biographie Générale*, published in 1824, in an article under the signature of D. Denne Baron, gives October, 1743, which seems more probable inasmuch as Louis XV had what amounted to a passion for exactitude in his habits and the Court regularly left Versailles in July for Compiègne, where it remained until the last week in August, returned to Versailles and then left again for Fontainebleau in the first week in October, to remain until mid-November.

"Choreography" is used by Noverre in this anecdote in the eighteenth-century sense of the art of writing down dances and the use which Jean Denis Dupré made of dance notation may perhaps explain Noverre's later impatience with all such systems.

⁶ Under the Electors of Brandenburg, French artists had been seen from time to time in Berlin and there is a reference in the accounts for the year 1684 to expenses paid to ballet dancers, probably members of a troupe who had halted on their way from France to Denmark or Poland. Queen Sophia-Charlotte, wife of Frederick I of Prussia, did much to encourage the arts and created, at her summer palace at Lietzenburg (now Charlottenburg), a court ballet composed of courtiers led by a few professional dancers. The name of at least one French choreographer, a certain Desnoyers, who arranged ballets for the opera *La Festa del Himeneo*, given in 1701 for the marriage of Charles Frederick, landgrave of Hesse, and Louise Dorothée Sophie, Princess of Brandenburg, is known to us.

With the death of Sophia Charlotte, on February 1st, 1705, however, interest in the arts declined in Prussia.

⁷ The dancers engaged included Babet Cochois, a second cousin of Marie Sallé, and Mlle. Simione, followed in 1742 by Marianne Cochois, who was seven years later to marry the Marquis d'Argenson, and the seventeen year old Mlle. Roland.

[8] We have no record of the date at which Noverre left Monnet to go to Berlin. It seems probable, however, that he obtained the engagement through J. B. Lany after the coming of Barbara Campanini when the *corps de ballet* was formed. In this case he probably remained at the Opéra Comique until its final closure in 1745, and appeared in Favart's various vaudevilles.

C. E. Noverre (op.cit.) says Noverre left Berlin in 1747 and, in 1749, obtained the post of *Maître de Ballet* at the Opéra Comique, whilst C. W. Beaumont (preface to Noverre's *Letters*) says "In 1747 he was appointed Maître de Ballet at the Opéra Comique". Permission to reopen the Opéra Comique was, however, not given until December 20th, 1751, and it did not in fact open its doors until February 3rd, 1752.

C. W. Beaumont (op. cit.) says: "Dissatisfied with his reception he went to Potsdam at the invitation of Prince Henry of Prussia. . . ." I would respectfully suggest, however, that, bearing in mind Frederick the Great's dominating character, it seems improbable that his brother would have taken into his service an artist discontented with his treatment at the Prussian Court and who may even have broken his contract.

Léon Vallas (*Un Siècle de Musique et de Théâtre à Lyon*, 1932, and *Un Centenaire, Noverre à Lyon*, Revue Musicale de Lyon, 27.11.1910—Year 8 No. 7) says he returned from Berlin in 1749.

It seems to me that, failing evidence to the contrary, it must be assumed that Noverre left Berlin with Lany for, in his reply to Angiolini which forms a foreword to the programme printed in Vienna for *Les Horaces et les Curiaces*, he states that he was composing ballets in Marseilles and Lyons in 1748.

[9] A letter to the Duc de Villeroy, dated June 25th, 1754, re the new theatre it was proposed to build at the bottom of the grounds of the Hotel de Ville, proves the fashionable vogue of the Terreaux district at the time:—". . . but that which seemed to me to decide the issue is, that in building a new hall for the purposes of entertainment, one must take into account the district and the means of ensuring its support and that it is certain that it will find support in the Terreaux district, which is the favourite residential area of the merchants and therefore groups most of the well-to-do persons in the city." (Arch. Dep. du Rhône, C.135).

I have been unable to trace when or where Noverre was married, but it would not seem to have been at Lyons. His wife, née Marguerite Louise Sauveur, a native of Malmédy, may have been related to the Sauveur et Dame Sauveur, dancers, referred to in the Strasbourg archives for the season 1751–2 and 1753–4 (Noverre and his wife also appeared in Strasbourg) and to the Nanette Sauveur engaged as a dancer at the Wurtemberg Court in 1760.

The record of the death of Antoine Noverre on April 14th, 1829, at the age of 78 years 4 months, states that he was born in Lyons.

The register of the Catholic church of St. Saturnin at Lyons, which is no longer in existence but stood in the Rue Paul Cheiravard not far from the Place des Terreaux, contains the following entry at January 25th, 1752:—"Claudine Gervaise, daughter of Sieur Jean Georges Noverre and Louise Sauveur his wife, born yesterday, place des Terreaux, has been baptized by the undersigned, vicar, this 25th January, 1752; the godfather was David Flachat, esquire and ex-magistrate, and the godmother Dame Claudine Gervaise Bruyzet, wife of sieur Claude Pierre Fuselier, esquire and secretary counsellor to the King, both of which have signed."

Signed: "Noverre"                                        "Colombier, vicar"
(Arch. Mun., Bibl. de la Ville de Lyon, No. 623, Fol. II Vo.)

A later entry in this same parish register throws an interesting light on the attitude of the Church to the stage:—"This day, 30th of January, 1758, Jean Arnaud, known as Durand, having recognized through divine mercy that the art of representation in the theatre is contrary to the profession of Christianity, and although he has not acted for six months past, promises, swears and proclaims before the altars, never to act or contribute directly or indirectly to stage representations in this town or elsewhere, in witness whereof he has signed in the presence of the undersigned, vicar, and made the said proclamation this said day, month and year."

[10] "Remarks by the Sieur Mathieu Belouard on the statement of expense and earnings

of the Comedy from Easter, 1751, to Easter, 1752 handed to Monsieur Perrichon, State Counsellor" (Arch. Dep. du Rhône, G.135).

"This statement would make it appear that the expenses amounted to 87.572 livres, 6 soles, 10 deniers and the receipts to 69.533 livres, a loss of 18.039 livres, 6s. 10d.

There have been omitted from the expenses the salary of the Sieur Bertrand amounting to 1.000 livres. Also there have not been included a payment made to the Sieur and Dame Noverre to break off their engagement for a good and sufficient reason— L.2.800. There has also been omitted in the expenses the bonus paid to the Sieur Noverre for several ballets agreed at 120 livres for each, a total of 10, which makes L.1.200 of which the Sieur Bertrand has paid 288 and the balance was paid by the Sieur Mathieu—912."

11 Jean Monnet made his way to London on August 6th, 1748, and opened at the Little Theatre in the Haymarket on November 9th, 1749. On the opening night there was a free fight between the French Protestant refugees, aided by the unemployed English actors in the gallery, and Monnet's patrons who filled the boxes, and officers with drawn swords had to protect the artists on the stage. The next night the noble lords arrived with an escort of Thames watermen and the riots recommenced with renewed bitterness. After the fourth performance the Lord Chamberlain banned any further representations and Monnet was fain to close down. It was at this time Monnet met and struck up a life-long friendship with David Garrick, who gave a benefit performance to help him recoup his losses.

12 *Observateur Littéraire*, 1759, pp. 274-5.

13 Charles Collé (1709-1783), *Journal* (1868 and 1911)—Vol. II, p. 3. Mlle. Gauthier, actress; Mlle. Beauménard, known as Gogo, actress; Marie-Anne Dangeville, actress; B. J. Saurin, dramatist and critic. *Mercure de France*, March, 1755, p. 159. Mme. Noverre appeared as the "Soubrette" in Molière's *Tartuffe* and Regnard's *Les Folies Amoureuses*, as "Cléanthis" in Regnard's *Démocrite Amoureuse*, and as "Finette" in Destouches' *Le Philosophe marié*.

14 Collé, op. cit., July 1754, I.248. & J. A. J. Des Boulmiers, *Histoire de l'Opéra Comique*, 1769, II.323.

It would seem that the ballet was to have formed part of *Le Chinois poli en France*, opéra comique in one act by M. Anseaume (a parody of the *intermède* "Chinois" at the Bouffons). *Le Chinois poli* was, however, postponed owing to the illness of some of the actors and was not given until 1754.

It has been stated that the scenery was by François Boucher. The earliest suggestion to this effect which I have been able to trace is in Emile Campardon's *Les Spectacles de la Foire*, published in 1877, where the scenery is attributed to Guillier, Moulin et Leuse after the invention and drawings of Boucher. None of the contemporary sources to which I have had access, however, make any reference to either Boucher or Leuse, and Campardon, alas, does not give the source of his information.

Des Boulmiers states that the ballet was given in Lyons, Marseilles and Strasbourg before it was seen in Paris. Noverre (*Lettres sur la Danse et sur les Ballets*, Ed. 1782, Let. VI) states:—"my ballet" (*Les Jalousies ou les Fêtes du Serail*) "was all the more successful than that entitled *Ballet Chinois*, and which I revived at Lyons . . ." and he appends a footnote "This ballet has since been given in Paris and London . . ." It would appear therefore that the ballet was first created in neither Paris nor Lyons but possibly in Marseilles or Strasbourg.

There is also a letter in the Arch. Mun. de la Bibliothèque de la Ville de Lyon (GGXVI, 476, 22K, item 169), dated March 17th, 1752:—"The Sieur Noverre asks me, Sir, to give you all the information I can as to the settlement I made between him and the Sieur Mathieu. The latter is in error when he thinks that in the amount which I fixed as the sum to be paid to Noverre, was included anything which might be due to a painter for a Chinese Ballet. I recollect quite well that there was never any question of this painter nor that Noverre had to pay him anything, so that the sum awarded him was to be free of all encumbrance." The signature is illegible.

15 The triangle would seem to have been first introduced with the side drum by Gluck in his *Iphigénie en Tauride* (1779), whilst he used the bass drum and cymbals in

his *Pilgrims of Mecca* in 1764. The term Turkish Music is probably derived from the Sultan of Turkey's famous regiment of Janissaries, founded in 1326 and finally disbanded in 1825. Eastern military music began to be known in Europe as a result of the Crusades and gradually came to be introduced into European military bands. Instruments known under this heading must have had a definite eastern connotation in the minds of an audience in 1754, which would explain their use in this ballet.

[16] *Cythère Assiégée* by Fagan and Favart, vaudeville with songs and dances, based on Longus' *Daphnis and Chloe*, originally created as *Le Pouvoir de l'Amour ou le Siège de Cythère*, 1.7.1743. Revived in a one act version by Favart alone, Brussels 7.7.1748. It is this latter version which was given at the Opéra Comique with ballets by Noverre, and again in Vienna in 1757 and served as a basis for Gluck's opera of that name. Angiolini also composed a ballet to music by Gluck, *Citera assediata*, in 1762.

[17] Des Boulmiers, op. cit., II. 335. There had been an opera of the same name and subject by Carolet et Dupuy at the Foire St. Laurent in 1721, which was a failure.

[18] op. cit. II. 486.

[19] This is the first reference we have to his sister who does not reappear at a later date. Was she in fact Nanette Sauveur, his presumed sister-in-law, who may have been described in the English programme as Miss Noverre to reduce the number of French names in view of the anti-French feeling which was abroad?

[20] The Opéra Comique in the Foire St. Germain was situated on a property belonging to the Abbaye, to whom it paid dues as well as to the Académie Royale de Musique (for the year 1769 dues to the Abbaye amounted to as much as 23,520 livres).

[21] Noverre's insistence that Garrick shall appear in person at his benefit is a matter of considerable financial importance to him and he is obviously well informed on the subject. In a letter to Voltaire in March, 1765 (Marigné, *Vie de David Garrick*, pp. 158–160), he explains how, in addition to their salaries, the actors at Drury Lane had a benefit performance:—
"Their salaries varied accordingly as they had more or less talent. The leading actors drew very large salaries. Two and a half months of the season, which lasted for approximately eight, were largely devoted to the benefits of the actors, that is to say performances for their profit. Those of the most esteemed actors were worth up to five hundred guineas to them and Garrick played in some of these benefits either according to their contract or as a favour. This kindness was even extended to the most obscure class of this theatre, that is to say the stage hands and the supernumeraries had performances which were always excellent. Garrick had one of which it would be all the more difficult to estimate the amount, inasmuch as some paid ten and fifteen guineas for their tickets and that a box was worth twenty-five and sometimes thirty to him. Furthermore, Garrick was the barometer of the takings; when he played all the boxes, all the seats were booked and at five o'clock★ the auditorium was full and the box offices were closed.
I have only one more word to say on the subject of benefits. The authors who distinguished themselves by a continued success had a performance for their profit, apart from the fees attributed to them, and the resulting proceeds were worth infinitely more than anything we (*i.e. in France*) grant to taste and imagination."
★The curtain was usually taken up at six, but it was customary to send servants to occupy seats until their masters arrived, when the servants were given seats in the gallery where they all too frequently created a disturbance.

[22] Noverre's religion seems to have been largely a matter of convenience. He was certainly baptized in the Protestant faith and, during the first London season, he allows Garrick to advertise the fact that he and his family are Protestants. His brother, Augustin, is buried in a Protestant church in Norwich and the latter's descendants were baptized, married and buried in the Protestant faith. Jean Georges' daughter, Claudine Gervaise, was, however, baptized in a Catholic church. He himself lived for a time in the Catholic Abbaye of St. Germain des Près and was persona grata at the very Catholic court of Maria Theresa of Austria and was awarded the Papal order of the Golden Spur. Both he and his wife were buried in a Catholic church.

[23] This letter is unsigned, but in Noverre's hand on a slip of paper as though penned

in great haste. From this and from the correspondence between Patu and Garrick given hereafter, it seems clear that Noverre did not arrive in London before mid-October, 1755, and Arthur Murphy's memory must be at fault when he states (*Life of Garrick*, I. 277), "Noverre arrived in London in the month of August with a band of no less than a hundred chosen for his purpose."

[24] Postage was at the time a very expensive item as it was calculated according to the distance at so much per sheet; thus, towards the end of the century, the postage from London to Edinburgh was $1/1\frac{1}{2}$ per sheet. Envelopes had not yet been invented and the sheets were folded and sealed so that the postal contractors could easily check the number of sheets.

[25] Arthur Murphy, *Life of David Garrick* (1801).

[26] *Public Advertiser*, 8.11.1755.

[27] Late in the 17th century, the practice was started of sending over from Paris, once a month, life sized dolls dressed in the latest fashions. Even wars did not interrupt the custom and, until the advent of Napoleon, enemy generals nearly always permitted the dolls to pass that the English ladies might study the latest creations from Paris. See M. von Boehn, *Modes and Manners*, 1935, II. p. 150.

[28] *Journal Etranger*, December, 1755, II. 233. The programmes referred to were as follows:—
November 8th, *The Fair Quaker of Deal*, with Garrick, and the *Chinese Festival*.
November 12th, *The Inconstant or the Way to Win Him*, with Mrs. Clive, and the *Chinese Festival*.
November 13th, *The Provok'd Wife*, with Garrick and Colley Cibber, and the *Chinese Festival*.
November 14th, *As You Like It* and the *Chinese Festival*.
November 15th, *Much Ado about Nothing* and the *Chinese Festival*.
November 17th, *The Orphans, The Lilliputian Sailors*, with Miss Noverre, and *The Lying Valet*.
November 18th, *The Earl of Essex*, with Murphy, Mrs. Cibber and Mrs. Pritchard, and the *Chinese Festival*.
A bill of the first performance is preserved in the Victoria and Albert Museum, London, and reproduced in full in C. E. Noverre's *The Life and Works of the Chevalier Noverre*, p. 12. It will be observed that, in an effort to placate the public, Noverre and his family all have their names prefaced by Mr. or Miss instead of the usual Monsieur or Madame. The Mr. Noverre, junr., is, of course, Augustin Noverre. The first Miss Noverre is presumably his sister (or his sister-in-law, Nanette Sauveur, see note 19) and Mrs. Noverre is his wife. The second Miss Noverre, who seemingly heads a group of children, may have been his daughter, Claudine Gervaise, by then almost six years of age.

[29] Printed R. Griffiths in Paternoster Row, 8vo. 6d. See also the Monthly Review for December, 1755.

[30] The Monthly Review, January, 1756, p. 76. Pamphlet published Robinson, 8vo. 1s.

[31] Augustin Noverre was advised to take refuge in Norwich which, although a town made prosperous by the weavers and silk spinners, refugees from religious persecution in France, Austria and the Netherlands, was isolated and some distance from London. He took a house in the Chauntry where, after being attached for some time to the ballet at Drury Lane, he finally retired and taught in the adjoining Assembly Rooms. He was long known as "Dancing Froggy" and, although he endeavoured to anglicize his speech by interspersing it with "goddem, goddem, goddem", he never succeeded in acquiring a good English accent. That he earned the affection and esteem of his fellow citizens is shown by the obituary notice in *Bell's Weekly Messenger* for Sunday, September 1st, 1805:—
"On the 23rd ult., at his house in Norwich, Augustin Noverre, Esq., aged 73, brother of the celebrated Writer and Ballet Master, the Chevalier Noverre. Mr. Noverre was a native of Switzerland, and invited to this country by Garrick, whose protection and friendship he enjoyed in the highest degree to the last moment of the life of that eminent man. He was considered the most finished, elegant and

gentlemanly minuet dancer that ever appeared. He quitted the Stage nearly at the same time as his Patron, for the private exercise of his profession as a Master; and by his simple and scientific method of instruction, has done more to advance the art than any man. He was esteemed by his pupils (among whom were most of the Nobility of the Kingdom), respected by his acquaintance, and beloved by his family and friends."

His son, Francis, born in the Parish of St. Clement Dane, London, on July 19th, 1773, who married Harriet Burton (1778-1859), the daughter of John Burton (1741-1822), manager and proprietor of the Norwich Theatre Royal, carried on in his father's footsteps and, according to the Norwich Mercury, "obtained the most extensive repute as a teacher, and has been of course, the instructor of a very large portion of the existing generation. By his pupils he was universally regarded and in all the relations of life there never was a more amiable man." He was also a pioneer in British insurance and was one of the original directors of the Norwich Union Fire Insurance Society (Founded in 1797) and of the Norwich Union Life Insurance Society (Established in 1808). He died in 1840 and was buried alongside of his father in the family vault in St. Stephen's Church, Norwich.

Of his six children, Charles Cornelius Noverre carried on the profession of a teacher of dancing in the neighbourhood of London, whilst Frank Noverre (6.6.1806-1.6.1878) carried on the school in Norwich. The latter was greatly interested in music and was founder and hon. secretary of the Norwich Philharmonic Society from 1841 to the day of his death, hon. treasurer of the Norwich Choral Society, as well as taking a prominent part in the promotion and support of the Norfolk and Norwich Triennial Musical Festival, which had an unbroken existence from 1824 to the outbreak of the first world war in 1914.

His sons Frank William Bianchi (born 1843) and Richard Percival (born 1849), assisted for a time by the former's daughters Mary and Ada, continued to teach the art of dancing but found that their interest in music prevailed. Frank William Bianchi, in fact, continued his father's connection with the Norwich Triennial Musical Festivals. He also founded the Norwich Ladies' Orchestral Society.

It was not until I had been working for some time with Miss O. F. Abbott, to whom I am indebted for much of the research carried out in Paris, that I discovered the happy coincidence that she had, in her youth, been taught to dance by the Noverre Brothers and, in a letter to me, she has recorded her impressions as she looks back across the years —". . . the classes were held in a historic building, a large Tudor room, with a low ceiling and a beautiful parquet floor. All that is fifty years ago and at that time I was much more interested in the Grammar School boys who were our dancing partners than in the Noverre family. I seem to remember, however, that the Noverre Brothers" (presumably Frank and Richard) "wore tail coats and knee breeches, silk stockings and buckle shoes, and we certainly did learn to waltz and reverse beautifully. Also, we knew at the time that their ancestor had been ballet master at the French Court."

Another brother, Charles Edwin Noverre, a Justice of the Peace of the County of London, who made a brilliant career in the insurance world, becoming first Chairman of the London board of the Norwich Union Fire Insurance Society, and President of the London Insurance Institute in 1912, has left a biography of the Chevalier Noverre which is a remarkable work when it is considered that the author was not versed in dance history.

I have been privileged to make the acquaintance of several members of this remarkable family, and I found in them that mixture of old-fashioned courtesy and erudition which must have been one of the outstanding characteristics of the Chevalier Noverre, and I am deeply indebted to them for generously giving me access to records compiled by the late Charles Edwin Noverre and other members of their family, for permission to reproduce a number of family portraits and also for acquainting me with a number of facts which have been handed down by word of mouth.

The Assembly Rooms, in which Augustin Noverre probably gave his classes, and the right wing of which was inhabited by his descendants from 1812 to 1905, still stands in Theatre Square, on the site of the old Collegiate of St. Mary in the Fields which was destroyed when the monastic orders were dissolved. This beautiful red brick building, flanked on either side by wings, painted white, with its old tiled roof and its fine iron railings and gate was, as it were, rediscovered by Mr. Oliver Messel who by good fortune found himself billeted there as a member of the camouflage corps during the war. He saw through the alterations which had been made in the years since it had passed out of the hands of the Noverre family, its beautiful proportions, and it is now being restored and will serve as a municipal arts centre.

The left wing gives on to a loke, known as the Chauntry, but I have been unable to determine with any degree of certainty in which of the houses in the loke Augustin Noverre actually lived. The dancing classes were subsequently held in what are known as Noverre's Rooms which were built on to the right wing.

A plate in the chapel where the font now stands in St. Stephen's Church, is inscribed:—

"To the memory of Augustin Noverre who died 23 August 1805 aged 76 years, also of Francis Noverre, son of the above who died 5th of January 1840 aged 67 years. Both buried in the family vault under the altar in the church, also of Frank Noverre, son of the last named who died 1st June 1878 aged 71 years all of whom worshipped in this ancient chapel."

Augustin Noverre has left a book, "Twelve Cotillons, two favourite Allemandes and Six Minuets, with the Figures adapted by Augustin Noverre, Marlborough Street, London, Printed for Willm. Napier, the corner of Lancaster Court, Strand, Price 2s. 6d.", of which the only copy I have been able to trace is in the possession of Mrs. M. Farebrother, a direct descendant. The Cotillons are often given titles taken from his brother's ballets, from which they may have been taken: *La Fontaine de Jouvence, La Toilette de Venus* . . . There is also *Miss Garrick's Minuet* and a number of Minuets presumably named after Society ladies who were his patrons, *Lady Charlotte Bertie's Minuet, The Hon. Miss Thynne's Minuet* . . .

[32] T. E. Marignié, op. cit. pp. 172 *et seq.*

[33] J. G. Noverre, *Lettres sur la Danse*, V.

[34] "Magasin"—this probably refers to a shop he owned, possibly a wine shop since we know he distilled spirits, or to his ballet wardrobe, which he would not require whilst working for Garrick who provided all costumes and scenery.

[35] The account, seemingly in Garrick's hand with certain additions by Noverre, together with the other correspondence referred to, is in the Forster Collection, Vols. XXII and XXVI, in the Victoria and Albert Museum, London. The petition is signed but undated and bears no address.

[36] They are quoted in full, together with three letters from Voltaire to Noverre, in Noverre's *Lettres sur les Arts Imitateurs* and in T. E. Marignié, op. cit. p. 125 *et seq.*

[37] Letter in the Forster Coll. Victoria and Albert Museum, London, undated but presumed written *circa* end of 1764 or early 1765, when Noverre was at Stuttgart, since he refers to Garrick's decision to return to the stage.

Garrick had for some time been in indifferent health and was weary of the continual diatribes of his enemies, led by a certain Fitzpatrick, who attacked the actor in pamphlets and articles culminating, in 1763, in the "half price riots". It had long been the custom to admit the public at half price to see the pantomime at the end of the play Early in 1763, Garrick sought to abolish this privilege during the run of a new play. The new regulation was applied in January, with the staging of a version of *Two Gentlemen of Verona* with additions by Benjamin Victor. Public resentment, fanned by Fitzpatrick, grew in intensity from night to night culminating on the tenth night in riots reminiscent of those over the *Chinese Festival* and Garrick was forced to give in or see his theatre wrecked once more.

Tired and disillusioned, he retired temporarily from the stage and departed for the Continent, with Mrs. Garrick, on September 18th, 1763, leaving his theatre in the charge of his brother, George, and his partner, Lacey.

[38] Affiches, Annonces et Avis divers de Paris, 1758, November 1st, 8th and 15th. These communiqués are interspersed with statements such as "the ballet is a painting, the scene is a canvas", which Noverre uses in his *Lettres sur la Danse,* and it is possible that they were written by Noverre himself who, anxious to obtain an appointment at the Paris Opéra, was glad of an opportunity to publicize his name in the press of the capital.

[39] J. G. Noverre, *Lettres sur la Danse et sur les Ballets*, XIV.

[40] J. G. Noverre, *Lettres sur la Danse et sur les Ballets*, VI.

[41] There were many members of the Hus family connected with the French stage and it is uncertain which of them was at Lyons at this time. For a complete analysis of the known data see M. Fuchs, *Lexique des Troupes de Comédiens au 18 ème. Siècle*, p. 117, *et seq.*

[42] Favart, *Mémoires et Correspondance*, Ed. Collin, 1808, p. 10.

[43] The date of publication is given as 1760, but it was reviewed in the *Affiches de Lyon* for December 29th, 1759, which suggests that it was in fact published in 1759.

[44] J. G. Noverre, *Lettres sur la Danse et sur les Ballets*, V.—Claude Bourgelat (1712–1779).

[45] With the dismissal of his prime minister, Hardenberg, in 1755, and the divorce the following year of his wife, Elizabeth Frederick Sophia of Brandenburg Bayreuth, the last restraining influences in his entourage disappeared and he was free to lavish the contents of the ducal exchequer on the satisfaction of his pleasures.

[46] Noverre was engaged as Ballet-master and his wife as *comédienne* on the first of March, 1760, for a period of six years, at a joint salary of 5,000 florins plus 200 florins each for travelling expenses. On the 6th of July following he was given a fresh contract for fifteen years with a tax-free salary of 3,500 florins for himself, free lodging and forage for two horses, plus 130 florins shoe money and, for his wife 2,500 florins free of tax. At the same time his sister-in-law, Nanette Sauveur, was given a fifteen–year contract to Easter, 1775, with a salary of 1,500 florins tax free plus 130 florins for shoes.

On April 25th, 1761, his contract was revised again to give him 4,000 florins salary plus ten buckets of wine, 20 measures of wood and 100 florins for the ballet-copyist, out of which Noverre had to supply the latter with writing materials, wood, light, etc. On May 5th he was further allocated, as from St. George's day, 400 florins to pay for his quarters in Ludwigsburg in lieu of the free lodging previously promised him.

In addition he drew special allocations from time to time and we find in the Ducal Household accounts on August 31st, 1762, a payment of 600 florins to cover a journey to Paris, probably to recruit new dancers, and on December 15th, 1764, his salary is again increased from Martinmas to 8,800 florins. In November, 1765, there is a payment of 225 Gulden for finding a new *danseuse*. In January, 1767, 625 florins is deducted from his salary to pay his rent outstanding in Ludwigsburg.

Notes from the *Wurtemburg Landschreiberrechnungen und Rentkammerprotokollen*, K.44.F.18 and *Oberhofmarschallamt* 43.18.590, quoted Niedecken, op. cit., appendix 3, and J. Sittard, *Zur Geschichte der Musik und des Theaters Wurtemburgischen Hofe*, p. 59 and appendices 6 and 11. These two writers also reproduce the following entries from the Ducal private and state archives:—

April 25, 1761:—Dancer Vestris, jr., from Paris for six years to Easter 1767 as first *danseur sérieux*. Yearly salary 2,200 florins plus 130 florins shoe money, tax free, plus 25 carolins for his journey there and 25 for the return.

May 5, 1761:—Pietro, father and son, supernumeraries for a further six years. For the two, 2,400 florins tax free to include shoe money.

May 5, 1761:—The supernumerary Le Picq to be re-engaged to Easter 1767. Yearly salary 600 florins and 100 florins shoe money tax free. It being made clear that it is intended that Le Picq shall be trained by M. Noverre in the serious dance and perfected in that art, for which purpose the Ballet-master has been promised 15,000 florins to be paid as soon as possible.

July 27, 1761:—The *danseuse* Nency Lévier to be re-engaged from Easter for so long as she wishes to remain in the Service at a new yearly wage of 2,200 florins tax free instead of 1,000 florins hitherto but to include the shoe money she has always drawn.

October 14, 1761:—Dancer Baletti, under a new agreement for 6 years to St. George's day, 1767, at 2,000 florins yearly and 130 florins shoe money and 200 florins for his return journey. In addition a bonus of 500 florins in part payment of his debts.

May 5, 1762:—The Dancer du Poncel for 3 years from Candlemass of this year at 800 florins plus 120 florins for shoes.

the *danseuse* Lotti, 300 florins.

the *danseuse* Armery for a further year on the same terms as before.

September 3, 1762:—The *danseuse* Antonia Guidi for one year to June 1763 at 1,000 florins to cover everything and 200 florins journey money.

November 1, 1762:—The dancer Jean Dauberval, as *premier danseur*, at 2,500 florins yearly and 130 florins shoe money to Easter 1764 and 25 golden louis for his journey there and the same for his return.

November 1765:—Madame Lolli shall from Candlemass get a yearly increase of 500 gulden. To the dancer Simonet a bonus of 400 gulden.

N.B. Of Baletti we know next to nothing, although he must have been a dancer of merit to command in Stuttgart a yearly salary of 2,000 florins. Possibly he is N. Baletti, a son of Joseph Baletti known as Mario, who made his début at the Théâtre des Italiens in Paris on February 1st, 1742, as *premier amoureux* but of whom Parfaict (Dictionnaire des Théâtres) remarks that he dances with considerable lightness. He may also be connected with the Balletty or Baletti who appeared in Strasbourg in 1752-3. There was also in Strasbourg at this time a Delaistre with his wife, also a dancer. It is possible that they were both, with Nanette Sauveur, engaged at Stuttgart through the good offices of Madame Noverre-Sauveur. The Pietros, who appeared in the *corps de ballet* in Stuttgart, may have some connection with the Pietro who appeared at Lyons in 1761-2.

[47] Joseph Uriot, *Lettres Wurtembourgeoises ou La Vérité sans fard opposée à la pire vérité telle qu'elle est*, Freiburg, 1766. Letter VI, Stuttgart, July 12th, 1766.

[48] *Description des Fêtes données pendant quatorze jours à l'occasion du jour de naissance de son Altesse Sérénissime Mgr. le Duc Régnant de Wurtemberge et Tech . . . le 11 février 1763*, J. Uriot.

[49] First given in Rome in 1747. Revived in a new version, Stuttgart, 1751.

[50] First given Padua, 1743—libretto Metastasio, German translation Cajet Neusinger.

[51] The Biographie Nouvelle des Contemporains also lists the following ballets as given at Stuttgart:—*Les Amours d'Henry IV, Antoine et Cléopâtre* and *Venus et Adonis*, C. E. Noverre (op. cit.) adds *Le Jugement de Paris* to the list.

[52] Grimm, Diderot, Raynal et al., *Correspondance littéraire, philosophique et critique*, Ed. 1813, V. p. 50 et seq.

[53] Report of the Ministry to the Duke Karl Eugene of Wurtemberg concerning the claims put forward by Jean Georges Noverre after the termination of his contract. From the Privy Council records, Ludwigsburg, p. 41. No. 14:—

*Secondly*

The ballet director Noverre in the account he gives of the assurances given him by your Serene Highness and in the references he makes to documents which are in the country but which to date he has been unable to produce, thinks he is entitled to a further 15,410 florins approximately made up as follows.

(1) 2,175 fl. over and above his salary for the quarter from Candlemass to St. George's day, 1767. Unless your Highness made any special promise to Noverre, he has already been paid by us according to the terms of the instructions we received. Noverre's salary was agreed with the deputation of the Theatre personnel and with your Highness and since he had already received an extraordinary payment, he had no claim to any further salary for the period after Candlemass unless your Highness should change his views on the subject.

(2) 240 fl. to cover various disbursements which Noverre made on the occasion of the ballets presented on the arrival of Prince Frederick. He can however prove nothing and says that he gave the receipts of the Wardrobe inspector Bourgoin and Jud Seeligmann to your Serene Highness personally.

(3) 55 fl. for 9 golden louis to the elder Vestris on the orders of your Serene Highness but which he cannot substantiate.

(4) 1,100 fl. or 100 golden louis according to a letter which your Serene Highness wrote to Noverre and which is in the hands of the Duke; but on requesting this from him, he apologizes and states that this document is still in the hands of the Minister, Thonn, in Paris, and that he should have been paid by the Minister on the occasion of a journey which he made to Paris and since this was not done, this amount is still outstanding.

(5) 275 fl. travelling expenses. He claims that he spent this sum in the course of a journey to Metz and Lothringen made on the orders of your Serene Highness on the occasion of the death of King Stanislas, but he cannot produce any vouchers.

(6) Noverre claims, without being able to substantiate this, that he gave a bonus of 100 fl. to the dancer Favier out of his own pocket-case and on the instructions of your Serene Highness.

(7) The sum of 121 fl. 39 cr., missing in the theatre account and

(8) 1,500 fl. which he asks for teaching the dancer Simonet and

(9) 3,850 fl. for teaching dancing to Mlle. Toscani during seven years at 50 golden louis per annum and

(10) 1,650 fl. calculated for three years for Mlle. Salomoni and also

(11) 1,650 fl. for Mlle. Nenci, which together with the four items above make a total of 8,650 fl. for which Noverre can produce no vouchers. There is no order in existence by which it could be established that your Serene Highness had given his consent to some consideration being given for the teaching of the dancer Simonet and of the Dlles. Toscani, Salomoni and Nency, and it is hardly to be supposed that this should have been the case, for Noverre might have had the intention to ask from time to time for increases in his already very large salary.

(12) Noverre asks for 40 crates of wine which he had sent from Lyons on the instructions of your Serene Highness but which he could not keep for himself. He refers to several persons who should be able to confirm that these liqueurs arrived addressed to your Serene Highness and that a part thereof was placed in the Ducal cellars and taken out again after six months to be returned to Noverre who, with a loss to himself of 4,300 florins, placed them with Roussonel in Warsaw. These transactions cannot, however, be confirmed and it is the same with

(13) a present which Noverre says was promised to him and which he has fixed at 825 fl. On the other hand in the settlement of December 15, 1764, which has been paid, is included 400 fl. for copying (*i.e. presumably music*) which Noverre has, however, never attended to and copies were made by the oboists of the guard and separately paid for. We leave it to your judgement as to whether a refund should be sought from Noverre or whether this should be left as it is.

Concerning all these points the undersigned await the Ducal decisions. Noverre has been paid according to the directives of the Minister Count von Montmartin and everything is settled except for the above matters on which the decision of your Serene Highness is awaited. Stuttgart, Privy Council of February 17th, 1767.

Signed Count of Montmartin, von Noeulten, E. von Kniessedt, L. von Volgstädt,

Renel, illegible, Boettger.

[54] C. F. Pohl, *Joseph Haydn*, II, 130.

R. M. Haas, *Die Wiener Ballet Pantomime im 18. Jahrhundert*, p. 27, gives the date as January 11th, 1767. Vestris came to Vienna on the sudden termination of his contract at Stuttgart. The entire Court attended and he was given the full takings of the evening.

[55] J. G. Noverre, *Lettres sur les Arts Imitateurs*, I. 359

[56] Wurtemberg House and State Archives, Oberhoffmarschallamt B.582—quoted Niedecken, op. cit., Appendix 5.

[57] The ballets were finally arranged by Noverre's successor at Stuttgart, Dauvigny

[58] Prince Khevenhueller-Metsch, High Steward of the Court of Maria Theresa, *Aus der Zeit Maria Theresas*, p. 264, 10.9.1767, refers to Noverre as Sieur Noverre de Hougard. He seems alone amongst contemporary writers to give the Ballet-master this title which may refer to Hougaerd, a town in what is now the province of Brabant, Belgium, but was at the time part of the Austrian Netherlands and of the old Kingdom of Lotharingia.

[59] Quoted Carlyle, *History of Frederick the Great*, VI, p. 260, from the pen of the Prince de Ligne, *Lettres et Pensées du Maréchal Prince de Ligne* by Baronne de Staël-Holstein, Paris, 1809.

[60] Although no copy of the score of the ballet has been discovered, it seems from sketches preserved in the Mozarteum, Salzburg, that Mozart must have composed the music for this revival.

[61] Margarethe Delphine is first mentioned as a pupil of Noverre in 1768. In 1770, Zinzendorf notes (*Tagebuch*, December 4), her performance in *Alceste*:—"I admired the dance of the Delfine. What strength, what precision, how she surpassed all the others". On her appearance in *Paride e Elena*, he notes (Tagebuch, December 15, 1770):—"What a gulf separates the dancing of the Vigano from that of the Delphine". The *Chronik*, the Vienna *Theaterkalendar* for 1772 and 1773 and J. Oehler's *Geschichte des gesammten Theaterwesens* in 1803, bear testimony to her great talent.

[62] Calzabigi and Angiolini were close friends and it is possible that the latter's later letters to Noverre may also be from the pen of the librettist. Noverre seems to hint at this in his programme notes to *Les Horaces et les Curiaces* and Ranieri Calzabigi, himself, in his *Lettera al S. Conte Alfieri*, p. 34, states:—"In 1762 when the Ballet Pantomimes of Médée, La Mort d'Hercule and others which caused surprise and admiration, had already been performed by Noverre at Stuttgart, there was given in Vienna the Convitato da Piedra, of the composition of Angiolini. The immortal Gluck wrote the music and I the French programme, in which I gave brief preliminary information on the art of pantomime in the olden days". See also Ghino Lazzeri, *La Vita e l'opera letteraria di Ranieri Calzabigi*, 1907, p. 213.

[63] Quoted R. Haas, op. cit., p. 29. The French ". . . et à tirer parti des plus mauvais sujets" could mean either "to make the most of the poorest themes" or "to get the best out of the poorest dancers". The two very bad ballets were probably *L'Orphelin de la Chine*, to Angiolini's own music, given on 1.4.1774 and found to be a "pantomime of deadly coldness, without any dancing", and a ballet added to Gluck's *Il convito d'Alessandro*.

[64] Recueil des Programmes de Ballets, à Vienne chez Joseph Kurzböck, 1776.

[65] Probably a reference to Calzabigi, see note 62.

[66] We have no indication as to the precise date on which Noverre was made a member of the Académie de Danse but, in the preface to *Renaud et Armide*, printed in Milan in 1775, he describes himself as a "Membre de l'Académie de Danse de Paris". The Académie, founded by Louis XIV in 1661, was made up in 1777 of Malter, doyen and chairman, Laval, director, Javillier, D. Dupré, Lany, Vestris, Lyonnois, Gardel, Dauberval, Malter (the younger) and Noverre.

[67] The French style of dancing and the ballets of Noverre caused a sensation in Naples. The Abbé Galliani, *Lettres à Madame d'Epinay*, coll. *Lettres du 17e et 18e Siècle*, Charpentier, Paris, 1881, II. 73, reported on July 24th, 1773:—". . . we have at present with us the celebrated dancer le Picq, who is giving the ballet Armide with its choruses and all that which could be given at the Opéra of your Palais Royal. One must admit that he is as good a dancer as Vestris and Dauberval. However he has found it harder to gallicize the Neapolitans than did Aufresne.* He thought at first that he would be booed for the Neapolitans, in a theatre as enormous and gigantic as ours, could not see that he was dancing since he did not jump. But, as he is very well built, he began by taming the Neapolitans and little by little the nation was converted."
The Neapolitans were used to a style of dancing in which the executants put into their sailors' dances, Chinese dances, etc., all the strength of movement of which they were capable and continued until they dropped exhausted, so that by contrast the French *terre à terre* style must at first have seemed so tame as to be uninteresting.

* Aufresne, actor born in Geneva, first ap. Comédie Française 30.5.1765, died *circa* 1806, appeared in Naples with a troupe of actors just before Le Picq was seen there.
See also *Archivio Storico per le Province Napoli*, An. XVI, p. 293, "I Teatri di Napoli", and Benedetto Croce, *I Teatro di Napoli*, VII, 219.

[68] Garrick Correspondence, Forster Coll., Vic. & A. Mus., London, Vol. XXI Add.

[69] Garrick Correspondence, Forster Coll., Vol. XXI Add.—This letter, although unsigned, is in the same hand as that of the same date to Garrick and contains a number

of opinions on various dancers which are of interest. Mr. Slingsby he considers most excellent but Le Fontaine is not worth much. Cortez is a beautiful woman, but she is being spoilt by the cavaliers of Turin. Ricci is beautiful, has little expression but a lot of execution, whilst her brother is worth no more than to be third dancer but she wants five thousand florins and a benefit, and her brother 150 guineas. Prince Esterhazy and his lords have spoilt her by giving her a lot of money. Of the two Dupetit, who are with him, one is feeble and the other strong and with a pretty face. He also has Terrades, her little sister and a certain Guiardet, who is young, tall and has talent.

The following list of dancers is balanced along the same lines as for the current Carnival except for Setrizza and the Forselly, with Franchy in the place of Corticcelli who is no good:—

| | | They demand in English money:— | |
|---|---|---|---|
| Mlle. Villeneuve earns 600 | | | |
| Mlle. Ricci | 700 | Villeneuve | 350 guineas |
| Her brother | 200 | Ricci | 400 |
| Guiardet | 500 | Franchy | 400 |
| Franchy received | 650 | Guiardet | 300 |
| Camille Dupetit | 400 | Mr. Ricci | 100 |
| Mariane Dupetit | 200 | Camille Dupetit | 250 |
| Terrades | 400 | Mariane Dupetit | 100 |
| Her sister | 150 | Terrades | 200 |
| Zechingilliaty, worth 11 French louis | | Her sister | 100 |

The Biographie Nouvelle des Contemporains, 1824, states that Noverre did in fact have a London season before he joined the Paris Opéra, but a study of the English press does not substantiate this. Furthermore, it is obvious from the short time between the date on which he left Vienna and that on which he was engaged in Paris that he cannot possibly have played in London in the interval.

[70] Bachaumont, *Mémoires Secrets*, IX, 261, 14.8.1776.

[71] Unsigned and undated note in the handwriting of Jean Papillon, dit la Ferté, Arch. Nat., Paris, No. 616.

[72] La Harpe, *Correspondance avec le Grand Duc depuis Empereur de Russie*, Vol. II. 9, Let. LV.—De Méricourt, *Le Nouveau Spectateur*, August 1, 1777, p. 30, footnote to art. "Des Pantomimes".

[73] op. cit. IX.

[74] Maximilien Gardel (the elder), 1741-1787, and Pierre Gardel (the younger), 1758-1840, who succeeded his brother as *Maître des Ballets* at the Opéra in 1787 and married the dancer Marie E. A. Boubert, known as Miller—1770-1833.
Letter quoted Grimm, op. cit., Vol. III, part ii, p. 227, Aug. 1776.—See also Bachaumont, op. cit., IX, 112.

[75] Grimm, op. cit., Vol. III, part ii, p. 274, 1.10.1776. See also La Harpe, op. cit. I. XXXIX, 311 and Bachaumont, op. cit. IX, 258.

[76] La Harpe, op. cit. II, 17, LVI.

[77] *The Diary of Madame Campan*, Jeanne Louise Henriette Campan, 1752-1822, first lady in waiting to the Queen, daughter-in-law to the officer of the chamber of Marie Leczinska and later secretary to Marie Antoinette. See also de Méricourt. *Le Nouveau Spectateur*, 2.7.1776, and Bachaumont, *Memoires Secrets*, IX, 261.

[78] Grimm, op. cit., November, 1776. Le Picq was making his first appearance at the Opéra.

[79] De Bachaumont, op. cit., X. 20–26. See also *Journal des Théâtres ou le Nouveau Spectateur*, I. 216 et seq., and *Journal de Paris*, II. 2, p. 1167, Jan. 22nd, 1777.

[80] *Journal de Paris*, II. 2, p. 1167, Jan. 30, 1778.—*Roland*, opera by Piccini to a libretto by Quinault revised by Marmontel, first performed 27.1.1778.

[81] Leopold Mozart, writing to his son from Salzburg on 16.3.1778 (*Letters of Mozart and his Family*, translated Emily Anderson, II. 760), noted "M. de Voltaire is in Paris

but whether M. Noverre (who as I see in the newspapers, has also received the Order from the Pope) is there, I do not know for certain".

It has been stated that Noverre was given the Portuguese Order of Christ, but a search of the records of the holders of this Order in Lisbon does not reveal his name, neither is there any mention in the Portuguese Court records of his ever having visited that city, as has sometimes been suggested. Noverre is, on the other hand, recorded on the rôle of holders of the Papal *Ordine Equestro di Cristo* (*Ordine dello Sperone d'Oro*) in 1778.

[82] *Letters of Mozart and his Family*, translated Emily Anderson, II. 766, April 5, 1778; II. 769, April 5, 1778; II. 782, April 20, 1778; II. 791, May 6–11, 1778; II. 796, May 14, 1778, and II. 822, June 29, 1778. The score of *Les Petits Riens* was discovered in the archives of the Paris Opéra by Victor Wilder in 1872.—De Vismes had been reappointed to the Opéra on Feb. 27th, 1778.

[83] *Journal de Paris*, II. 1. 437, Dec. 26, 1778.

[84] Cécile Dumesnil, known as Cécile, a pupil of Maximilien Gardel, entered the Opéra 1776, died in child-birth in 1781.

[85] See memorandum from J. G. Noverre to Papillon de la Ferté dated 1780 (Arch. Nat. Paris, 622). According to a MS. Family tree in the possession of the Noverre family, Noverre's daughter, N. Noverre, married a Colonel Gelami. Was this in fact Claudine Gervaise or was there a second daughter? I have been unable to trace any entry in the Paris records which would throw light on the marriage but many of these records were, of course, destroyed during the Revolution.

[86] The payrolls are preserved in the Arch. Nat., Paris, file AJ.XII.23.

According to the *Calendrier Historique des Théâtres ou Almanach Historique et Chronologique de tous les Spectacles de Paris*, the ballet personnel at the Opéra in 1776 consisted of:—

> *Maître des Ballets*—Vestris
> Assistants—Gardel, Dauberval
> *Danseurs Seuls*—Vestris, Gardel, Dauberval
> *Danseurs en Double*—Despréaux, Leger, Walter, Abraham
> *Danseurs figurants*—27, including Laval and Simonet
> Supernumeraries—8 men and 33 women
> *Danseuses Seules*—Peslin, Guimard, Heinel, Nidoux, Dorival
> *Danseuses en double*—4
> *Figurantes*——22

A total of 106 in all. In 1777, Noverre replaces Vestris as *Maître des Ballets* and the total number drops to 102. It is 110 in 1778, 79 in 1779, 92 in 1780 and 93 in 1781. The total wage bill was 56,100 livres for the year 1775–6, 66,400 for 1776–7, 72,600 for 1777–8 and 128,380 for 1778–9, out of which Noverre received each year 3,000 livres salary and 9,000 livres bonus. With the reduction in the number of dancers, it falls in the following years to 99,400 in 1781–2. In 1778 the elder Vestris was in receipt of 2,000 livres pension, 3,000 salary and 4,566 "feux", a total income of livres 9,566.

[87] Arch. Nat. O. I. 622.

[88] Métra, *Correspondance Secrète*, III. 27.

[89] Bachaumont, op. cit. XVIII, 94—Oct. 22, 1781.

[90] Mlle. Crépé, known as Théodore (?-1798), a pupil of Lany, entered the Opéra as a supernumerary in 1775–6. Her style of dancing was not unlike that of Mlle. Allard and she was noted for her *ballon*. She has been described as a "free thinker in short skirts" and a "philosopher in pink satin slippers" because she was said to be more interested in the writings of J. J. Rousseau than in dancing.

[91] Jean Bercher, known as Dauberval (1742-1806), married Mlle. Théodore in September, 1783. They both applied for reinstatement at the Opéra, she as *premier sujet*, he as joint *Maître de Ballet*. Their application was refused for fear of the trouble

187

their return might cause. He then accepted the post of ballet-master at Bordeaux where he created (and she danced in) his principal compositions including *La Fille Mal Gardée*, *le Deserteur* and *L'Epreuve Villageoise*.

[92] The Novestris may be a reference to Novosielski, the designer of the costumes and décor for Vestris' revival of *Jason et Médée* and not a pun on the names of Noverre and Vestris.

[93] *Public Advertiser*, 19.11.1781.

[94] François Hippolyte Barthélémon (1741-1808), has left a number of compositions for the violin of some merit, in addition to ballet music and at least one opera, *Le Jugement de Paris*, given in 1768. Lebrun, probably Louis Sebastien Lebrun or Le Brun (1764-1829) who composed a number of operas including *Marcelin* (1800) and *Le Rossignol* (1816).

[95] *Public Advertiser*, 25 and 27.2.1782.—See also Bachaumont op. cit. 18.3.1782.

[96] *Public Advertiser*, 12.4.1782.

[97] *Public Advertiser*, April 17 and June 10, 1782.

[98] *Public Advertiser*, 8.5.1782.

[99] *Public Advertiser*, June 6 and 10, 1782. *The Recorder*, June 7, 1782.

[100] Bachaumont, op. cit. 4.6.1780.

[101] Bachaumont, op. cit. XXXVI, 247—3.12.1787.

[102] *Public Advertiser*, 29.3. and 8.4.1788.

[103] *Public Advertiser*, 18.6.1789.

[104] *Public Advertiser*, 29.1.1793. Mlle. Miller, who in England changed her name to Millard, first appeared at the Opéra in 1786. She later married P. Gardel.

[105] *London Chronicle*, March 3–5, 1791, and *Public Advertiser* 28.4.1791 and 26.1.1793

[106] *Morning Post*, 11.1.1794.

[107] *Public Advertiser*, 27.2.1793.

[108] *Morning Chronicle* 24.4.1793—see also 29.4. and 14.5.

[109] Vol. II, p. 38–40. "Taisez-vous, bête"—shut up, fool!

[110] Arch. Nat. A. J. XIII, 46, 48, 49, 84.

[111] The inscription in the Castle Museum, Norwich, reads: "Silk dress worn by Queen Marie Antoinette of France, presented by Francis Gray Noverre Esq. This dress, in the dancer's family continuously since the execution of the Queen by guillotine on October 16th, 1793, was given to the Chevalier Jean Georges Noverre. Maître des Ballets en Chef,* Académie Impériale de Musique, Paris, as a souvenir of his royal pupil."

The dress, of heavy silk with narrow blue stripes on white streaked with silver, is high waisted with a shaped yoke, fuller at the back than in front, with long tight fitting sleeves and a narrow belt of the same material. The separate bodice, worn over the dress, is laced, with puffed sleeves to the elbow. Pieces have been cut from it, it is said by the Chevalier Noverre, to give away as tokens of remembrance.

* This is not, strictly speaking, accurate as Noverre was never *Maître des Ballets* at the Opéra under the Empire, he was *Maître des Ballets at the Académie Royale de Musique*.

[112] On the authority of Louis Racine and of Boileau, it is known that Louis XIV ceased to dance in the court ballets following on the production of Racine's *Britannicus* in a scene of which (Act IV, Sc. 4), Narcissus repeats to Nero the gossip to the effect that it is unseemly that he should seek to shine by talents unworthy of an emperor.

It has been assumed from this by ballet historians that the King made his last appearance in a ballet in *Flore* on February 13th, 1669. The first performance of *Britannicus* was not, however, until December 13th of that year. Furthermore the printed libretto of *Le Ballet des Ballets,* otherwise known as *Les Amants Magnifiques* or *Le Divertissement Royal,* printed by Ballard shows:—

"First *intermède,* second *entrée,* Neptune—The King" and there are verses to be recited by him in this rôle at the opening of Sc. 3, Act 1.

"Sixth *intermède,* fifth *entrée,* Apollo—The King", with appropriate verses for him to declaim.

The *Gazette* of February 7th, 1670, describes a "dance followed by that of the god, Neptune, interpreted by the King with that grace and majesty which shines forth from all his actions" and, further on, to Apollo again interpreted by the King.

This same *Gazette* for February 14th, however, reports that the Marquis de Villeroi interpreted Neptune and Apollo instead of the King, who did not dance.

A letter from one, Robinet, on the 15th notes, in a short poem, that the King did not dance and that he was in error in his letter of the 8th in indicating, seemingly on the strength of the libretto, that the King did appear. The libretto presumably would have been printed some time before the first performance. On the other hand, the edition of 1682, and the English translation of 1771, still show these rôles of Neptune and Apollo as being for the King.

Georges Monval, *Les Amants Magnifiques,* 1894, has put forward the thesis that Louis XIV may have danced in the first performance of Molière's ballet on February 4th, 1670, but that, having seen Racine's *Britannicus* in the interim, he decided not to dance any more and did not take part in the second performance some ten days later.

[113] de Pure, *Idée des Spectacles Anciens et Nouveaux,* 1668, Chapter XI and p. 235 *et seq.*

[114] There were of course exceptions such as *Bellerophon* in 1679 for which the libretto was written by T. Corneille, Fontenelle and Boileau.

[115] It has been generally assumed that the first professional *danseuse* was introduced in Lully's *Le Triomphe de l'Amour* in 1681, but this is specifically denied, in his *Lettres sur les Arts Imitateurs,* I. p. 68, by Noverre who may well have met eye-witnesses of the production:—

"On January 21st, 1681, there was given at St. Germain en Laye, in the theatre of the Château, le Triomphe de l'Amour, opera by Quinault to the music of Lully. It was in this magnificent spectacle that the *beau sexe* were seen for the first time in ballet. M. le Dauphin and Mme. la Dauphine, the princes and princesses of the blood, the dukes and duchesses, in a word all the great at Court, took part. To the nobility had been added the dancers and pensioners of His Majesty and all those of the Académie Royale de Musique. This prodigious assembly created the finest effects; the richness and elegance of the costumes, the sparkling diamonds and precious stones, gave in detail and as a whole the most brilliant spectacle in the world. Louis XIV did not dance in it . . .

Le Triomphe de l'Amour was as much talked of in Paris as it had been at court. The public wanted to see the opera. Lully and his partners gave them their wish and staged a first performance on May 16th the same year, that is to say about four months after the performance at the Château of St. Germain. A contemporary author has stated that in imitation of the Court, *premières danseuses* and *figurantes* were seen here for the first time in the ballets at the Opéra. This author did not see correctly. The women he thought he saw were but young *danseurs* dressed as women, for the dance was then cultivated at court and the King, having declared himself in favour of this art, which he practised with success, it was politic for persons of his court to imitate him in his tastes.

A simple factor, and which destroys the illusion of this author, is that it takes two or three years of study to form a good *figurante* and six or seven years of training to make a *première danseuse,* and that only provided she is born with some aptitude. The dance has never accomplished such prodigies and that of those days was much less learned and miraculous than that of today."

[116] Chevrier, F. A. de, *Les Ridicules du Siècle,* 1774, VI. 38.

[117] Angelo, *Reminiscences,* 1830, II. 319.

[118] The Académie de Musique et de Danse, formed in 1570 by Jean Antoine de Baïf, one of the poets of the Pleiade, and the musician Joachim Thibault de Courville, was designed to foster the fusion of poetry, music and movement after the fashion of the

189

13*

ancients and did in fact create spectacles danced to the rhythm of antique metres. Balthazar de Beaujoyeulx, in the printed account of his *Ballet Comique de la Reine*, given in 1581, described it as "a thing which had not been seen since antiquity" and explained how he had attempted to blend music, drama and dancing.

Molière, in the preface to *Les Fâcheux* in 1661, explained that "so as not to break the theme of the comedy" by the *intermèdes* inserted in the intervals it had been decided to "stitch" them to the subject and "to make one thing of the comedy and the ballet" and he went on to point out that this was "a mixture new to our theatres and for which a precedent might be sought in antiquity".

[119] J. Uriot, op. cit. VI.

[120] Balon, French dancer renowned for his lightness, entered the Opéra in 1691.

[121] *Lettres sur la Danse*, I et seq.—See also Footnote 139.

[122] *Lettres sur les Arts Imitateurs*, Vol. I. V. 71.

[123] *Lettres sur la Danse*, X. 261 et seq.

[124] *Lettres sur la Danse*, X. 269 et seq., *Lettres sur les Arts Imitateurs*, Vol. I. IX. 129.— The Abbé de l'Epée (1712-1789) invented a form of mime for the deaf and dumb which is thought by many historians to have formed the basis of the traditional mime used to this day in such ballets as *Le Lac des Cygnes*.

[125] Preface to *Agamemnon Vengé*, Vienna, 1772.

[126] *Lettres sur les Arts Imitateurs*, Vol I., Preface.

[127] *Lettres sur la Danse*, VI. 78 et seq.

[128] *Lettres sur la Danse*, VI, 90. The term "Sérieux" as applied to dancing and "la belle Danse" have been translated as "classical" which to the writer seems to give a truer equivalent of the meaning accepted in the 18th century than would a literal translation.

[129] Vol. II, VI. and *Lettres sur la Danse*, Ed. 1783, I. 2.

[130] *Agamemnon Vengé*, preface. These limits which a wise choreographer will not exceed, cause Noverre to write, in the *Lettres sur les Arts Imitateurs*, I. IX. 125, that after fifty years of research and work he found he had made but a few steps forward and had stopped where a seemingly impassable obstacle had appeared on his path. The *Maîtres de Ballet* who had adopted his *genre*, he further noted, had not been able to cross the barrier which brought him to a standstill.

[131] *Lettres sur la Danse*, VIII.

[132] *Lettres sur la Danse*, III. 30 et seq.

[133] *Lettres sur la Danse*, IV. 58 et seq.

[134] *Lettres sur les Arts Imitateurs*, Vol. I. XXIV and pp. 349, 350, 553.

[135] *Lettres sur les Arts Imitateurs*, Vol. I. XXV, p. 358.

[136] *Lettres sur la Danse*, V. 73 et seq. and VIII.

[137] *Lettres sur la Danse*, XII. 358 and VIII.

[138] *Lettres sur la Danse*, VII. 123.

[139] *Lettres sur la Danse*, VII.

The analogy which Noverre draws between the composition of a ballet and that of a painting is more than a mere figure of speech for, in the *Lettres sur les Arts Imitateurs*, I. IX. 125, he states that he has taken advantage of his visits to Italy, Germany and England to visit the finest galleries and has made a point of meeting the most famous artists and "it is to painting that I owe a part of my success".

[140] *Lettres sur la Danse*, IX. *Lettres sur les Arts Imitateurs*, Vol. I. IX. 124.

[141] *Lettres sur la Danse*, VIII.

[142] *Lettres sur les Arts Imitateurs*, Vol. II. p. 150.

[143] *Lettres sur la Danse*, XI and XII.

[144] *Lettres sur les Arts Imitateurs*, Vol. I. IX. 128.

[145] *Lettres sur la Danse*, IX. 239.

[146] Grimm, op. cit. II. 400, Jan. 1771.

[147] *Lettres sur la Danse*, XIII.—Françoise Prévost (1680-1741), held the stage of the Opéra for thirty years and excelled in passepieds. There were three Dumoulin at the Opéra, François (the elder), who entered in 1700, Pierre le second and David (the youngest), both of whom entered in 1705.

[148] *Lettres sur les Arts Imitateurs*, Preface.

[149] "Eclaircissements donnés à l'auteur du Journal encyclopédique sur la musique du Devin du Village."

[150] "Six Sonates pour un Violoncelle avec la basse continue dédiées à Monsieur Flachat de St. Bonnet, prévôt des marchands de la Ville de Lyon, par M. François Granier ordinaire de l'Académie des Beaux Arts. . . ."

[151] Letter XIV.

[152] Letter XV.

[153] *Le Dessinateur pour les fabriques d'étoffes, d'or, d'argent et de soie*, Joubert de l'Hiberderie, Preface dated 20.11.1764, published 1764, XV. 112.

[154] I have reconstituted the action from the various published scenarios of the ballet written by Noverre himself, quoted in inverted commas where I have been able to use his own text, amplified by contemporary criticisms. The musical notes are the result of a careful study of the scores in Paris and Vienna. The fitting of the music to the action is, of course, a matter of opinion but the programmatic nature of the score and references in contemporary criticisms makes the relationship of the passages noted to the scenario reasonably clear.

[155] For a detailed analysis of his ballet compositions see Lisbeth Braun, *Die Balletkompositionen von Joseph Starzer*, who found that his compositions prior to *Don Quixote* (1768), the first work he arranged for Noverre, are but a suite of character dances, whereas from the time of his collaboration with Noverre, they develop into a closely constructed dramatic whole.

[156] Dress worn by Mlle. Guimard as a "shepherdess" in the third act of *Jason et Médée*, in January; 1771. The dress, elegantly caught up to show a petticoat of a different colour, was in fact first introduced by actresses of the Comédie Italienne before Guimard adopted the style with the addition of garlands and pompons. However, as the "dress à la Guimard, it became the rage of Paris and replaced the traditional domino at the ensuing carnival.

[157] This would seem to be one of the earliest examples of the use of the word *choreography* to designate the composition of ballets as opposed to the more usual 18th century meaning of the recording of dances by dance notation.

[158] Noverre had kept through the years a contact with the theatre at Lyons where his name was still a certain draw. In 1777, his *Apelles et Campaspe* was staged there following the productions the previous year at Paris and Fontainebleau.* In 1781 there was given his *Les Amours d'Enée et de Didon*,† which met with little success. Whether he personally went down to Lyons to stage these two works we do not know but, in March 1787, he personally produced at Lyons *Adèle de Ponthieu*,†‡ *Apelles et Campaspe* and *La Foire du Caire* and the three works were given together at a performance for his benefit on the 28th of March.

*Libretto published in Lyons with a dedication to the Marquise d'Aurbert (Bib. de la Ville de Lyon, 351911).

† Scenario Bib. de la Ville de Lyon, 359444, 358711 and 313293. See also *Petite Chronique Lyonnaise*, Morel et Voleine.

‡ Libretto with a preface by Noverre dedicating the work to the ladies of Lyons. Bib. de la ville de Lyon 351966.

[159] "Extrait du registre des délibérations du Comité de Législation, Section des Emigrés, de la Convention Nationale, du 24 pluviose, an 3", in the possession of Mrs. J. Arnold, a direct descendant of J. G. Noverre.

[160] "Projet d'une Fête, par Mr. Noverre."

# BIBLIOGRAPHY

Abert, H.: Nicollo Jomelli als Opernkomponist    1906
    Gesammelte Schriften und Vorträge    1929
Albert, M.: Les Théâtres de la Foire 1660-1789    1900
Albouy Dazincourt, J. J. B.: Notice Historique sur Préville    1800
Anderson, E.: Letters of Mozart and his Family    1938
Angelo, Henry: Reminiscences    1828
Arteaga, Stefano: Le Rivoluzioni del Teatro musicale Italiano dalla sua origine
    fino al presente    1783-88
Bachaumont, L. Petit de: Marie Antoinette, Louis XVI et la famille royale    1866
    Mémoires Secrets    1781
Baron, M. A.: Lettres et Entretiens sur la danse ancienne et moderne, religieuse,
    civile et théâtrale    1825
    Lettres à Sophie sur la danse    1825
Batteux, Charles: Les Beaux Arts réduits à un même principe    1746
Boaden: Private Correspondence of David Garrick    1831-32
Borde, J. B. de la: Essai sur la Musique ancienne et moderne    1780
Bos, J. B. Abbé du: Réflexions critiques sur la poèsie et la peinture    1770
Boulmiers, J. A. J. des: Histoire de l'Opéra Comique    1769
Boyer, J. B. de: Lettres du Marquis d'Argenson au Roi de Prusse    1788
Breghot, C. du Lut et Péricaud Ainé: Biographie Lyonaise    1839
Brillant, M.: L'Amour sur les Tréteaux    1924
Burette, P. J.: Treize Mémoires sur la Gymnastique des Anciens    1839
Cahusac, L. de: La Danse Ancienne et Moderne    1754
Campan, J. L. H.: Marie Antoinette
Campardon, E.: L'Académie Royale de Musique au 18ième siècle    1884
    Les Spectacles de la Foire    1877
Capon, G.: Les Vestris    1908
Castil Blaze: De la Danse et des Ballets    1832
Chénier, M. J. B. de: Oeuvres Posthumes    1826
Chevrier, F. A. de: Les Ridicules du Siècle    1774
Collé, C.: Correspondance    1864
    Journal    1911
    Journal Historique    1805
    Journal et mémoires 1742-1772    1868
Cooper, Martin: Gluck    1935
Croce, B.: Scritti di storia letteraria e politica Vol. 7    1916
Cumberland, R.: Memoirs    1807
Despréaux, J. E.: Mes Passe-temps    1806
Diderot, D.: Oeuvres ed. Assézat Vol. VII    1875
Didot, A. F.: Souvenirs de J. E. Despréaux    1894
Favart, C. S.: Mémoires et Correspondance    1808
Fournel, V.: Curiosités théâtrales anciennes et modernes    1859
Frederick II, King of Prussia: Oeuvres Complètes, Vol. 15    1790
Fuchs, M.: Lexique des Troupes de Comédiens au 18e siècle    1944
Galliani, Abbé F.: Correspondance    1818
    Lettres    1881
Genest, Rev. J.: Some Account of the English Stage from 1660 to 1830    1832
Goldsmith, M.: Maria Theresa of Austria    1936
Goncourt, E. & J. de: La Guimard    1893
Graffigny, H. de: Lettres du XVIIe et XVIIIe siècle    1873
Gregor, J.: Kultur Geschichte des Balletts    1947
Grimm, F. M. von, Diderot, Taynal, Meister, etc.: Correspondance Littéraire    1813
Grosley, P. J.: Londres    1770
Haas, R. M.: Gluck und Durazzo im Burgtheater    1925
    Die Wiener Ballet Pantomime im 18. Jahrhundert    1923

Harpe, J. F. de la: Correspondance avec le Grand Duc, depuis Empereur de
    Russie                                                 1801-7
Hastings, B.: The Contribution of Gluck and Angiolini to the French Ballet
    Tradition, Article in "The American Dancer"              1947
Hedgecock, F. A.: David Garrick and his French Friends           1911
Heinse, J. J. W.: Heinses Stellung zur Bildenden Kunst and Ihrer Asthetik    1901
    Hildegard von Hohenthal                                  1838
Heulhard, A.: La Foire St. Laurent                          1878
    Jean Monnet                                         1884
Hiberderie, Joubert de l': Le Dessinateur                    1764
Hugounet, Paul: Notes et documents pour servir à l'histoire de la pantomime    1889
Iacuzzi, A.: The European Vogue of Favart                  1932
Jahn, O.: Life of Mozart. Translated P. D. Townsend         1882
    W. A. Mozart                                   1856
Jullien, A.: L'Opéra Secret au 18e siècle                   1880
Kelly, Michael: Reminiscences                          1821
Khevenhueller-Metsch, R.: Aus der Zeit Maria Theresas         1907
Klant, G. Fischer: Hat J. G. Noverre die Tanzschrift abgelehnt?—Der Tanz,
    Berlin                                          1940
Krauss, R.: Das Stuttgarter Hoftheater von den ältesten Zeiten bis zur
    Gegenwart                                      1908
Laban, R. von: Modern Educational Dance                  1948
Lalande, J. J. Le François: Voyage d'un Français en Italie        1769
Lazzeri, G.: La Vita e l'opera lettararia di R. Calzabigi         1907
Leroy, A.: Marie Antoinette                              1946
Lesage, Fuzelier et Dorneval: Théâtre de la Foire            1722
Lewiton, J.: J. G. Noverre—Theater der Welt, Vienna        1937
Ligne, C. J. Prince de: Memoirs and letters                 1899
Ligne, C. J. E. de: Lettres à Eugénie sur les Spectacles        1922
Loewenberg, A.: Annals of the Opera                    1943
Lynham, Deryck: Ballet Then and Now                   1947
Marignan de: Eclaircissements donnés à l'auteur du Journal encyclopédique sur
    la musique du Devin du Village                      1781
Metra, F.: Correspondance Littéraire Secrète              1787
Monnet, J.: Mémoires                                 1909
    Supplément au Roman Comique                     1772
Muller, J. H. F. N.: Genaue Nachrichten von beyden Kais. Kgl. Schaubuhnen    1772
    Abschied von den K.K. Hof und Nationale Schaubuhne        1802
Murphy, Arthur: Life of Garrick                         1801
Neimeitz, J. C.: Séjour de Paris                          1727
Niedecken, H.: Jean Georges Noverre                     1914
Nisard, M. L. C.: Mémoires et Correspondances historiques et littéraires
    inédits de 1726 à 1816                            1852
Noverre, C. E.: Life and Works of the Chevalier Noverre        1882
    Some Notes of the Norfolk Noverres and Bruntons        1916
Noverre, J. G.: Lettres sur les Arts Imitateurs en géneral et sur la Danse en
    Particulier                                   1807
    ★Lettres sur la Danse et sur les Ballets (Lyons)           1760
    Lettres sur la Danse et sur les Ballets (Vienna)          1767
    Lettres sur la Danse et sur les Ballets (Londres, Paris)      1783
    Lettres sur la Danse, sur les Ballets et les Arts (St. Petersburg)    1803-4
    Auszug aus Noverre's Briefen über die Tanzkunst (Transl. Lessing & Bode)    1862
    Letters on Dancing and Ballets (Translated C. W. Beaumont)    1930
    Médée                                          1804
    La Prima Eta dell' Innocenza                      1775
    Recuil des Programmes de Ballets de M. Noverre (Vienna)    1776
    Renaud et Armide                             1775
Olivier et Norbert: Une étoile de la danse au XVIIIe siècle, Barbarina Campanini 1910
Ollivier, J. J.: Les Comédiens Français dans les cours d'Allemagne    1901
Parfaict, F. & C.: Dictionnaire des Théâtres de Paris           1756

Pfaff, Carl: Geschichte Wurtembergs 1819-20
Pohl, C. F.: Joseph Haydn 1875
   Mozart und Haydn in London 1867
Pure, Michel de: Idée des spectacles anciens et nouveaux 1668
Rabbe: Biographie Universelle 1830
Ritorni, C.: Commentarii della vita e delle opere di Salvatore Vigano 1838
Schmid, C. H.: Chronologie des deutschen Theaters 1775
Schubart, C. F. D.: Schubart als Musiker 1905
Sonnenfels, J. von: Briefe von Sonnenfels 1769
Uriot, J.: Description des Fêtes 1763
   Lettres Wurtembourgeoises 1766
Verri, Pietro: Lettere e scritti inedite di Pietro e di Alessandro Verri 1879
Vallas, Léon: Un siècle de musique et de théâtre ` Lyon 1688-1789 1932
   Noverre à Lyon, article Revue Musicale de Lyon 27.11.1910
Vossius, I.: De Poematum cantu et viribus Rhythmi 1673
Weaver, J.: An Essay Towards the History of Dancing 1712
  ★ All references to and quotations from the "Lettres sur la Danse et sur les Ballets" refer to the 1760 edition unless otherwise stated.

### Periodicals

Affiches de Lyon 1759-60
Ausgewählte Ballette Stuttgarter Meister aus der 2. Hälfte des 18. Jahrhunderts.
   Vol. XLIII, XLIV (J. J. Rodolphe) 1892 etc.
Bells Weekly Messenger 1805
Dancing Times, The
Deutsche (Teutsche) Merkur, Weimar 1774-6
                                    1789 (III)
Journal Etranger 1755
Journal de Paris (Abrégé de) 1789
Journal des Théâtres ou Le Nouveau Spectateur (T. de Méricourt)
London Chronicle 1791
London Daily Post and General Advertiser 1752-94
London Evening Post 1755
Mercure de France 1755-60
Monthly Review 1754-6
Observateur Littéraire, Abbé de Laporte 1759
Oracle 1789-95
Oracle and Public Advertiser 1794-5
Public Advertiser 1755-93
Quarterly Musical Magazine and Review 1818-28
Wiener Instrumentalmusik vor und um 1750. "Gesellschaft zur Herausgabe der Denkmaler der Tonkunst in Oesterreich" XV2 1908

# Index

For greater convenience all Ballets have been listed in italics under "Ballets" and in the same way all composers and musicians will be found under "Composers", all dancers and choreographers under "Dancers", scenic artists under "Designers", librettists under "Librettists", operas under "Operas" and theatres under "Theatres".